porn, politics and punishment:

The Madness of Joe Francis

"I Thought We Were All Just Having Fun … I Was Wrong."

David L Angier

Cover photograph by Robert Cooper and The Panama City News Herald.

ISBN-10: 0615705804

EAN-13: 9780615705804

To the girls who make my life a little more wild:
Angela, Rachel, Vivi, Chris, Heather,
Nica and Aubrey.

Chapter 1

"I thought we were all just having fun."

The seed that would take root in Joe Francis' mind and blossom into a full and flowering madness was planted on a beautiful winter morning with a phone call.

He had just parked his car and was walking across the lot of Paramount Studios in Los Angeles to do an interview with Entertainment Tonight, when his cell phone vibrated in his pocket.

He recognized his publicist, Bill Horn, and the humor in Horn's voice.

"You're gonna love this," Horn said. "I just got a call that there's some wacky mayor out in Panama City Beach who is running his mouth and saying all this stuff about Girls Gone Wild and how he's gonna put your cameramen in jail if they get girls to lift their shirts in public."

The words "wacky mayor" immediately resonated with Francis. It was the type of phrase that got the media's attention. He intended to use that, and a wide, crooked smile broke across his tanned face.

He had a scheduled Pay-per-View event in Panama City Beach, and Francis immediately thought of the marketing potential of a public battle with Southern officials.

The threat didn't bother him; he never for a minute thought the mayor was serious. Politicians were in the marketing business just like him. They were constantly on the lookout for high-profile squabbles to get their righteously indignant faces before the television cameras and win over conservative voters.

"He was the perfect character, the perfect adversary," Francis said years later. "I thought we were all just having fun. I was wrong."

Francis had taken marketing to a new level with his Girls Gone Wild brand and late-night infomercials, making him a millionaire in his mid-20s. Never before had a porn empire been built through the use of volunteer actors. He paid girls with T-shirts, cheap plastic beads and the occasional hundred-dollar bill to star in his videos, then sold hundreds of thousands of the DVDs for $19.95 a piece.

He'd been sued, but usually won. He sometimes paid out six or seven figures in settlements, but even that was chump-change compared to what he was bringing in.

Francis had recently won a federal case in Central Florida in which a judge had made it clear that public nudity, without sexual activity, was not illegal.

Francis felt untouchable.

But Francis wasn't entirely stable. He'd struggled with attention deficit hyperactivity disorder since he was a child and was borderline bipolar, meaning he experienced wide mood swings.

He was personable and funny, in a manic sort of way, but quick to anger as well.

"Things always seem to go a lot smoother when Joe's not around," a cameraman would say after the cameraman's arrest in Panama City.

Years later, another cameraman, Ryan Simkin, described Francis as: "a child molester; jail-baiting pervert; pimp; sick bastard; sleaze-peddler; tax cheat; rapist; sleazehole; the epitome of a true misogynist, coked-out amoral direct marketer; violent thug; juvenile smut-peddler; sexual predator; one of the 50 most loathsome people in America; and the Douche of the Decade."

The last one wasn't one thought up by Simkin. Francis had won the title "Douche of the Decade" from voters on a website poll.

Radio talk show host Howard Stern once asked him, "So you're thinking there's money in this nudity thing?"

Francis told Stern he'd gotten his start selling the video "Banned from Television," spliced together scenes of death shot by television reporters that were too graphic for mainstream TV.

"'Banned from Television', that was my start. You remember when the lady got hit by the train?" Francis said.

"Oh yeah, I love that video," Stern said. "You are so rich now from, let me get the name right, the 'Girls Gone Wild' videos and from the chick getting hit by the train?"

Francis was making $10-20 million a year, and Girls Gone Wild was fast on its way to becoming a cultural phenomenon with the words "Gone Wild" being used to describe any out-of-control situation.

On April 2, 2003, two months after that fateful phone call, Joe Francis was arrested in Panama City and charged with racketeering. He would be jailed in 2007 by a federal judge in Panama City, and suffer a crying, screaming breakdown that had two psychologists predicting a complete mental collapse.

The problem for the rest of us was knowing when Joe Francis actually did lose his mind.

Chapter 2

"I look forward to seeing how this resolves"

"Mayor, let me start right with you," Fox News' Greta Van Susteren said to Panama City Beach Mayor Lee Sullivan. "You don't want them in your city, do you?"

"No ma'am, I don't," Sullivan growled. It was March 7, 2003, and Sullivan, a Vietnam War vet, former police chief and future television news commentator, had perfected his simple, deep, gravely Southern drawl and no-nonsense answer.

Sullivan, Joe Francis and lawyers Tom Julin and Joe Tessitore had agreed to appear on Van Susteren's "On the Record" to discuss Girls Gone Wild's plans to film Spring Break 2003 in Panama City Beach. Sullivan had been outspoken about the pressure he was putting on local cops to aggressively enforce public nudity ordinances in regards to Girls Gone Wild.

"The concept of having a commercial peep show operated in our community is not only offensive to our community, to our industry and to our government, but it is also against the law and we will not tolerate it," Sullivan said.

"Is your position that it is immoral, what this company does?" Van Susteren asked.

"No, ma'am, it's illegal," Sullivan said. "It may be immoral to some. The issue for us as a community and an industry is it is illegal."

"It's not illegal at all," Julin said.

Public nudity was not against the law in Florida. The nudity had to be accompanied by a lewd or sexually suggestive act. A woman exposing her breasts to a cameraman was perfectly legal – even a minor. Francis maintained that they were just shooting a documentary.

"It's a little farfetched to call it a documentary," Van Susteren said. In 2004, the Court of Appeal of California would describe Girls Gone Wild as a "documentary videotape series."

"What's the difference between a girl, you know, in a bikini and a girl without a bikini?" Francis replied.

"Then why sign a waiver?" Sullivan countered.

Francis, ignoring the question, told Sullivan that a planned Pay-per-View Spring Break party was still going to be shot in Panama City Beach.

"And if the mayor thinks he's going to stop us, he can come arrest me on stage," Francis said. "He can come arrest me with Snoop Dogg, and he can put a bunch of half-naked girls in handcuffs as well because it's going to happen.

"It's probably worth the $19.99 on Thursday night to watch that happen," he finished with a wide, lopsided grin.

"What a class act," Sullivan snarled.

"Mr. Mayor, we're not doing anything illegal," Francis said. "My cameramen and myself will not be pushed around by a local tyrant, or his city police, who barely won an election by 90 votes."

"Seven votes, my friend," Sullivan said. "If you can count that high."

Sullivan came to the Panama City Beach Police Department in 1970, when Northwest Florida was the state's wild west. Biker gangs dominated the beach at certain times of the year and drug smugglers moved trade in shrimp boats along the mostly undeveloped coast.

Thirty years later, the coastline had added a skyline, but there were areas where the jungle still touched the waves. The Panhandle was called the "Forgotten Coast" mainly because developers had ignored it.

Sullivan, who was the youngest police chief in the state in 1977, joined the police department after being "shot twice and blown up once" in Vietnam.

"As bad as being shot is, it pales in comparison to being blown up," he once told The Panama City News Herald.

Sullivan once stood on the hood of a police cruiser with a shotgun in hand and faced down a mob of Hell's Angels. He called it a prayer session. He said he told the bikers that they would probably kill him that night, but he was sure to take a couple of them with him.

"Now, let's pray," he said, bowing his head. He says when he looked up, the bikers were leaving.

By the time Sullivan resolved to face down Girls Gone Wild his reputation had grown larger than the man himself. And Sullivan was a formidable man who always wore a cowboy hat pulled down low on his brow.

The hat was as much for image as it was to keep Sullivan's sandy brown toupee from blowing away.

Sullivan ended his speech on Greta Van Susteren's show by saying Francis was not welcome in Panama City Beach or anywhere in Bay County.

"He runs a commercial peep show and the community doesn't welcome him, the businesses don't welcome him and if he cares to take exception to that or if he thinks that he finds a welcome in any area of our community, he's mistaken."

"I look forward to seeing how this resolves," Van Susteren finished with a smile.

Joe Francis and Girls Gone Wild first appeared on the Bay County Sheriff's Office radar in 2002. Capt. Jerry Metz, head of the sheriff's special investigations unit, says Joe Francis came to his attention when he happened across Girls Gone Wild advertisements on late-night TV with Panama City Beach in the background.

When officers were gearing up for Spring Break 2003, an event that brought between 500,000 and one million visitors to a county of less than 150,000 people, Metz told his men to be on the lookout for GGW crews.

"I orchestrated a meeting with all of the people that worked for me to be aware of this group on Panama City Beach and for them to contact their informants, any of their citizen contacts with hotels and motels, and document some activity that may be occurring," Metz told Joe Francis' criminal defense attorney Aaron Dyer in a deposition.

Metz insisted that officers were simply watching the GGW crew, keeping tabs on them.

"Were they supposed to follow the Girls Gone Wild vans?" Dyer asked him.

"If they thought that the vans were on the move and that they were headed to a specific location as opposed to just riding the strip like most of the time is what they did, well then I would have asked them to note where it went and so forth," Metz said.

Lee Sullivan's interviews with Greta Van Susteren and the local newspaper, The News Herald, brought Metz's investigation into the public light.

"After Lee Sullivan got the publicity he did, it was pretty widespread knowledge through Panama City Beach that there was an investigation ongoing," then-Bay County Sheriff Guy Tunnell told Dyer in a 2005 deposition.

Once word got out that the cops had their eyes on GGW, the public got involved and Tunnell started getting calls from residents.

Tunnell and Metz both insisted that officers weren't harassing GGW employees, only monitoring them. Francis filed a lawsuit claiming otherwise. It said on March 7, 2003, a sheriff's helicopter hovered outside a residence leased by Girls Gone Wild, with a spotlight trained on the cameramen. The cameramen, doing what they do, filmed themselves looking skyward into the rotor wash and blinding light, blinking and looking bemused.

Officers on bicycles – it's hard to look tough while wearing a bicycle helmet and shorts – circled GGW cameramen as they "interviewed" girls.

"Based upon recent news articles, plaintiffs have a legitimate apprehension that defendants intend to arrest plaintiffs and other Mantra representatives for exercising their constitutional right to document on film events taking place in public places," the March 10, 2003, lawsuit claimed.

Mantra Entertainment is the company, owned by Francis, that puts out the Girls Gone Wild videos.

The police harassment, according to the lawsuit, prevented the film crews from taking as much video as they would have liked and rendered them unable to "film truly spontaneous conduct due to the apprehension of the individuals being filmed."

The "spontaneous conduct," the sudden flashing of breasts that epitomized the Girls Gone Wild brand was very often a torturous process of begging or negotiating by the cameramen that was rewarded with beads and T-shirts.

But that's not to say that Girls Gone Wild was not welcomed by beach goers. At times, Francis, his silver Ferrari and Girls Gone Wild van were mobbed by screaming fans.

In March 2003, Francis rented the SunDancer nightclub on Thomas Drive. SunDancer, a former dance club popular with black patrons had been another target of the Sheriff's Office when the predominantly white residents of the neighborhood behind the club started complaining about the noise and club goers urinating in their bushes and parking on their lawns.

Years before, deputies had raided the club, the helicopter hovering overhead and beaming that spotlight down on the parking lot. The owners were arrested and eventually the club closed for good.

On the night of the GGW party, the editors at The News Herald anticipated a similar raid. They assigned a reporter and photographer to monitor the live Pay-per-View event – from a television set in the reporter's home and do a story about it – especially if the place was raided.

It was a disappointingly uneventful show, prompting one editor to dub it "Girls Gone Mild," but it was far more interesting to local cops when Francis boasted during the show that he was "bigger than city officials" who wanted to stop him from filming in Panama City Beach. Sullivan made a point to bring that up a few weeks later when Francis was arrested.

"Mr. Francis made a comment that he was too big to be run out of Panama City Beach," the mayor told News Herald reporter Daniel Jackson. "I can assure you they found a cell big enough for him at the jail."

• • •

Bay County Deputy Adam Buff stands 6-foot-6 and has, at times, weighed in at more than 300 pounds. His friends call him "Buffy." A few investigators at the sheriff's office have similar nicknames, like "Buttercup" and "Petunia," but it wouldn't be wise to use those names unless you were very good friends.

On the morning of April 2, 2003, Buff got assigned to the Princess Condominiums to watch for Francis and arrest him on sight. Francis had gone to World Gym to work out that morning and Buff waited for his return in the condominium's parking lot.

When Francis finally arrived he was dressed in typical workout attire, T-shirt, shorts and a ball cap. Buff watched him get out of his car and as he started toward the condo's elevators Buff moved to intercept him.

Francis saw him coming and it was clear this was not a fan.

"Hey Joe," Buff called out, "I'm with the Sheriff's Office. I've got to take you in."

Francis started looking around, instantly nervous.

"I haven't done anything," he said.

Buff saw all the signs of someone about to "rabbit" – run. Francis was inching away, looking for ways out. When he turned toward the elevator, Buff grabbed his arm. After a moment's resistance, Francis allowed himself to be led to a car. Buff leaned him over the hood, cuffed his wrists and searched him. Other officers arrived, led Francis to a car and locked him in the back.

Francis couldn't stop talking. He kept asking what he'd done to be arrested. Buff kept telling him he didn't know and he'd have to talk to a superior.

"How about him, is that someone I can ask?" Francis would ask about every officer that arrived on the scene.

Buff would just shrug. He was new to the division and had no authority. It wasn't his job to comfort Francis or answer his questions. He'd been told to take him into custody and that's what he'd done.

Eventually, investigators Faith Bell and Richard Bagwell did arrive but they also felt little need to respond to Francis' questions. They wanted to know where his film crews were, and Francis eagerly gave them everything he knew about his employees' locations.

"Why do you need a search warrant?" he asked Bell, who told him she had several warrants to search the condos he and his crew were using. "You can search. I've got nothing to hide."

Officers seized everything when they went inside: T-shirts (some of them saying "Joe Francis for Panama City Beach Mayor"), beads, rental movies, cell phones and more than 175 hours of uncut footage the crews had shot during the last month.

They also found a birthday card from the day before when Francis had turned 30.

"Joe, celebrate your 30 with a couple of 15's," cameraman Ryan Simkin had written. Another note on the card, this one from Dana Pustetta, said, "Hey Joe, make sure she's 18 tonight, would ya."

In a shaving kit, officers found several tablets of hydrocodone and one Viagra.

Later that day, Buff took his German shepherd, "Hunter," to search the Girls Gone Wild jet.

Hunter sniffed around the tires and wheel wells, a few times rising up on his hind legs to sniff the air closer to the fuselage, before sitting and looking at the underbelly of the plane. Sitting was the way he indicated his detection of drugs.

The rumor was, and it was a rumor that made it all the way to Francis' defense team, that someone put Hunter on the roof of a truck and drove him slowly around under the fuselage in an effort to get him closer to the cabin. According to the story, Hunter was so unnerved that he did nothing more than cling to the rooftop and whimper until the ride was over.

But just sitting by the wheels was enough probable cause for a search warrant. Bagwell reported that he found a silver serving platter that had cocaine residue on it.

Francis, meanwhile, was being booked in a small, concrete block room in the basement of the Bay County Jail. He'd been led down a gray-walled hallway, over gray floors and doors to the temporary holding cells and drunk tanks also painted gray. These cells were usually crammed with men waiting for processing, release or relocation to a cell block.

A few pathetic faces stared at him through the narrow slits in the cell doors.

Francis smiled for the booking photo, but his eyes were dull and distant.

He was charged with racketeering, conspiring to commit racketeering, promoting the sexual performance of a child, conspiracy to promote the sexual performance of a child, using and conspiring to use a child in a sexual performance, procuring and conspiring to procure a person younger than 18 for prostitution, sale or distribution of obscene material and prostitution.

The racketeering charges were first-degree felonies and carried a 30-year prison term. The rest were various levels of misdemeanors and felonies. Francis potential penalty added up to more than 100 years in prison.

The racketeering and conspiracy charges were significant, they implied an intent to use minors in "Girls Gone Wild" videos.

• • •

The next morning Francis went before County Judge John O'Brien for first-appearance and the setting of a bond.

Prosecutor Mark Graham asked for Francis to be held without bail. He argued that Francis had all the money and resources he needed to leave the country, including access to a private jet.

Short of no bond, Graham told O'Brien, a bond had to be set so high that Francis would never forfeit it.

O'Brien was new to the bench, having been appointed in 2001. He'd spent the previous 30 years as one of the best defense attorneys in the area. Since taking the bench, he'd made a reputation as a defense-friendly judge who set low bonds.

In Francis' case, O'Brien wouldn't consider keeping him in jail without bond. Nothing short of a murder charge would warrant such a measure.

O'Brien also reasoned that an outrageous bond was unnecessary, because if Francis wanted to bond out and run very little would stop him. He decided $50,000 was enough.

Joe Francis posted bond and was leaving the jail, but Investigator Bagwell arrested him at the jailhouse door on drug charges he'd failed to file the first time.

Bagwell told Aaron Dyer, Francis' criminal defense attorney, that he had not purposely waited to see if Francis would be released before serving the second set of charges. He also wasn't trying to force Francis to spend another night in jail before he could bond out again.

Bagwell said it simply took him some time to process the hydrocodone, weigh it and prepare the paperwork charging Francis with trafficking drugs.

Dyer asked him how long it took to weigh the pills. Bagwell said a minute or two. He asked how long it took to fill out the paperwork. Bagwell said 10 to 15 minutes. Francis had been held for roughly 24 hours.

Dyer asked Bagwell if he had a history of holding back charges to file on defendants he knew would bond out. Bagwell said he'd done it before, but he didn't consider it holding back intentionally.

Judge O'Brien was not amused by Bagwell's re-arrest of Francis and quickly allowed him to bond out for an additional $15,000 without another night in jail.

Francis was charged with trafficking drugs and possessing prescription pills without a prescription. Both charges would be dropped when a state lab found no trace of cocaine on the silver platter and Francis produced the prescription for his pills.

Francis' other charges, racketeering related to prostitution and commercial sexual exploitation of children, would stick around a little longer. Cameraman Mark Schmitz was charged with racketeering, and two crew members, Ryan Simkin, 26, and Noah S. Tannenbaum, 24, were charged with drug possession. The racketeering charge for both Francis and Schmitz carried a 30-year prison sentence.

Bagwell wrote in the official report that Francis coerced two 17-year-old girls, Christina and Darlene, into having sexual contact with each other for $100 each. Schmitz filmed the two girls kissing and doing other things in a motel shower. Bagwell also claimed that Francis paid Vanessa and Brittany, 17, $50 each to jerk him off.

"The named defendant did procure Christina to commit a sexual act with another female," Bagwell wrote. "On March 31, 2003, the named defendant did procure Christina to commit the act of prostitution. The named defendant then did video tape this act for the purpose of marketing this sexual act for commercial gain."

He wrote about Vanessa's allegation: "on March 31, 2003, the named defendant did procure Vanessa to commit the act of prostitution. The named defendant did video tape this act for the purpose of marketing this sexual act for commercial gain."

He went on: "On March 31, 2003, the named defendant did produce and/or direct a video tape, which in whole or in part, depicted Vanessa involved in sexual conduct."

On the day of Francis' arrest, several officials gave News Herald reporter Daniel Jackson a statement for his article.

"One of the girls was feeling guilty over it and she confessed to her parents," Sheriff Guy Tunnell told Jackson. "We contacted the others. They were extremely embarrassed. This is more than someone flashing their breasts. This is pretty hard-core pornographic production ... and it involves minors, which is most alarming to me."

Tunnell told Jackson that Francis knew the girls were underage, filmed them anyway then made them sign waivers after the shoot saying they were adults.

Panama City Beach Police Chief Robert Harding told Jackson, "Francis is a maverick. He thinks he's untouchable. We told them all along that if you film in public without breaking the law, we don't have a problem. This has nothing to do with constitutional freedoms. It's just not something that we're going to tolerate on the beach."

In addition to the charges, the sheriff's office seized Francis' private jet and his 2003 Ferrari, then began forfeiture procedures to have them turned over to the department if Francis was convicted.

For the time being, Francis and the other three men were free on bond.

But this was just the beginning of the charges.

Chapter 3

"Girls Gone Wild, Whoo!"

"I don't think I need to see anymore," Circuit Judge Dedee Costello cringed, held her hands up and turned away from the television screen. She'd watched a little more than an hour of raw Girls Gone Wild footage: Lots of girls flashing their breasts and the first showing of what would become known as "the shower scene."

Then there were the tapes of Joe Francis and his Ferrari cruising Front Beach Road in Panama City Beach, picking up giggling girls, cajoling others to expose themselves.

One blonde, oval faced girl sitting in the passenger seat of a car, lifts her sweater and says a catch line for Girls Gone Wild. The cameraman's voice comes from off-screen while the camera remains focused on the girl. He asks her how old she is.

She is 17.

"If I say I'm 18, does it make a difference?" the girl asks. The disembodied voice tells her they'll shoot it again, and this time she has to be older.

The girl lifts her sweater, shows her breasts, says the line – "Girls Gone Wild, whoo!" Then, when asked, she says she's 20 years old.

"This is just the tip of the iceberg," attorney Franklin Harrison said as he clicked off the videotape, releasing Costello from her agony. Costello had once chastised a female defendant for 15 minutes because she wore a t-shirt to court with "Porn Star" written across the chest, imagine how she felt about watching the real thing in her own courtroom.

It was May 13, 2003, a little more than a month after Francis' arrest and the first time anyone outside the investigation had seen the videos taken as evidence in his case.

This hearing was to determine if officers had the legal right to hold the jet and Ferrari pending the resolution of the case. Investigators said the vehicles were used in Francis' criminal enterprise and therefore fair game for seizure.

The defense said seizing the $2 million jet and $100,000 car proved that the arrest, the case itself, was all about extorting money. The sheriff's office, they said, saw an opportunity to legally steal Francis' toys.

They decided to take the issue to Judge Costello. What was supposed to be a half-day hearing went two days. Two days of porn in Judge Costello's courtroom and the room was packed.

Harrison, the sheriff's lawyer, had several of the tapes on hand to show Costello, including the shower scene, which he cued up next.

The judge shifted uncomfortably in her seat. There were several dozen reporters and lawyers in the room, all of us doing our best to appear disinterested, clinical in our observations.

Not everyone considered it strictly evidence though, and more than a few snickers could be heard coming from the crowd. I suddenly realized that I'd picked an unfortunate spot to watch the show. Costello allowed lawyers and the occasional reporter to sit in the jury box when it wasn't being used, so there I was, in my favorite seat, which happened to put me closest to the television screen besides the judge. Once the videos started, I felt very exposed and slid down in my seat, until I was on the verge of falling out. Straightening up would bring unwanted attention so I tried to stay still, chin almost touching my chest.

Luckily, there was no reason to take notes.

The girls on the tape were obviously driven by something other than passion, lust or even curiosity. They were urged on by the cameraman's constant pleading and direction.

Costello, who never kept her feelings off her face, watched with squinted eyes and one corner of her lips turned up in a menacing, disgusted sneer. Trim and meticulous, her black hair cut short and characteristic bright red lipstick carefully applied, Costello didn't have much patience for what she was watching.

She'd seen a girl stretched out naked on a bed, her head hanging over the edge looking upside-down at the camera, with another woman straddling her, talking about how she'd been 16 or 17 the year before when she'd done a sex scene for Girls Gone Wild.

Costello had seen a video of the rapper Snoop Dogg sitting in front of a camera, rolling what appeared to be a cigar-sized joint while apparently in the jet. The camera shot was tight on him and while his head bobbed to the music, his hands with the rolling paper and herb stayed perfectly centered on the screen. He appeared to be giving a tutorial on the finer points of rolling a blunt.

All the videos, which were just tiny snippets of the hours of footage, were intended to convince the judge that there was probable cause that criminal activity had occurred during GGW's short stay in Panama City Beach in March and April 2003, and the company's private jet and Ferrari were integral parts of that criminal behavior.

Harrison argued that the jet was used to transport the people and equipment needed to carry out their illegal deeds. He said the Ferrari was a lure.

"It's all a part of the scheme," Harrison said. "Francis is a part of all of this. He's not a disinterested businessman. He's right in the middle."

If the judge agreed, the sheriff's office would keep the jet and Ferrari, at least until the conclusion of the criminal case.

Apparently, Harrison had not burdened Costello with some of the more unsavory tapes.

"Some of these cameramen have the worst taste," a bleary-eyed Aaron Dyer told me sometime later, after watching hours of uncut video.

It was at this hearing that Harrison summed up the prosecution's case: "They (the defense) are saying that it's these children who are at fault. We are in the business of protecting children in Florida."

Children, he argued, were unable to make good decisions when it came to predators like Joe Francis. They were vulnerable, easy targets, and Francis was quick to pounce.

The defense attorneys also made a statement, but it was not nearly as quotable.

Attorneys Jim Fensom and Robert Griscti put into evidence the statements of all the girls who were the named victims in the worst charges against Francis. In each statement, the girls told authorities that they'd lied to GGW cameramen about their ages. All had said they were 18 and even signed releases stating they were 18.

That's all.

Girls Gone Wild had been lied to despite their best efforts to be responsible.

"To think that Mantra Entertainment is targeting 17-and-a-half-year-old girls, finding them more attractive than these wrinkled 18-year-olds, is ridiculous," Fensom said.

Costello, who was trying to leave town for the weekend, ruled late on a Friday afternoon that Girls Gone Wild could have its jet back, but the sheriff's office would keep the Ferrari a little longer.

She didn't explain her ruling. She simply wrote it and sent it to the lawyers. The lawyers speculated that there was next-to-nothing tying the jet to any of the crimes Francis faced.

Francis was at least driving the Ferrari when he picked up girls.

Harrison appealed to the First District Court of Appeal. He argued that the sheriff's office had presented more than enough evidence showing not only Girls Gone Wild's coast-to-coast illegal operation, but the integral role the jet played in it all.

Besides the obvious struggle to keep the jet, this appeal was the beginning of the fight over the basic argument in the criminal case, the legal concept of "strict liability."

Harrison told the appeals judges that, "The state does have a compelling interest in protecting under-aged persons from being sexually abused or exploited."

"When presented with charges of procuring children for prostitution or sexually exploiting children, it should not be a defense that the child or children misrepresented their age or that the defendant did not know the true age of the victim," Harrison wrote in his brief. "In other words, these crimes against children are strict liability offenses."

Strict liability, in essence, makes sexual contact between an adult and a minor illegal regardless of whether the adult tried to determine the child's age and was misled. In strict liability cases, it didn't matter if an adult male had picked up a girl who looked like she was 30, at a bar where she had been served beer on a fake ID, had sex with her and the next morning found out she was only 15. It is illegal.

In Francis' case, criminal intent, knowledge that the girls being abused or exploited were minors, would be unnecessary to prove guilt if the charges against him were found to be strict liability offenses.

Griscti, the lawyer arguing on behalf of the jet, spent much of his 58 page answer talking about strict liability. He admitted Harrison produced precedent to support his argument, but asked the appeals judges to ignore them.

"They are wrong," Griscti wrote.

He said none of the criminal charges against Joe Francis were strict liability. On the contrary, he said, intent was essential.

Dyer put it more succinctly later when he said the idea of strict liability in a racketeering case was bewildering. Racketeering is setting up an illegal practice within a legal business; in GGW's case it would be knowingly including illegal child pornography within its legal pornographic videos. But, he said, that would have to mean that the GGW cameramen knew the girls were underage. How else would they know to illegally include them?

Harrison's appeal was denied, without comment, by a three-judge panel. It's called "per curium affirmed" and is essentially the death knell of any appeal. Without a written reason from the judges, there was almost nothing the lawyers could do to appeal it to the state supreme court. Harrison said later that it was an abrupt and disappointing dismissal of a complex argument.

At this stage in the proceedings, Costello was simply the judge in the seizure issue. Circuit Judge Michael Overstreet had the criminal case.

Chapter 4

Secret information

Part of my job as courts reporter for the News Herald was to check daily filings in criminal cases at the courthouse. In 2003, there were 12 clerks in that office, all women.

They looked at me as a little brother and gave me unprecedented freedom within the building.

I walked in the door of the clerks' office on October 14, 2003, past Angela's desk and Laura's desk, but stopped short of Joanne's. I could see through the clear plastic wall of her cubicle that she wasn't there.

"Where's Joanne?" I asked. "I need a file."

I'd gone online earlier in the day and seen a new filing in the Girls Gone Wild case. It appeared to be an amended "information" – a new set of charges based on changes in the evidence.

"Her files are on her desk," one of the girls answered without looking up from her work.

Right on top was the information I was looking for. It was thick and had a lot more names on it besides Joe Francis.

"Can I make a copy of this?" I asked no one in particular, my head nearly touching the pages as I leafed through them.

Someone told me to go ahead.

"You know where it is," she said.

Five minutes later I walked down the hallway, past security and into the parking lot without taking my eyes off the document. The exchange at the clerk's office was typical, but there would be nothing typical about what would happen later.

For months, there had been talk of additional charges being filed and here they were.

As soon as I got back to the office I called State Attorney Jim Appleman and asked him a few questions about the amended information. It was easy to hear the amusement in his voice.

"At our last hearing, the judge ordered us to go through all the tapes," he said. "We said at that time that we anticipated there would be additional charges, and that's what happened."

Francis was now looking at 43 charges, instead of the 22 originally brought, and was facing 335 years in prison. Nine employees also were charged, all of them with racketeering – a 30-year felony that implied a conspiracy to operate an illegal business.

"How much of this is just trying to pressure some of these employees into testifying against Francis?" I asked.

"Would we do that?" Appleman coyly asked. Then he dropped his voice into his official on-the-record tone. "We feel like we can prove all of these crimes were committed by the persons charged."

I asked him to give me some details about the type of work these employees did for Mantra.

"I think most of them are cameramen, but you'd have to ask the company what they specifically do," he said.

I told him I'd already sent an email to Mantra spokesman Jim Horn and Aaron Dyer. I asked Appleman if it was all right to call prosecutor Mark Graham if I had any technical questions. He said that would be fine.

A few minutes into the story I ran into something that I needed guidance with. The language in the information was formal and vague. So I called Graham.

"Hey Mark, I'm doing a story about the amended information against Francis and the Girls Gone Wild employees. I checked with Appleman and he said it would be OK for me to talk to you about it," I said.

Graham stammered for a second, before he could wrap his mind around the three or four alarming pieces of information I'd just given him.

"How did you get the information?" he finally asked. "And Jim talked to you about it?"

"It's online," I told him. "And Jim didn't have any problems giving me an interview."

"Jim gave you an interview? About the amended information?" Graham continued to spit out. "When are you running this story?"

"It's gonna be in tomorrow's paper. But look, I'm running into some problems making this thing understandable," I said, not quite grasping what was bothering him so much.

"Tomorrow?" he said, a note of panic entering his voice. "Look, that information was supposed to be sealed. I don't know how you got a copy of it, but we're trying to keep it under wraps until we get some of these guys in custody. We don't want any of them to be tipped off and try to leave the country."

"Well," I started, not sure how he would take this last bit of news, "I already emailed Mantra to get more information about these employees and what they do for the company."

"You sent them the names?" he asked, still not angry, just amazed that his day had come crashing down within the span of a five-minute phone call. "I gotta go."

He hung up. Now it was my turn to be amazed.

I checked my email and found a response from Jim Horn. He wanted to know if I would send him a copy of the charges. He didn't, however, answer any of my questions about the employees.

I ignored the email and went back to writing my story.

The phone interrupted that. It was Jimmy Judkins in Tallahassee, another one of Francis' Florida lawyers. He wanted me to fax him a copy of the charges. I told him I'd have to talk to my editors and got off the phone after he told me he couldn't answer any of my questions until he got the charges.

Graham called a minute later.

"I know I can't ask you to hold this story," he said, meaning he'd like me to volunteer to hold the story. "I checked with Joanne and she said she did put the information online. I know you didn't do anything wrong in getting it, but if you could just do me one favor and keep the employees' names out of this story?"

I told him I'd have to talk to my editors and got off the phone.

I didn't really need to talk to my editors, even though I would to let them know what I was doing. What I really needed was a few minutes to think.

The defense didn't have the charges, and they wanted them badly.

Graham, I knew, didn't have any way of keeping me from reporting the story. I'd gotten the document legally and the paper would be on solid ground with any story we ran. I also knew I didn't have to withhold the names.

But, I had this story all to myself. If I wanted to sit on the names for a day or two I could, but Graham would have to give me something in return.

After filling in my editors, I called Graham back.

"I'll hold the names," I said, "for now."

I didn't say anything about what I wanted in return. Graham made me an offer.

"They're supposed to turn themselves in within the week," he said. "I'll let you know when that happens."

That'll work.

I called Judkins back and told him, reluctantly, that the editors had decided that we couldn't provide him with the charges. I said it wasn't our place to do that if the state wouldn't.

"I understand," Judkins said, clearly meaning the opposite. "You've got to work with the prosecutor. But I wonder what your colleagues in other newspapers in this state would think of your collusion with the state?"

It was a surprisingly effective jab. There's no denying that small and midsize newspapers in Florida work under the considerable shadow of papers like the Miami Herald and St. Petersburg

Times. Newspapers in the Panhandle also have to deal with the reputation of being unprofessional.

Despite the immediate doubt Judkins was able to plant, I stuck to my plan.

"I don't honestly know how this would be viewed by other papers," I said, "but this is our decision. You'll just have to get the information from the State Attorney's Office."

Graham had already filed a motion to close the charging document from the public. I was now guaranteed that I would not only have the only other copy, but I would also have first notification when the GGW employees started appearing at the Bay County Jail.

The next day, when Judkins and the defense team were unable to get the information from the clerk's office they weren't any happier with the News Herald when I called for comment.

"How can you file something in the public records then say it's not public?" he asked. "How can you, David Angier, get it and we can't get it?"

The defense team was especially annoyed that Appleman had given me an interview before Graham moved to have the document sealed.

"The State is seeking only to withhold information from the Defendants, but not the media," Jacksonville attorney Henry Coxe, one of a battery of lawyers working with the defense, wrote in his response to Graham's motion.

Unfortunately, Joanne in the clerk's office was caught in the middle of this skirmish. Even though she had done nothing wrong in posting the information and the clerks had done nothing wrong in releasing it to me when they did, Joanne was questioned by her boss, Clerk of Court Harold Bazzel.

Bazzel also asked me about it, especially the part about my taking the document off Joanne's desk without her being there.

"Harold," I said, "it didn't matter if Joanne was there or not. It wouldn't matter if it had been locked in her desk. It is against the law for you to deny me a public record."

The next morning, though, I stopped at a bakery and bought twenty-four fresh muffins. Bazzel saw me coming into the courthouse with the two batches of muffins in hand walking toward the clerk's office.

"You're a smart man," he said, grinning.

Later that week, and over a two-day period, all of the GGW employees named in the new information reported to the Bay County Jail. They were quickly booked and allowed to leave on a preset bond.

The first day, the News Herald had the exclusive, with photographers roaming the jail's parking lot. I showed up late in the morning to watch the show and met up with one of the photographers. A clerk who was taking a break came out to complain to me about how aggressive the photographers were being. She could see the jail parking lot from her office window.

"Why do they have to chase them?" she asked, not realizing one of the photographers was standing next to me.

"Because they ran," the cameraman said.

Chapter 5

"I'll be your lawyer today"

As they came before Circuit Judge Michael Overstreet's bench on November 20, 2003, Assistant Public Defender Matt Meredith met each Girls Gone Wild defendant with the same handshake, smile and greeting, "I'm Matt Meredith, I'll be your lawyer today."

Meredith couldn't represent all nine. A defendant's lawyer has to be free to make decisions that would be in that defendant's best interest without worrying about the impact on a co-defendant.

The Public Defenders Office itself could only represent one defendant because of the same conflict of interest. So private attorneys, paid by the state for their work on this case, would be assigned to eight of the nine Girls Gone Wild employees.

After Meredith introduced himself he stepped aside and let Overstreet assign a private attorney. Only cameraman Charles Rapp would have a public defender as his lawyer: Brantley Clark Jr.

Clark, who would years later become circuit judge, was a burly man with thick eyebrows and forearms. He was not only physically imposing, but he also had a sharp legal mind which he disguised with a friendly and soft-spoken demeanor. Clark was as typical Bay County as Aaron Dyer was Southern California, and always looked ready to ditch his suit, grab a rifle and dive into the woods to hunt deer.

Rapp, who was 28 when he was arrested, was a part of the production crew, a "camera-toter" as one lawyer put it. He was trying to start up his own production company in New York when he was hired to do some work for Girls Gone Wild.

For doing one day of camera work and some odds and ends over a six-week stint in Panama City Beach, Rapp got charged with racketeering, conspiring to commit racketeering and two misdemeanors. He was looking at 30 years in prison.

Most people who are assigned a public defender think they'll get subpar legal service. Of course, the public defender's office is where many recently graduated law school students go for a first job. These fresh-faced, even pimply, kids are asked to stand with career criminals against 20-year prosecutors and state-minded judges.

But public defenders grow up fast, and they have an office full of experienced trial attorneys to help them. They have twice the caseload of a private attorney and half the chance of striking a favorable deal for their clients. Private attorneys lose money if they go to trial – it is essential to their reputations and their bottom line to be able to work out good deals.

Brantley Clark was a seasoned public defender. He worked evidence creatively and doggedly and even had a good trial record. So when he inherited Charles Rapp's case, he began working the evidence.

Rapp was the only Girls Gone Wild defendant to see his charges dropped. Prosecutor Mark Graham cut him loose in October 2004 after Rapp agreed to testify against his co-defendants if called upon.

Two weeks later, David Youngpeter, another "camera-toter," pleaded no contest to two misdemeanor charges – with his 30-year felonies dropped – in exchange for his testimony. Youngpeter was represented by Waylon Graham, one of the hardest-working, most expensive and personable private attorneys in the circuit.

Youngpeter only had to pay a $500 fine and Waylon Graham vowed to have his record expunged.

He said on the day the plea was signed that the prosecutor had to look at "the big picture" to realize that it was unfair to charge such "low-level" employees with 30-year racketeering charges.

Lead prosecutor Mark Graham probably was looking at the big picture when he worked out the plea agreements and that picture was of Joe Francis' smiling face. Graham was lining up the pawns to take down the king.

Every employee except Noah Tannenbaum and Mark Schmidt entered a plea before Joe Francis' case was over. None went to jail and all agreed to testify against Francis.

Tannenbaum spent only two weeks working for Girls Gone Wild before his arrest. At the time, he was a student at the University of Southern California, had already earned a Master's degree from the University of Florida and in 1999 was named an Anderson Scholar for Outstanding Academic Achievement. His stepfather, Harvey Watnick, a lawyer out of Miami, posted his $250,000 bond and represented him.

Tannenbaum was 24 at the time he was charged with racketeering, conspiring to engage in racketeering activity, conspiring to promote the sexual performance of a child, possessing to sell obscene material and several misdemeanors. His job at GGW had been to seek out girls in the crowd who might want to be in the videos, and he did a little camera work.

Watnick reluctantly agreed to talk to me after a bond hearing.

"Contributing to the delinquency of a minor," he read off one of the charges against Tannenbaum, his voice heavy with distress. "How can you have that on your resume?"

He said even the allegations were going to affect Tannenbaum's future.

"It was a fluke job," Watnick said. "He didn't have any experience working a camera. He was coached and given advice on what to do."

Four years later, Tannenbaum, even with his case still open and hanging over him, was able to move on. He got married, had a child and landed a good job. In 2008, after Francis resolved his criminal case, Tannenbaum entered a plea of no contest to a single misdemeanor count of contributing to the delinquency of a minor. He was sentenced to 60 days probation and a $500 fine. The state dropped all other charges.

• • •

On October 8, 2003, six girls filed suit in federal court against Joe Francis and Girls Gone Wild for child abuse. The complaint read: On March 31, four of the plaintiffs and an unidentified 16-year-old girl were stopped by a GGW van and solicited into flashing their breasts.

"Defendant Schmitz was then and there informed that the four girls who'd just flashed were under the age of 18." But, according to the lawsuit, the cameraman went ahead and offered to pay the girls to accompany him to a motel room where they'd be videotaped having sex with each other. They went to the motel, where Joe Francis met them.

Francis was then told the girls were underage, according to the lawsuit, but he ignored that fact and offered two of the girls $100 each to have sex with each other and allow a cameraman to film it.

Those two girls went with the cameraman to the bathroom. The girls disrobed and got into the shower together and the "shower scene" was born. Two other girls remained in the other room with Francis, who promptly offered them $50 each to masturbate him.

The four plaintiffs claimed child abuse, sexual promotion of children, racketeering, infliction of emotional pain and coercion into prostitution.

Panama City attorney Dixon Ross McCloy Jr., who never uses his first name and complained to me once that even his mother didn't know who I was talking about when I wrote out his full name in a story, filed the lawsuit along with Chicago attorney Tom Dent.

A few months later, a federal judge ordered that all work on the lawsuit come to a halt until the criminal case involving the same girls came to an end.

• • •

Well away from Panama City, in the early morning hours of January 22, 2004, Joe Francis became the victim of a crime himself. As he walked in his front door after a night out, a masked man with a gun came out of his kitchen.

Darnell Riley took Francis on a "shopping spree" in Francis' house, picking out things he wanted to steal and putting them into two designer bags. Riley then took Francis into a bedroom and with gun in one hand and a video recorder in the other, he made Francis lay face down on a bed, with his butt exposed, a sex toy next to him and tell the camera that he liked taking it in the ass. Riley then demanded $300,000 or he'd put the video on the internet.

Riley wasn't caught until almost a year later, though for the next six months he called Francis and tried to extort money from him. Riley was caught when Paris Hilton, Francis' ex-girlfriend, overheard some people talking about the incident at a party.

Riley was arrested and charged with burglary, robbery, kidnapping, extortion and carjacking. Convicted at trial, he was sentenced to 10 years in prison.

Chapter 6

"Insidious and depraved"

The afternoon of March 3, 2004, Circuit Judge Michael Overstreet had a sentencing scheduled before hearing the first of the key motions in the Girls Gone Wild case. Off the bench, Overstreet was soft-spoken, cerebral and deeply Zen man who took Chinese herbal supplements to ward off disease. He stayed slim by climbing mountains and paddling a kayak around the bay on weekends.

On the bench, Overstreet was a patient judge as long as the lawyers worked on his schedule. He expected them there on time and ready the minute he was.

On this day, George Thrasher, a thoroughly pathetic old man, was in Overstreet's court for sentencing on 78 counts of possessing child pornography.

Overstreet had thought long and hard about Thrasher's sentence and had written what he wanted to say. Now, he leaned forward and looked down from the bench. His voice cracked with emotion and he stared hard at the stooped, thin, graying man standing before him.

"When evaluating the shortcomings of the human condition it's difficult to find more insidious and depraved behavior than the child porn trade," he said.

"I saw these pictures," Overstreet continued. "There were babies, infants, adolescents in these photographs. And what I found incredible was, almost to the last child, their eyes gave away everything.

"I saw horror in their eyes. I saw their fear, their physical pain – physical pain. And I saw the look of betrayal in their eyes."

Thrasher was looking at a maximum sentence of five years in prison for each charge – 390 years total. He was remarkably unfazed.

His attorney argued that the Websites that produced the images were still in business, still producing photos that could be accessed by anyone with a computer.

Overstreet said customers like Thrasher kept the child pornography business thriving.

"No one who intentionally participates in this market, either as a producer or a consumer such as Mr. Thrasher is entitled to anything less than the most severe sanction this court can lawfully impose."

Thrasher was looking at 390 years in prison and that's what he got. It was the longest sentence ever handed down by a Bay County judge. In Bay County, they don't expect a defendant to be able to complete a sentence like that, only do the best they can.

In the hallway outside the courtroom, the Girls Gone Wild defense team waited.

They stood in a circle in an alcove that had photographs of the circuit judges going back to the late 1800s. Tall, lanky Aaron Dyer was at the center of the team, directing the conversation in his easy, comfortable way. He was dressed for court, gray suit, yellow tie, briefcase, but as always he gave off an impression of such ease that he could have been arriving at a small get-together with friends.

I walked out of the courtroom, having covered Thrasher's sentencing for the next day's newspaper. I needed a break before changing gears for the GGW hearing.

"Be careful," I told Dyer. "He just sentenced a guy to 390 years in prison."

"What was the charge?" Dyer asked.

"Possession of child pornography."

"I think we'll tread as lightly as possible," Dyer said.

Dyer was preparing to argue the first big motion in the criminal case. He wanted the judge to acknowledge that there was no law in Florida prohibiting the public exhibition of female breasts, even underage female breasts.

It was a theory that he'd broached early in the proceedings, but now the defense had run into a stone wall and they needed a ruling. The lawyers wanted to have copies of videotapes. The sheriff's office and prosecutors were refusing, saying most of the tapes were contraband – obscene material or child pornography that they couldn't legally copy and disseminate.

The only way to resolve the matter was have Overstreet decide what was illegal about the tapes.

"If it's a minor it doesn't matter," Dyer said in an earlier hearing. "It doesn't become child pornography when you're just dealing with nudity."

Overstreet had previously rejected that argument, but he'd left the door open for the lawyers to raise it again. Five months later, the lawyers were ready to do just that.

The Thrasher crowd cleared out and Dyer led his group in. Overstreet returned to the bench and looked down at the group. He was composed and at ease. The Thrasher sentencing was behind him and he'd moved on.

Dyer started the hearing by saying the issue had already been decided by a federal judge in Orlando, who ruled in a GGW lawsuit that there was no law in Florida that made simple public nudity, above the waist, illegal even if the one who was nude was younger than 18.

The nudity had to be accompanied by some act that could be considered sexual conduct.

Overstreet asked prosecutor Dustin Stephenson about the statute, which was pretty clear in stating that there had to be some kind of touching associated with the exposed breasts to make it illegal.

Stephenson, who was filling in for lead prosecutor Mark Graham, acknowledged that there was no touching, but argued that the circumstances were sexually suggestive.

"We're talking about more than just a sterile viewing of the female breast," he said.

Dyer showed Overstreet the video at the center of the hearing. It showed the cameraman's first meeting with the four girls who would later go to the Chateau Motel and become the center of the criminal case. He was trying to get one of them to flash. Her friends, in the background, harassed and teased her about how willing she is to expose herself in other situations.

Dyer said he needed to have that tape so the audio could be enhanced. For one thing, he said, the girl lied about her age to the cameraman, claiming to be 18. It's defense evidence, Dyer said, and he wants to be able to examine it outside the watchful eyes of deputies.

Overstreet didn't rule that day. He said he wanted a chance to review the law and arguments.

Less than a week later, he issued an order in favor of the defense. The wording of the ruling indicated that he wasn't happy with what he had to do. He wrote that there were harmful consequences to a minor who has been videotaped this way and an argument could be made that there should be a law against it.

"To date, our Legislature has elected not to criminalize the promotion or possession of images of this nature," Overstreet wrote in his ruling.

"This is a really big ruling for the case," Dyer told me a short time later. "It eliminates 90-percent of the state's so-called evidence.

"Eventually, I'm sure this will lead to motions to dismiss charges. But the real issue is that the main charge brought by the state, the racketeering charge, is based upon conduct that is entirely legitimate. When a girl lies about her age and flashes for the camera, the cameraman and the company have no liability whatsoever."

Actually, the ruling had very little immediate impact on the case. Dyer didn't even ask for the tape.

But he made the most of the positive press, to the point where Mark Graham felt the need to write a letter warning him that talking about the material facts in a pending case could lead to serious consequences.

Graham sent the letter to judges and lawyers in town, but not Dyer. He knew, eventually, the letter would make it to the newspaper. And it did.

"I'd like to comment on the letter, David," Dyer told me when I called for a quote, "but I haven't seen it."

His interviews on national television seemed to indicate that the ruling was essential, but Dyer didn't asked for any of the charges to be dropped.

"You're going to drop the flashing charges?" I asked Mark Graham sometime later. We were in court for a case that had nothing to do with Girls Gone Wild, but Joe Francis had been placed on the docket for that afternoon. Placed, then removed. That had happened more than once in the months following Judge Overstreet's ruling.

Graham said it bothered him that he wouldn't be able to pursue charges against Francis that involved underage girls exposing themselves to the cameras in public.

Many, many charges would have to be abandoned. Graham recognized this, but reluctantly. Then he shrugged off those thoughts and got back to the conversation.

"We're going to concentrate on the filming in the motel room."

"But you're going to drop the flashing charges?"

"We're going to concentrate on the filming in the room," he said again, making it clear that I could ask the question all day and he'd answer it the same way every time.

"Is Francis charged with a lewd and lascivious, with the two girls that he paid?"

"No. He's charged with soliciting minors for prostitution."

"Why not? I figured L and L was a given because of the contact."

Lewd and lascivious is, essentially, sexual contact between an adult and a minor. Ignorance of age isn't a defense.

"L and L applies to victims under 16. The girls in the room were both 17," Graham said. "Even the soliciting charge has some interesting legal argument. Apparently, the language applies to a third person, like a pimp, soliciting a minor for prostitution with someone else."

"This case is full of interesting arguments," I said.

"Yeah, for you," he said, walking away.

In July 2004, the circuit judges had a redistribution of cases. Instead of two judges handling all of the felony cases in Bay County, four judges would now split the duties.

Judge Dedee Costello, who had until then been on the civil forfeiture case, also took over the Girls Gone Wild criminal case from Judge Overstreet.

The switch from Overstreet to Costello was more than just a name change.

Overstreet had been on the criminal bench for a little less than two years. He'd spent most of his career presiding over civil cases, which is usually more orderly, predictable and cerebral than criminal court. Overstreet was certainly a thinker, but he was also more emotional than Costello – especially when it came to matters dealing with children.

At the time of the GGW case, Overstreet was in his second marriage. His first wife died tragically, leaving him to care for their daughter. A few years later he met Paula Barbieri, the one-time girlfriend of O.J. Simpson. The mountain climbing, boyish-looking Overstreet and the beautiful model started an odd-couple relationship that led to marriage and another daughter.

Overstreet was a man surrounded by and protective of women.

He was also unpredictable on the bench.

In 2004, Overstreet did the unthinkable in Bay County – he gave a man convicted of first-degree murder and facing the death penalty a new trial. Unthinkable because the normal course of action for local judges was to deny controversial motions and send them on to the appeals court. If the ruling was overturned, the local judge – who is an elected official – could blame the "liberal" appeals court.

After the ruling, defense attorney Walter Smith – who spent more than a decade specializing in defending accused murderers – said he'd experienced two firsts that day: He'd never had a local judge grant him a new trial and he'd never before been struck speechless by a ruling.

Costello was also a smart judge, but many Panama City defense attorneys thought of Costello as a "second prosecutor" in the courtroom. For many years, she was also the judge in the circuit that was most often overturned by the appeals court.

Costello was the first woman to practice law in Bay County. She came to the area in 1962 from Miami and took the bench in 1981 – becoming the first woman judge in the circuit.

Costello's behavior in trial was legendary. She would roll her eyes and cough in her fist if she thought the defense attorney's opening argument was ridiculous. She'd glare pointedly at the prosecutor if he didn't object to a defense line of questioning and was known to make her own objections if the prosecutor was reluctant.

Costello was known for issuing the maximum sentence to defendants who took their cases to trial – especially if their defense was weak. If they wasted her time, she'd make them pay at sentencing.

Costello once sentenced a man to five years in prison for stealing a monkey from a zoo. At his sentencing, Costello heard from the monkey's owner that the animal was now afraid of the dark and had suffered emotional trauma from the incident. Costello gave the maximum sentence for stealing a monkey, saying in her ruling that she was doing it, in part, because of the monkey's distressed state.

Costello was not afraid of controversy and could make tough rulings when properly convinced. She was one of the most prepared judges in the circuit when she came into a hearing and up to date on changes in the law.

Joe Francis was facing a judge who would throw the book at him – possibly sentencing him to every one of the 300-some years he was facing.

• • •

On July 30, 2004, the Federal Trade Commission sent out a press release saying Francis and Girls Gone Wild paid $1,089,627 in fines and reparation to consumers. The FTC said beginning in 2000, some customers had been put on a continuity program without their knowledge after they'd purchased a DVD. It meant that they'd receive a new GGW video every month and the cost was automatically charged to their credit or debit card.

The FTC said many of these customers didn't agree to a continuity program and GGW didn't clearly explain the program before signing them up. The settlement required GGW to pay $548,392 to these consumers. It also resolved the case without anyone admitting they did anything wrong.

• • •

2004 was State Attorney Jim Appleman's last year in office after holding the position for 24 years. He announced his retirement in 2002, well before the GGW case began, but he'd hoped to make Joe Francis' trial the exclamation point on his career. He took an active role in the case late in 2003 and early 2004, but when it became clear that the trial wouldn't happen in '04, he backed out.

"They came to me and said they'd go ahead and plea him out," Appleman said of Francis' defense attorneys. "But it would be for a misdemeanor and no jail time. I told them, 'Bullshit.' So they told me they didn't care because they wouldn't take the case to trial while I was in office anyway."

Assistant State Attorney Steve Meadows was running against defense attorney Martha "Sister" Blackmon-Milligan in a nasty race to take Appleman's office.

Meadows was a good trial attorney and for some years had been responsible for prosecuting high-profile cases.

Many of the prosecutors were intimidated by Milligan and vowed not to work for her.

I called Aaron Dyer. He said, on the record, that the defense had been busy with the discovery and wasn't purposely stalling to await the result of the election.

"Now, off the record, how did that sound to you?"

"Well," I said, "it was politically well spoken and makes perfect sense, but I think it's a load of horseshit."

Dyer was laughing before I finished.

"Yeah," was as close as he came to confirming my assertion. "We can't control what goes on with the election and how it will affect this case. I don't know if it will make any difference who gets elected, whether it's Steve or Sister."

Milligan was getting a lot of money from out of the state, even California, but none of it suggested ties to GGW.

She'd also been on Meadows' case from the beginning about his record as a prosecutor – that he made too many deals, especially for the right people. It was politics, but it put Meadows in an interesting position when it came to how he would be able to resolve GGW if he got elected.

Lawyers both in and out of the prosecutors' office were talking about how weak the case was. They thought Meadows, if elected, wouldn't hesitate to drop it.

But the case was one of the most notable and expensive in county history. Just dropping it could be food for Milligan if she wanted another try in 2008.

The race didn't turn publicly dirty until the News Herald interviewed both candidates in October. The editors made a decision to do a series of articles, letting the candidates say what they wanted and getting out as cleanly as possible. Behind the scenes, both candidates had been saying some pretty nasty stuff about each other.

Meadows came first, meeting with me and two editors in a small meeting room off the newsroom floor. Meadows is about 6-foot-1 and his weight fluctuates wildly from around 220 to 260, depending on how many lunch meetings he's having.

When giving interviews, Meadows would sometimes adopt a soft tone of voice as if he was explaining everything to an easily spooked 6-year-old.

The 90-minute interview was little more than rhetoric.

Milligan insisted on being called "Sister" and asked the paper to just call her Sister, instead of Milligan, when they did stories on her.

About 5-foot-7 and sturdily-built, with short blonde hair, Milligan owned and rode horses regularly. She was a formidable woman: fierce, intelligent, direct and persistent. People regularly gave her what she wanted because they knew they would have to eventually.

The interviews produced two fairly interesting topics, both dealing with spouse abuse. Sister accused Meadows of hitting his first wife. Meadows said Sister had choked down her ex-husband in his office.

The incident with Meadows' first wife was documented in his 1977 divorce papers. He apparently hit her in the chest with a pager during an argument. Meadows denied that he ever "hit" a woman.

"Are we gonna let the race denigrate to this level?" Meadows asked in response to the question about the domestic violence. "Am I going to bring in an affidavit from somebody who says they had to call the police because Sister was choking her ex-husband down in the law office? I could do that, but I don't want to do that because this race is more important than denigrating it with that kind of mud that has nothing to do with our professional record."

That was typical Steve Meadows, throwing out obvious accusations, while at the same time trying to claim the moral high ground.

Milligan denied choking her ex-husband, former State Attorney Leo Jones.

"Whoever was saying I choked my husband is lying," she declared. She threatened lawsuits.

Jones, however, was more amused than intimidated by Milligan's threats.

"It did happen. The story is legendary," he said. The interview with him was by phone and Jones was in his home, which was apparently filled with exotic birds. They squawked, chirped and talked constantly in the background.

He said she didn't exactly choke him, but grabbed him around the neck and bent him backwards over his desk. It happened while they were discussing the dissolution of their marriage.

"She's a strong woman," Jones said. "I wasn't concerned about her getting hurt and me getting blamed for it, I was concerned about getting hurt."

Jones then asked about Milligan's wealth. She'd placed her worth in the millions in tax documents.

"How'd she get all that money?" he asked.

"I figured she got it from you," I said.

"Not me. That's why she was so mad. We had an ironclad prenuptial agreement."

In November, Meadows won by roughly 3,500 votes out of about 70,000 cast. There were also 3,500 people who declined to vote for either candidate. In interviews outside polling stations, many people said the race was just too dirty.

• • •

In 2005, Joe Francis turned 32. His attorneys in Los Angeles and Tallahassee were working his state criminal and federal civil cases without much interference from him.

In Northwest Florida, 2005 was all about hurricanes. Four hit the northern Gulf coast, including Katrina which flooded New Orleans and sent thousands of refugees into Panama City.

December ended with a small group of residents calling the News Herald to make sure we would be adhering to a strictly Christian observation of the holidays – namely that we would have the words "Merry Christmas" across the front page on December 25.

Executive Editor Phil Lucas found the calls amusing at first, until they showed an organized effort on somebody's part. Lucas assured the callers that the paper had no policy on the banner, which had been Merry Christmas for a few consecutive years.

He told callers that a decision on the wording would be made at the appropriate time.

On the big day, the newspaper ran "Peace on Earth" in Arabic script, something the copy desk found hilarious.

The Girls Gone Wild case was showing no movement in court, but things were happening behind the scenes. The lawyers were busy scheduling, then canceling depositions.

On January 19, 2006, an assembly of judges, lawyers and dignitaries gathered at the Martin Theater in downtown Panama City. Federal judges in black robes sat on the theater's secondary stage, called the Backdoor Theater, while several hundred spectators filled the rows of seats towering over the stage. Richard Smoak, a longtime civil lawyer, former Green Beret and Vietnam War veteran, was scheduled to be sworn in as Panama City's first sitting federal judge. Judge M. Casey Rodgers, whose office was in Pensacola, about 100 miles to the west, sat in the front row of the judges. This should have been a joyous day for Rodgers, who would certainly see her trips to Panama City cut down significantly, but Rodgers looked bored and annoyed throughout the process.

An investiture is like a judicial roast, followed by a ceremonial robing and oath of office.

"I set out to find something humorous about Dick. I called lawyers and even secretaries and there was nothing. Absolutely nothing," Ross McCloy told the gathering. "Dick, some of them wouldn't even return the call. Most lawyers would tell you that Dick is as naturally funny as a colonoscopy."

McCloy read the letter he wrote to President George W. Bush recommending Smoak's appointment as federal judge, but then spent the rest of the ceremony trying to find something funny to say about a man who, by almost all accounts, did and said nothing funny.

McCloy said that Smoak's cleanliness and posture made him an ideal candidate for federal judge.

"He was born standing at attention," McCloy said.

Smoak smiled, laughed and seemed fairly comfortable.

"Welcome aboard," U.S. District Judge Robert Hinkle told Smoak. "I knew when I heard about your appointment that you'd be a wonderful judge and would fit right in. I didn't realize until I heard the remarks of Mr. McCloy that you are a humorless dullard like the rest of us."

• • •

On August 1, 2005, Pam Smoak died. She was a tall, determined woman with piercing eyes under wavy white hair, but she softened tremendously when she smiled. She and Richard Smoak had met and married in the 1970s and raised two daughters together, which spoke volumes for the type of man Richard Smoak was. Pam Smoak was not the type to suffer fools.

She'd worked in the State Attorney's Office for 20 years and had considered running for the top spot until cancer rearranged her life. Even from her deathbed, she was directing the creation and organization of the Gulf Coast Children's Advocacy Center, where victims of abuse would be cared for.

After her death, now-Federal Judge Richard Smoak continued to work and take his usual miles-long walks at a military pace along Panama City's most scenic street, Beach Drive, which is bordered by magnificent homes on one side and St. Andrew Bay on the other. But now he kept his eyes fixed ahead of him during these walks, and stomped the pavement as if he was trying to level the ground.

• • •

The evening of January 26, 2006, I was playing poker with a group of lawyers when I overheard a conversation between two attorneys about Joe Francis' state criminal case.

"What nixed the plea?" someone asked.

Those words got my attention. I hadn't heard of a plea. I hadn't heard of a plea offer.

Turns out, the deal was supposed to have gone through that afternoon.

The prosecutors' office had even scheduled a celebration at a downtown restaurant. They kept the date, even though the plea had fallen through. When I called Joe Grammer, the office spokesman, it was obvious that he was at his daughter's soccer game.

"So Joe, what killed the Joe Francis plea?"

"The family," he said.

"The victims' family?" I asked

"If you want to call them that," he said. "Seems they've hired a publicist."

The rest of what he said was drowned out by the roar of the crowd. Somebody must have scored.

"You'll have plenty to write about when the motions start getting filed," he said. "Looks like a trial is unavoidable at this point."

I hung up and turned back to the poker table.

Chapter 7

Forward again

They had threatened to go to Oprah.

In March 2006, Joe Francis' lawyer, Tom Julin, filed a motion in the federal lawsuit accusing Panama City lawyer Ross McCloy and Chicago attorney Tom Dent of sabotaging the plea in the state criminal case to keep the upper hand in the lawsuit.

Francis had worked out a plea and was on his way to Panama City in January 2006 to enter into it, when the deal suddenly fell apart.

Dent, Julin said, wanted the criminal case in place so he could use it as leverage in negotiations for a multi-million dollar settlement.

Julin said Dent called him in March and offered his clients' help with Francis' criminal problems in exchange for several million dollars.

Julin also included Dent's Panama City law partner in this case into his motion –McCloy, a respected lawyer in the area and the judge's close personal friend.

On April 28, 2006, federal Judge Richard Smoak convened a hearing to hear Julin's argument. The hearing started poorly for Julin and only got worse.

Smoak entered the courtroom and took his seat. Close-cropped salt-and-pepper hair framed a square face. He favored bow ties, often in reds or yellows, that perched over black judicial robes. The robes were fitted to Smoak's blocky frame and didn't swish as he entered the room. Smoak wasn't a swishy kind of person, and he took his seat quickly without looking at the assembly.

A lawyer for 32 years and a life-long military man in thought and actions, Smoak took matters of honor and decorum very seriously.

Smoak had been on the bench for less than a year when he was assigned Joe Francis and the Girls Gone Wild lawsuit.

"I'm very concerned," Smoak repeated numerous times at the end of the 2006 hearing. He was concerned by Julin's motion, which accused Dent and McCloy of some serious ethical failings. And he was concerned by the lack of evidence Julin produced at the four-hour hearing, especially the fact that Julin didn't call any of the prosecutors to the stand to back up his allegation.

Dent denied threatening the prosecutors. He said it was actually one of his client's parents who told the State Attorney's Office that she'd take her complaints to Oprah Winfrey if they went through with the plea.

Dent said he'd heard that prosecutors Mark Graham and Larry Basford had agreed to throw out all the felony charges against Francis if he'd cop out to a single misdemeanor. The family member was outraged that the State Attorney's Office would offer such a favorable deal.

State Attorney spokesman Joe Grammer denied that to me. He said at least one of the 42 felonies was included in the deal.

Whatever the case, at the end of the day, Smoak denied Julin's motion to disqualify McCloy and Dent.

He then asked Julin's law partner, Barry Davidson, if their firm had an ethics board. Davidson said he was in charge of that board.

Smoak instructed Davidson to take a close look at Julin's actions and review them for ethical violations.

He then went a giant step further. He re-opened the civil case and told the lawyers they were going to get this case resolved.

The lawsuit had been put on hold in November 2003 so the criminal case could be resolved without interference from the civil lawyers. But as the criminal case dragged into its third year, Dent became restless.

He asked three times for the stay to be lifted so they could resolve the lawsuit. He punctuated his most ardent motion by saying he had a client that was so distraught by the long stay that she'd cut her wrists and had to be rushed to the hospital.

Two federal judges, Smoak and U.S. District Judge M. Casey Rodgers, both denied his requests to re-open the case.

But after Julin's motion, Smoak's irritation with Francis' lawyer carried over to this other issue and, without being asked again, Smoak said "We'll get this case on the road."

That decision probably had less to do with Julin questioning his opponents' integrity and more with the way Julin wrote his motion – and the fact that Smoak's clerks had told him that I knew about the motion in advance and was waiting for its arrival on the day it was filed.

To Judge Smoak, it looked like smear tactics.

Smoak's voice became menacing when he asked if Julin or anyone associated with his defense team had tipped the media to the pending motion.

Julin said he hadn't and couldn't say if someone else had.

He hadn't. Dyer had called me the day the motion was to be filed and tip-toed around the issue.

He called while I was engrossed in a story about red snapper regulations in the upcoming fishing season. I answered the phone automatically, but was really concentrating on the snapper story. These things can be somewhat complicated.

"Did I catch you at a bad time?" Dyer asked after several minutes of a fairly one-sided conversation. I was hesitant to tell him what I was so distracted by – I felt I should have a better excuse.

"No, no. Just working on a story. I'll get out of it."

"I can call you back," Dyer said, his voice carrying that ever-present note of humor.

"No, no. I'm okay now. What's up?"

He wouldn't tell me what was in the motion, but said it had to do with the plea agreement.

"Check out the motion," Dyer said. "I think you'll find it interesting."

Julin had devoted six pages to blasting the alleged victims' character and reliability as witnesses. He wrote that the girls were changing their stories now, making them seem more like victims.

In the beginning, three, possibly four of the girls admitted lying to a cameraman about their age and signing a release saying they were 18. Now they were backtracking, saying the cameraman made them lie.

Julin wrote that Girls Gone Wild was the real victim here – victims of fraud.

A year later, over blackened tuna and fried oysters on the deck at Uncle Ernie's restaurant in Panama City, Dyer and Mantra corporate attorney Michael Burke talked about the real issue behind that motion.

McCloy's law partner was Franklin Harrison, who was representing the Sheriff's Office in the forfeiture issue with Joe Francis. Burke said McCloy and Dent got access to the Sheriff's Office's files through Harrison and were able to add three plaintiffs by going through investigative files.

Not only that, when the plea deal was set to happen, McCloy sent notice to the Sheriff's Office and State Attorney's Office that they would require those agencies to keep all their records to be turned over to the plaintiffs as soon as they resolved the criminal case.

The notice was significant in its timing because there was a stay on discovery in the case. Burke said that meant nothing was supposed to happen. He said it looked more like the plaintiffs were trying to intimidate law enforcement into canceling the deal.

McCloy said at the hearing that they were just making sure the Sheriff's Office and State Attorney's Office didn't dispose of valuable records after resolving the case.

Julin's motion, however, continued to irk Smoak even a year later, when he put Francis in jail for contempt of court.

Chapter 8

"Aaron Dyer was giddy"

Aaron Dyer called again when I was deep in thought, but this time I was working on a GGW story. A big one.

"Watcha doin'? Workin' on anything interesting? Got any hot stories goin' on out there?"

"You're giddy. I'm gonna write that in the story: 'Aaron Dyer was giddy.'"

"That's how most people describe me: giddy," he laughed.

Dyer had every right to be happy. It was July 25, 2006, and Circuit Judge Dedee Costello had just thrown out all the evidence the Bay County Sheriff's Office gathered in raids of the condominiums. The videos, which made up all the tangible evidence, were gone.

If the State Attorney's Office wanted to go forward, it would have to rely heavily on the testimony of victims who they were quickly losing faith in.

"They've got problems of their own with the girls in this case," Dyer said.

He refused to give me anything good for the next day's story. He knew he was close to ending this case and he would do nothing to upset that.

"When this is all over, we'll sit down and chat," he said.

The next day would decide a lot about how the criminal case would play out.

When I called State Attorney Steve Meadows he sounded relieved that it might be over.

A plea was the prosecutor's last best chance to justify three years of expense and investigation.

Girls Gone Wild was the most voluminous, most talked-about case in Bay County history. It seemed so close to resolution, no one could have imagined that the case would drag on another three years.

The next day, Judge Costello signed and released her official ruling. The order itself was written by Aaron Dyer and Larry Simpson. It was scathing.

"All I want to know," I told Dyer, "is who wrote the inflammatory things about Richard Bagwell."

Sheriff's Investigator Bagwell had been in charge of the investigation and had applied for the warrants at the time of Francis' arrest to search the four condos being used by Girls Gone Wild employees.

The defense motions were strongly worded concerning Bagwell's warrants, but the order was brutal. The judge said that either Bagwell had lied to the judge who signed the warrants – which, by the way, had been Costello and County Judge Elijah Smiley – or had been recklessly unconcerned by the facts.

"That was the court's wording," Dyer answered. "Well, most of it was taken from the motions."

Under Florida law, there have to be at least two criminal incidents to support a probable cause affidavit for racketeering. Prosecutors were saying that Francis had supplemented the legal part of his video business by targeting minors to include in the tapes.

So when Bagwell applied for a search warrant alleging Girls Gone Wild was involved in racketeering by selling videotapes that included underage girls – basically they were selling child pornography – he was telling the judge he had allegations of at least two incidents where cameramen had taped underage girls in sexual situations.

Problem was, he didn't have two. He had one – the shower scene. The other allegation, that Francis had paid two girls to masturbate him, was never videotaped.

The judge was saying if Bagwell knew there was only one tape and told the signing judge – her – there were two, he was intentionally misleading the court. If Bagwell had mistakenly told her there were two tapes, she said, he was being reckless with the facts.

Either way, one tape was not enough to justify a search of the condos for evidence of racketeering. Therefore anything that came out of that search was inadmissible.

There went the evidence.

When Dyer called me at the office he was just fishing for my take on the story. He called back a few hours later in full quote mode, meaning he had planned out a series of useless statements that would do nothing to illuminate the issues. He started off with a bland, monotone, obviously rehearsed explanation of where the case would go from this point forward.

"You're talking like I'm looking for a quote. You think I'm quoting you, right?" I asked.

"Did you already put your story to bed?" he asked. "Good. That's what I was hoping for."

I was actually out walking my dog, Hiaasen, a 5-year-old, 95-pound German shepherd who was trudging through the late afternoon heat.

"He smells like cats," a 10-year-old boy said, coming up to pet the dog.

"He smells like cats?" I asked, moving the cell phone away from my mouth. "He should smell like dirty dog, because that's what he is."

I got back into my conversation with Dyer.

"Sorry," I said, "my dog gets a lot of attention when we take walks."

"Now I can tell you what's really going to happen next," Dyer said. He thought there were going to be some charges that would survive the motion, but probably none of the felonies.

As Hiaasen sniffed around the base of a telephone pole, I told Dyer that Meadows thought the felony charges of promoting the sexual performance of a child could be proved through testimony only.

Dyer said he was going to look at that next, but thought that charge would go away too. The only counts that might survive, he said, were the ones dealing with the two girls who Francis had paid to masturbate him. They'd always been based solely on testimony.

The girls, though, were killing their own case by changing their testimony to improve their standing in the lawsuit. But the more they tried to boost the suit the more damage they did to both the criminal and civil cases.

I finally pried Hiaasen away from the telephone pole and we continued walking through the waves of late afternoon heat. We both kept our heads down as we moved, both eager to return to the air conditioning.

A few months later, and a few degrees cooler, on December 4, prosecutor Mark Graham filed his answer to Aaron Dyer's and Larry Simpson's motion to dismiss the charges.

He admitted he didn't have the evidence to go forward with 32 of the 42 criminal charges. But said there were four charges of using minors in sexual performances and four charges of promoting the use of minors in sexual performances, eight felonies, all dealing with the shower scene, he thought he could take to trial.

The first four, the use of minors charges, Graham said, were his strongest.

He said the promoting charge had a stronger definition of sexual performance and he might have to call cameraman Mark Schmitz, who was charged along with Francis, and an unnamed photographer to testify that they witnessed the shower scene. He argued that an audience of two or three could support the elements of a performance.

Larry Simpson fired back two weeks later with his own written reply. He again argued that all the charges should be tossed. He then said that Graham's desire to convince Schmitz, who had not resolved his own case and was, at that point, not in a position to testify without incriminating himself, and the photographer to testify wasn't a good enough reason for the judge to let Graham keep those charges.

Simpson said the girls shouldn't even be allowed to testify now because they'd been shown the tape to refresh their memories, and their testimony would now be tainted by illegally obtained evidence.

The sides returned again to the issue of strict liability – whether ignorance of age was a defense against these remaining charges. Graham cited three cases which, in no uncertain language, supported his claims that ignorance was not a defense.

Simpson, however, said Graham's cases preceded a 2004 Florida Supreme Court ruling that said all strict liability crimes must be stated as such in the statute. If use or promotion of a minor in a sexual performance doesn't specifically classify itself as strict liability, then it wasn't.

Right before Christmas, I got word that Judge Costello was planning to issue a written order on the dismissals.

I stopped by her chambers to see her. She was doing a small, understated salsa dance in front of a tiny CD player on a table behind her desk and singing quietly in Spanish. She was in a festive mood from the prospect of a weeklong winter's break.

"I just stopped by to see how my favorite judge was doing," I said.

"Fine," she said without hesitation. "What do you want?"

"You think you might have an order for me this week?"

"You've got spies everywhere," she said. "Who told you I was going to have an order."

I just shrugged

"Was it across the street?" she asked, pointing to the State Attorney's Office. "I know it didn't come from (Simpson in) Tallahassee. Or did it?"

"You got a 50/50 chance of getting it right."

"Hmph," she uttered, giving me a sideways glance. "If I get something done today, you'll be the first to know."

"I doubt that, but I wouldn't mind being one of the first to know."

"We'll call you."

• • •

Even while the criminal case was falling apart, the man who started it all – Panama City Beach Mayor Lee Sullivan – was running for state representative and his supporters were circulating a flier touting Sullivan's famous 2003 verbal battle with Francis.

"When the porn peddlers known as 'Girls Gone Wild' arrived in Panama City to take advantage of our young women Lee Sullivan told them where they could go … Straight to Jail!" shouted a circular distributed by Panhandle Veterans. "And they got his message. Lee's tough, swift action got these predators out of our community. There's no place in our town for immoral pornographers who try to exploit young women. And thanks to Lee Sullivan anyone who participates in this ungodly behavior will find themselves behind bars."

Sullivan was pictured in a stark white cowboy hat pulled down low over his brow. On the front of the flier was a sad looking little girl clutching a Teddy bear.

• • •

"Joe Francis, the founder of the 'Girls Gone Wild' empire, is humiliating me. He has my face pressed against the hood of a car, my arms twisted hard behind my back. He's pushing himself against me shouting: 'This is what they did to me in Panama City!'"

That was Claire Hoffman's experience with Joe Francis in the summer of 2006 and the first words of a story she wrote about it in August 2006. At the time, Hoffman was an entertainment reporter for the Los Angeles Times and had traveled with Francis for a short time as he did his thing.

It was pretty obvious that three years after his arrest, Francis was still pretty angry about it. Hoffman's article was titled "Joe Francis: 'Baby, give me a kiss'."

"He snatches at my notebook. He is amped, his broad face sneering as he does a sort of boxer's skip around me, jabbering, grabbing at my arms and stomach as I try to move away, clutching my notebook to my chest. He stabs a finger in my face, shouting, 'You don't care about the First Amendment. I care about the First Amendment, but you are the kind of reporter who doesn't care.'"

Hoffman caught Francis at the turn of his career, when he was transitioning into mainstream industries. His companies were still being funded by the aggressive distribution of soft-core pornography, but Francis was starting a line of clothing, backing a movie and opening a string of restaurants.

But all the while Francis was still working the nightclubs and traveling with cameramen.

Chapter 9

Respect for the law

Judge Smoak ordered Joe Francis to be at the Panama City federal courthouse for the sentencing of his production company, Mantra Films Inc., in December 2006. The judge said it would instill in him some respect for the law.

The company had agreed to a deal before it had even been indicted on charges that it failed to keep the proper paperwork showing that the girls in its sexually explicit videos were of legal age. The lawyers had been told the indictment was coming, so they worked out a plea as quickly as possible. In the federal system, the faster a defendant admits guilt the lighter the sentence.

Mantra President Scott Barbour had been designated as the company's representative, but Smoak wanted Francis to be present at the hearing. Mantra lawyer Michael Burke said later that Smoak's request was improper because Francis wasn't a defendant in the case. Burke said they could have simply kept Francis at home and the judge wouldn't have been able to do anything, but they agreed to the judge's request.

Joe Francis walked into the tiny six-pew courtroom on the second floor of the Panama City federal courthouse and looked for a place to sit. He went to his right and inched past an AP reporter and took an empty spot next to her and in front of me. She slowly turned her head and shot me a grin over her shoulder.

One of Francis' lawyers spotted him in the audience and motioned him forward. He got up and was passing through the knee-high swinging gate when a bailiff stopped him.

"You can't sit up there," the bailiff said. "That area's just for lawyers and defendants. Are you a defendant?"

"No," Francis answered.

"Then you can't sit there. You have to sit out here," the bailiff said.

Francis inched his way back down the row and returned to his seat, but before he'd settled onto the wooden bench another bailiff came through the gate.

"You have to sit up here," the second bailiff told Francis, indicating the defendant's table where Francis had been going seconds before.

"He's not a lawyer and he's not a defendant," the first bailiff said to the second. "He can't sit up there."

"He has to. The judge said he wants him sitting at the defendant's table."

"But he's not a lawyer and he's not a defendant."

Aaron Dyer, who was preparing some paperwork at a podium, looked around for Francis and cut the bailiffs' conversation off.

"Where's Mr. Francis?" he asked. "He has to come up here."

The second bailiff eyed the first as he held the gate open for Francis to walk through.

"He's not a lawyer and he's not a defendant," the first bailiff said, but the fight had gone out of his voice. He turned and walked to a chair at the back of the room.

Judge Smoak came through a door behind the judge's bench. He took his seat and called for Dyer, Larry Simpson and the Girls Gone Wild company officers to come to the podium. Smoak never commented on the fact that Francis had shown up 10 minutes late.

Assistant U.S. Attorney Dixie Morrow got things started.

"We're here, your honor, because the federal law intends to protect sometimes 17-year-olds against their own impulses;

requires people like Mantra Films and Mr. Francis to make sure that they are old enough to do what they are being filmed doing," she told Smoak.

"We ask the court to keep in mind, your honor, that this isn't just a one-time proverbial big mistake. This is not just an aberration."

There were others, several others who had been filmed when they were underage. Some had made it into videos that were then sold worldwide.

Morrow told Smoak that he had a statement from one of the 17-year-olds who had been filmed and he could see for himself how her life had been impacted. This girl would file her own lawsuit against Francis a year later, known as the "Plaintiff B" lawsuit.

"At the young age of 17" the statement from a girl identified only as B.S. started, "I was manipulated and deceived and ultimately exposed sexually. To this day I am tormented by the event and have suffered from feelings of shame, guilt and even social anxiety.

"Since the release of the video I have endured a tremendous amount of humiliation because of the way friends and family saw me portrayed. It was difficult for them to look at me the same way and it has taken years to restore those relationships – relationships that are special and dear to my heart.

"Years have gone by, but the memories of being sexually exploited still surface and traumatize me."

Francis rocked from foot to foot and rolled his head from side to side as he stood behind his lawyers. He didn't know what to do with his hands so he put them in his pockets, took them out, clasped them behind his back and put them back in his pockets.

Smoak asked who ran Mantra Films. Dyer said Francis was the CEO, Scott Barbour was the president, Eric Deutsch was vice president.

Smoak then turned his attention to Francis.

"Mr. Francis, did you read the victim impact statements?"

"Yeah, I did. I read some of them."

"Mr. Francis, I want you to step up to the podium. I want to make sure you've read this," Smoak said, holding B.S.'s statement. "I want you to read it out loud."

Francis hesitated.

"I just want you to know that my policy has always been, and will always be, not to use girls under the age of 18 in any of our videos," he told Smoak. "Because these girls lied about their age, they were able to get in our videos and that's what happened here."

"You know that might happen, don't you?" Smoak asked.

"I never would have dreamed this would have happened with all the things we had in place to prevent this from happening."

Smoak asked him if he'd read a study that was released within the last year that indicated the human brain isn't fully developed until a person's mid-twenties.

"Doesn't take a real brave man to go out and corner some young female who has had four or five beers in the middle of Spring Break and convince them to do something dumb," Smoak growled. "Now read the statement, please, so we make sure that you have read it and presumably understand it."

"We go to war at 18 years old, your honor," Francis said in a quiet, unconvincing voice.

"Mr. Francis read the statement," Smoak said, his voice remaining even.

"I don't think those kids are dumb," Francis mumbled.

"Read the statement," Smoak roared.

Francis read it.

Smoak then set out the details of the sentence. He went through every aspect meticulously.

He questioned the size of the fine, saying $1.6 million represented just 3.5-percent of the company's profit since 2002.

"Now, I am concerned whether the fine alone as provided in the plea agreement adequately carries out the stated requirements of sentencing," Smoak said.

Dyer asked him to defer to the wisdom of the government in coming to that amount.

"They have conducted an intensive investigation and came to the conclusion that this is the fair result in this case," he said.

Dyer asked the judge to take into account that Girls Gone Wild was in its "fledgling" stage when the offenses occurred.

"Three of them were actually filmed at a time when they were just developing their filming techniques, their policies," Dyer said. Since then, he said, the company had ramped up its efforts to comply with the law.

Smoak imposed the fine, but then went a step farther. He ordered Francis and the three highest officers in his corporations to do eight hours a month of community service work in Bay County for the next 30 months.

The AP reporter was holding her breath at the thought of Joe Francis picking up garbage along Panama City's highways.

Smoak said Francis could step up and do 16 hours a month and that would let the others off the hook.

"Or, if he decides otherwise to essentially dump on them, then it will be his challenge to maintain their morale," Smoak said. "It makes no sense for this service to be performed in California. The offenses occurred in this community and these offenses have had a profound effect on this community.

"It is going to be a challenge for Mantra Films to possibly persuade some deserving organization, or needy organization, that it can somehow help them and help their community goals. And it's going to be a challenge for them to demonstrate that they can give back to this community in some positive fashion."

The reporters were the first ones out of the courtroom door when Smoak was finished. We walked out of the courthouse and indicated to the waiting photographers and cameramen that Francis would be out soon.

A few minutes passed and Francis came out with Dyer. They walked to a waiting SUV and Francis got in the front passenger side. Dyer went to close the door, but noticed Francis' hand sticking out waiting for a shake. They shook hands and Francis left.

Dyer turned to the waiting reporters.

He said they wouldn't appeal, that probation and community service were customary parts of a sentence like this.

He joked around with the reporters for a few minutes, gave the TV reporter a soundbite, then he was off to the golf course for a quick 18.

I called him as we were both driving away.

"Hey, didn't you want to set me up with that exclusive interview with Francis since he's in town?"

"He's gone. He's already been to the airport and left," Dyer said.

Chapter 10

Dirty feet

Joe Francis was four hours late to a scheduled three-day mediation beginning March 21, 2007, but finally arrived at the Bay Point Marriott in Panama City Beach. He was there to meet with the lawyers in the civil lawsuit for settlement negotiations.

When the lawyers were brought to him, they found Francis seated at the table in shorts and baseball cap playing a handheld video game.

When Larry Selander started his pitch, Francis leaned back in this chair and crossed his bare, dirty feet on the table top.

"Don't expect to get a fucking dime," Francis told Selander in a quiet, relaxed, conversational tone. "Not one fucking dime. I will not settle this case. I am only here because the court is making me be here."

Francis called this "strategy," establishing his position clearly and strongly. Selander, Tom Dent, Ross McCloy and Rachael Pontikes called it intractable and got up to leave.

Francis jerked his chair forward until all four feet were on the ground, shot out of the chair and intercepted them at the door. He put his face dangerously close to Selander's beard.

"We will bury you and your clients," Francis said, his voice tinged with the rage he'd always felt in this case. "I'm going to ruin you, your clients and all of your ambulance chasing partners."

Pontikes said Francis did make one offer before the lawyers left the room: "Suck my dick," Francis shouted to their backs and they filed out past him.

Two days later, Pontikes filed a motion asking Federal Judge Richard Smoak to hold Francis in contempt for not mediating in good faith as the judge had ordered.

Smoak set the issue for a hearing a week later.

On March 23, he told Francis' attorney, Mike Dickey, to send his client to charm school before bringing him back to court.

"Tell him to pack a bag," the judge said, "sanctions in this case might mean his going to jail."

Selander asked Smoak in a pre-hearing brief to at least make Francis bathe before resuming mediation.

Dickey wrote his own brief, saying he couldn't understand how a group of battle-hardened lawyers could act so intimidated during a heated mediation. He said it was more likely that they were just frustrated that they couldn't reach a settlement.

He said, at worst, Francis displayed "bad manners" and shouldn't be jailed for contempt of court. Dickey said if anyone had acted improperly it was the plaintiffs' lawyers, for breaking the rules of confidentiality that are ingrained in the mediation process and going to Smoak with their complaints.

"Taking plaintiffs' allegations at face value for the purpose of discussion," Dickey wrote, "one cannot condone the behavior of Francis during his ill-advised three-minute exchange with plaintiffs' lawyers. That, however, is not the point. His words and behavior may have been vulgar and extreme at times, but they were also protected as a matter of law."

On March 30, Francis walked into the small courtroom on the courthouse's second floor to face Smoak.

He stopped inside the door and looked around. He was wearing a dark blue suit and pink tie. His black hair was spiked to give him a casual, just-got-out-of-bed look.

He turned to scan the crowd, looking for someone; when he saw me, he broke away from his company's lawyer, Michael Burke, to walk over.

"Hey David?" he said, holding his hand out. "I'm Joe Francis."

I stood, smiled and shook his hand.

"Can we talk for a few minutes after this?" he asked.

"Sure. No problem," I said, continuing to smile. He turned and walked back to the defense table.

Bailiff George Dobos sidled over to me as I sat back down and whispered: "Media whore."

He meant me. I'd known Dobos since his days with the Panama City Police Department and he'd always been quick to tell you exactly what he was thinking.

Smoak came out to take the bench and the hearing was underway.

Selander told the judge that he could still remember Francis' face, his eyes, as Francis sprang from his chair to confront him at the door to a conference room.

"I thought he was gonna haul off and slug me," Selander said. He said Francis had started shouting soon after the plaintiffs' lawyers had entered the room. Three minutes later, as the lawyers were leaving, Francis was screaming at them: "Suck my dick."

Smoak looked at Francis. The expression on the judge's face was not kind. Smoak told him he'd squandered his best opportunity to settle the lawsuit. He said Francis had also willfully disregarded his order to mediate in a meaningful way.

He told Francis to stand.

"You get up and you tell this court on the record what you said," Smoak said. "And then I want you to tell me why you think those comments were appropriate. Take your hands out of your pockets!

"My question is: did you say what is quoted in the motion?"

"Most of it, I did. But it's taken out of context, your honor. I was posturing."

"What was the first sentence you said?"

"First sentence is, 'Do you realize what the lying of your clients have put me through?' Your honor, I said, 'I am the victim here.' That's the first thing I said."

Francis said there was some additional banter after that.

"We're going to do it sentence by sentence," Smoak said. "What was your third sentence?"

Francis repeated that he told them he was the victim and that their clients had lied.

"No," Smoak said, "that's not my question. What did you say in your third sentence?"

After a minute more of this exchange, Smoak told him to read what Pontikes had written. "Look at paragraph 9 of the motion. Read the paragraph."

"Your honor, do I have to read it?"

"Read it."

"Okay. 'Don't expect to get' – and I did not use that expletive. I said, 'Don't expect to get a dime' and then I said, 'not one fucking dime.'"

Francis insisted that he did not say that as his second sentence, but it was actually much later in the exchange. Smoak directed him to another paragraph.

"Read it verbatim, Mr. Francis."

"This right here? 'Francis then made (the only) offer that he was to make that day, 'suck my dick,' Francis shouted repeatedly as plaintiffs' counsel left the room.'"

"Did you make that statement?"

"One time, yes."

Francis insisted that his words were part of a heated exchange between the parties. He said Selander was cussing at him and Pontikes called him an "a-hole."

"The thing is, you've read one side of this whole thing, which is like the whole case. And it really frustrates me."

Smoak ordered a short break, and Joe Francis found me in the hallway outside the courtroom.

"We really need to have a sit down. I want to tell you the whole thing," Francis said to me. "Do you have a card?"

I didn't. I never did. But that was opportunity enough for two TV reporters to step up.

"Can we get a few words from you on camera?"

"Sure. Sure. No problem. I'll give you something."

Francis grinned, but shifted his feet and put his hands in his pockets. I touched his elbow and told him I'd get him a card from my car.

A few minutes later he trotted down the concrete stairway outside the courthouse. He took the last three steps like Bo Jangles dancing with Shirley Temple, his suit coat billowing open and a grin spreading across his face.

I was standing with photographer Robert Cooper, who was ready with camera in hand and two others slung over his shoulders. He wore a vest that bulged with lenses and pockets.

Cooper had stepped back as soon as Francis came out the front door and was shooting pictures in rapid fire.

I held out a business card and Francis pocketed it without a glance.

"I'd really like to tell you what's really going on," he said. "Like I said in there, I am the victim here. If it wasn't for these girls lying about their age to my cameraman, I wouldn't be here today. I mean, I was out of the country when they did that, I wasn't even around."

"Sure, we'll talk whenever you want."

"I mean, I'm the victim here. And all that at the Marriott? That was posturing. I mean, I went in there and they went in there and it was posturing."

He glanced at Cooper, who was shifting from side to side, his shutter firing continuously. Francis gave him a quick grin and snapped out of his thoughts.

"You want a picture. How about a picture together?"

He wrapped an arm around my shoulders and Cooper hesitated for a beat before realigning and firing off two more frames.

"You could bottle that grin," Cooper told me after looking at the pictures. I couldn't help it. He'd taken me so off guard that I was smiling like a fool.

I felt like an idiot.

• • •

An hour later, I came through the courthouse's glass doors to the metal detector and conveyor belt. Several men in suits were grouped at the end of the conveyor; a few were hopping on one foot as they put a shoe back on. Others were inserting belts back through loops. Security officers at the courthouse took great pleasure in stripping lawyers of anything that would set off the overly sensitive metal detector. Some of the wealthiest, most influential attorneys in the state have gone through the machine in socks, while holding their pants up.

If I know I'm going to be in federal court, I usually wear shoes that don't set off the alarm and pants that don't need a belt. I walked past the hopping, overly-scented lawyers and turned the corner toward the elevator. Francis, who'd apparently led the way for his attorneys, was standing in the hallway, hands in pockets, studying the elevator doors. He ignored me as I walked up. I turned toward the metal door, looked over it as if there was a floor indicator. Since there were only two floors, the designers felt it was a waste of time to install an indicator. If the elevator wasn't on your floor, it was on the other.

I looked at the door, down at my note book, back at the door. I was doing my best to be cool.

"You know, the whole story isn't getting out," Francis said, not looking away from the elevator.

"Well, the criminal case should be resolved soon and you'll be freed up to talk then," I glanced his way.

"Oh yeah, they're going away. It's bullshit." He looked up at the ceiling and past it to the second floor, where Smoak awaited him in the courtroom. "This is bullshit. You know, I'd think I was an asshole too if I read all that stuff that's been written about me in the media."

Francis' entourage finally caught up with us in time for the elevator door to open with a groan. We filed in, no one saying a word, and rode up in a fog of cologne, hands in pockets.

An hour later, Smoak adjourned the hearing for lunch, but this time with a warning to Francis. He said he had sanctions in mind and suggested that Francis could avoid them by settling the case.

"If you come back this afternoon," Smoak said, "somebody is going to be real unhappy, probably, with my ruling. That's fair warning and I think that you need to put a dollar figure in your mind on what it's worth to you to avoid what may be a sanction that you weren't counting on."

Francis bounded down the stairs this time and went to a waiting car. His lawyer couldn't find the keys and Francis was stuck standing there with the cameras rolling. He finally went around and grabbed the lawyer's bag to search it himself.

One of them found the keys and they drove off. They spent the next hour working with the plaintiffs' lawyers, Larry Selander, Ross McCloy, Rachael Pontikes and Tom Dent, to work out a settlement. They did not resolve the case and returned to court.

Francis began the proceedings by asking to clarify some things he'd said before the break. Some of the things he'd said during mediation had actually happened before the other lawyers entered the room – like saying he was the victim in this case.

He also wanted to clarify that Selander hadn't cussed at him.

But Francis insisted that Rachael Pontikes did call him an "a-hole" or something like that. She took the stand and denied it.

Francis' lawyer, Mike Dickey, wrote to the judge later saying she had said something to Francis, but he didn't offer that information during the hearing. The discrepancy would lead to a charge of criminal contempt against Francis that would ultimately be dismissed.

Smoak said Francis was going to have to spend the weekend in jail. He insisted that Francis participate in meaningful mediation, as originally ordered. Since they couldn't immediately arrange that with a mediator, Francis would have to sit in jail until the mediation could be scheduled.

Burke stood up rather stiffly, walked to the podium and asked Smoak if Francis could avoid the jail term by beginning mediation immediately. Smoak said no, because he wanted meaningful mediation, not just negotiations. He said the only way Francis could avoid the weekend jail term was to settle the case.

"One of the things that the court made clear in its order, as I heard it reported, is that the discharge of the contempt, civil contempt and confinement, was – it could only occur upon both Mr. Francis participating meaningfully in the mediation and the certification that at least two offers had gone back and forth, offers and counter-demands, by the parties and certification by a mediator," Burke told the judge.

He explained that the sides had met without a mediator over lunch and one offer had been discussed.

"Let me suggest this, Mr. Burke," Smoak said. "We still have time today. I will, can, delay Mr. Francis surrendering to the custody of the U.S. Marshal until 4:30, and that will give you all the opportunity to meet wherever you want. But at 4:30, if there doesn't seem to be substantial progress, then he is to surrender here at the Marshal's office."

"Appreciate that your honor," Burke said. "Would an affidavit or declaration by Mr. Dickey, filed under seal, in the absence of Mr. Caparello or another mediator – my understanding is that Mr. Dickey is a certified mediator, would that affidavit comply with the court's instruction?"

"If you all can resolve this this afternoon, if I get a phone call from Mr. Dickey and Mr. McCloy, then we've solved the problem," Smoak said.

"By resolve, you mean that the court's order has been complied with, that two offers have gone out and two responses have come back?"

"I'm looking for you all to resolve this thing finally," Smoak said. "If you can get it resolved this afternoon, fine. If you're not able to do it by yourselves then we need the mediator."

And with that, "settle or jail" was born. To Burke, Judge Smoak's order was clearly that Francis would have to settle the case, "resolve this thing finally," in order to avoid a weekend in jail waiting for the mediation to be arranged.

Smoak's stance softened as the day went on, and Francis was allowed to stay out of jail without settling the case. Both sides got together with mediator Dom Caparello by phone and began the process immediately.

Chapter 11

Settled

The headline the next day was: "Judge tells Francis: Settle or Jail." That rankled the judge, who would insist in later hearings that "settle or jail" was not what he had intended.

Smoak did not incarcerate Francis that night. He put off the sentence until 4:30, then 5:30 when he was told that negotiations were progressing. Smoak then postponed it until Saturday afternoon, and ultimately let Francis out of the jail sentence when he was told that Francis had made a settlement offer.

I found Francis that Saturday evening at Dickey's law office, a brick building overlooking the serene Massalina Bayou.

Francis and Dickey were standing outside. It was pure luck that I found him when and where I did. He watched as my Nissan Pathfinder pulled into a parking spot, then walked over with his hand outstretched.

"You're that reporter that did the story today," he said as if we hadn't talked the day before. We shook hands.

"I liked your story today. I guess you heard."

"Heard what?"

"The judge. He cut us loose."

"You've settled?"

"I guess you came here for the whole story."

"Actually, I just need to know what's going on so I can write my story and get to my basketball game."

That's when Francis noticed the University of Florida T-shirt I was wearing. The Gators were hours away from playing UCLA in the Final Four.

"I'd like to be up two beers by the time the game starts," I said.

"Oh yeah, you're a Gator huh? Well, I hope the Gators kick the shit out of UCLA – but that's totally off the record."

Francis had a business degree from the University of Southern California, the natural enemy of UCLA.

He started down a wooden pathway toward a deck at the back of the office.

"You wanna get the story?" He waved me along, inviting me to the deck.

I hung back with Dickey and asked him what was going on. Dickey said they'd been in mediation since Friday. Late Saturday afternoon, he and Ross McCloy found Judge Smoak in his yard and explained to him that Francis had engaged in meaningful mediation, just like the judge ordered.

Smoak suspended the contempt order and was letting Francis go.

"Hey, you gonna come sit down or not?" Francis yelled from the end of the pathway. Waving me over again.

Francis sat down at a wrought-iron table and stretched out his long legs. He leaned forward and laced his fingers, then leaned back and put his right elbow on the chair's arm.

"So, you went to the University of Florida," he said. "How'd you get here?"

"I grew up in Tampa."

"I like Tampa. I like the diversity."

"When I left UF, I spent some time working in St. Louis, but I got homesick. When I saw the advertisement for here, I applied."

"So have you worked in courts for long?"

"My whole career, 15 years in three states."

"Three states? So have you ever seen anything like that before? Have you ever heard of a judge threatening to put a defendant in a civil suit in jail if he didn't settle?"

I seemed to have his full attention and I weighed how truthful I could be. I needed to get an interview and expressing my opinion, especially when I disagreed, wouldn't necessarily facilitate that interview.

"If you had any other judge," I began, "like, Casey Rodgers for example, she would have put you in jail the day she found out about what you'd done and kept you in jail a week before she even asked you for your side. Then she would have put you back in jail for another week. She would have lit you up.

"Overall, I'd say the judge was pretty evenhanded."

"Evenhanded," Francis repeated. His face, usually animated and boyish, was blank. I waited.

Before he could go on, Francis' corporate lawyer, Michael Burke, looked out the law office's sliding glass doors and saw us talking. He bolted for the handle and was at Francis' side in two strides.

"Your story was a fair recitation of the hearing," Burke said, deadpan. "I liked it."

"Sarcasm will get you nowhere," I replied, pointing my pen at him.

He looked surprised, then smiled, "No, no, I mean it. I liked it."

"We were just talking about the judge's ruling," Francis said. "I was about to give David here the whole story."

Burke had both of his hands on the table and his head sagged between his arms before he looked up and smiled at his boss.

"You can't talk about the mediation," Burke said.

"I can talk about it. They're the ones that broke the rules about confidentiality."

"No, Joe, you can't."

Burke went into a dry and general description of the mediation process and the judge's decision to release Francis from the contempt order. I had all of it already and interrupted Burke to ask some questions. He prefaced his answers with a good three minutes of explanation of the rules limiting contact between press and lawyers in federal cases.

"I'll ask. Whatever you can't answer, you just say so. I won't get my feelings hurt."

"Just understand that it's not that I don't want to answer your questions; I just might not be able to."

I nodded.

"Are the sides very far apart in their negotiations?"

"I can't answer that."

"Is it likely that we're headed for trial?"

Same answer. I wasn't surprised. I was starting to have some fun; Burke seemed genuinely uncomfortable.

"I want to say something," Francis started.

"Joe," Burke warned.

"No, I think I can say this. The judge asked a question to me on Friday that I couldn't answer. He asked, if we were sitting around our mother's table would we use the kind of language I used in the mediation? My answer is: If my mother was suing me for $20 million, you better believe I'd use that kind of language."

Francis had more to say, but Burke and Dickey were issuing a steady stream of warnings to drown him out. Finally, Francis gave up and held out his hand.

"I hope the Gators do really well tonight," big grin. "I hope they kick the shit out of UCLA, but that's totally off the record."

Joe Francis left Panama City that Saturday night. The next day, April 1, he turned 34.

Three days later, Judge Richard Smoak called another emergency hearing and reinstated Francis' jail sentence. He ordered Francis to turn himself over to federal authorities in Panama City no later than noon the next day.

Chapter 12

"Judges gone wild"

The bells of First Baptist Church in downtown Panama City chimed out the noon hour on April 5. I was parked across the street from the federal courthouse, watching the empty lot. Joe Francis was nowhere to be seen.

At one minute past noon, he was officially a fugitive.

In a hearing the day before, federal Judge Smoak had ordered Francis' surrender and indicated that he would consider criminal charges against him.

What Francis had done was add conditions to an unconditional settlement offer he'd made on March 31, the Saturday that he left town. The girls had accepted the unconditional offer, and then Francis said he wanted to pay the amount over time.

Smoak said it was a very, very long payment plan.

Smoak decided that Francis had been insincere when he made the offer. All he was doing, the judge said, was making a false offer so he could get out of town.

"He may have snookered us and gotten out," Smoak said, "but he's coming back."

Ross McCloy cautioned the judge not to overreact. He said it was possible that Francis was just goading him into a rash decision that would result in a viable appeal, a motion for the judge to recuse himself or a change of venue.

Mike Dickey didn't help much by shrugging his shoulders and saying he was stumped by Francis' behavior.

The order went out – Francis must surrender himself in less than 24 hours.

The deadline came and went. Francis appeared on the Geraldo Rivera show by phone and said he would certainly honor the judge's order.

He told the AP that this was a case of "judges gone wild."

Francis' spokesman, Ronn Torossian, echoed that. When I asked him if Francis intended to turn himself in that Thursday, Torossian said Francis was "very busy" running a business. I took that as a no.

Burke and Aaron Dyer, in private, were outraged. The judge had denied that he'd ordered Francis to settle the lawsuit or go to jail – "Settle or Jail," the News Herald's big headline that the judge had so objected to.

But now, this was exactly what they'd feared. Burke said they made an unconditional monetary offer that was accepted. After that, the terms were negotiated actively over the next few days. When McCloy ran across a term he didn't like, he went to Smoak and told him Francis wasn't negotiating in good faith.

Smoak responded by ordering Francis to jail.

The plaintiffs now had a powerful negotiating tool. Scott Barbour, Mantra's president, said the threat of jail was an issue in future negotiations, which ultimately settled the case.

• • •

On April 10, 2007, Francis flew in to the Panama City-Bay County International Airport around 7 a.m. and was promptly arrested by airport police. He was five days late in complying with the judge's order to turn himself in.

As he was being booked in at the Bay County Jail, Mantra Films Inc. President Scott Barbour and Francis' personal attorney Bret Saxon waited on metal-and-plastic chairs in a corner of the jail's basement public area. Barbour stretched his legs in front of the Lance's peanut, cracker and hot fries snack dispenser. Saxon sat hunched over with elbows on knees.

"Hey Shirley," I said to Shirley Brown as I walked up to the notched and scarred plastic window. Brown had worked at the jail's public window for some 20 years.

"Hey David. Long time no see."

"I know. I don't get down here as much as I used to. Don't take this the wrong way, but I don't really like it here too much."

"I don't blame you," she laughed. "What can I do for you?"

"I need to see if you can get a message to Joe Francis, see if he wants to give me an interview."

Barbour, who I hadn't met before, spoke up from his corner seat.

"Are you David from the News Herald?"

He introduced himself and said Francis would almost certainly give me an interview once he'd been booked and had a chance to talk to his lawyers.

A few minutes later, Michael Burke came out of the jail and escorted Barbour and Saxon in to see Joe. I waited.

Barbour had said they had two hearings to attend that day, a 10 a.m. status conference in Judge Smoak's chambers, and a 1:30 hearing for some unexplained purpose.

After an hour of waiting in which I committed the contents of the junk food dispenser to memory, Barbour came out and said Francis would meet with me after the 10 a.m. hearing.

A few minutes later and a few blocks away at the federal courthouse, Burke and I looked over the criminal contempt complaint that Smoak had filed that morning. This was why Francis was coming back at 1:30, for an arraignment on that charge.

Smoak said Francis committed contempt of court by lying during a March 30 hearing and compounded it by not turning himself in as ordered on April 5.

"It's interesting that the judge relies on the plaintiffs' filings to write this out," Burke said, pointing to the instances where the judge said Francis lied. "He's got a transcript of the hearing."

Barbour and Saxon had resumed their positions from the jail waiting area as they sat in the hallway outside the courtroom. Barbour was stretched out and Saxon hunched over, in wooden chairs under group pictures of the sitting federal judges and magistrates.

I stood in the hallway, leaning against a door jamb, and waited for them to ask me a question, to get the conversation started. It didn't take long.

"Let me ask you something. Have you ever seen anything like this?" Barbour asked, echoing Francis' question to me from less than a week before. He wanted to know if I'd seen a judge hold someone in criminal contempt of court in a civil case, a charge that carried a six-month jail sentence. What he really wanted to know was if I'd ever seen anyone jailed because they wouldn't settle a lawsuit.

Smoak's orders over the last week had amounted to just that.

Luckily, Barbour dove into the real issue, the mediation, without waiting for an answer. He said settlement talks – exactly what Smoak had demanded in their last hearing – had been ongoing for two weeks. Offers and conditions in the offers were flying across desks every day.

"You've probably written, what, 20 settlement drafts in the last two weeks?" Barbour said to Burke.

"I wouldn't say 20."

Turns out the number was six. And a settlement had been agreed to in principal and was just awaiting final approval.

"The plaintiffs included two conditions just yesterday that if I didn't accept it would have killed the deal," Burke said.

Francis was in jail because he'd made an unconditional settlement offer and when the plaintiffs accepted it, he then added terms which the girls found unacceptable. Smoak said Francis had only made the offer to appease the judge and it wasn't an honest effort to resolve the case. He demanded that Francis surrender himself to begin a contempt of court jail term.

Smoak's decision was fueled by Francis' then-attorney Mike Dickey telling the judge he was "stumped" by Francis' actions.

"I don't want you to throw anybody under the bus," I said to Burke and Barbour, "but do you think if Mike Dickey had come out stronger in the April fourth hearing – told the judge that this was a part of the negotiation process – instead of saying he was stumped – you think this issue wouldn't have blown up the way it did?"

Burke looked away and didn't say anything.

Barbour tapped his fingertip against his nose and exaggerated a nod, but said, "I can't say a word."

That afternoon, Francis was taken out of an SUV behind the steps leading into the federal courthouse's holding area. Dressed in Bay County jailhouse blues, his ankles were chained together, allowing him little more than 12-inch strides. His wrists were shackled together and connected to a belly chain.

He smiled at the cameras recording his movements, then hop-skipped up the stairs.

He shuffled into the courtroom and grinned at everyone assembled. There were Bay County Sheriff's investigators, who came to all of Francis' court appearances, and lawyers – lots of lawyers.

He sat next to a thickset guy in a jail jumpsuit with a proud mullet and looked around the room. He leaned over, said something to mullet-guy, who snorted a short laugh.

U.S. Magistrate Larry Bodiford took the bench and ordered Francis held in jail until a bond hearing on Thursday. It was a shock to Francis, who had dinner plans for that night.

The next day I called Barbour on his cell phone and asked him if we could set up that interview. Barbour was already at the jail.

"Joe, this is David from the News Herald," Barbour said to Francis. "Other than the picture, he wrote a very nice story about you in today's paper. Do you want to meet with him today?"

Francis said something I couldn't catch.

"He'll meet with you. What's your deadline? Can we make it later this afternoon, say around 3?"

I hate working late.

"I was thinking more like right after lunch, say 1:30."

"How about 2? Can you make it at 2?"

"I'll be there."

• • •

I was led into a small room on the jail's first floor. Someone had managed to cram in a couple of shelves, desk and four small chairs.

Joe Francis opened the door and I walked in, moving out of the door's path and looking for a chair. Scott Barbour was seated behind the simple metal desk. Francis sat down in front of the desk with his back to the mason block wall.

"You want to sit here?" he asked, situating a chair to face him.

"How are you doing?" I asked, sitting down in the offered seat. "Really. How are you getting along?"

"I'm fine," he said, looking surprised at the question. He had bigger issues to address with a reporter.

"I guess you heard we settled."

Francis always assumed I knew everything. I hated to let him down and I didn't like to lie, so I just stayed silent and let him assume.

He tried to cross his legs but the space was too cramped and he kicked the desk instead. He put both feet back on the floor and started talking about the settlement.

"Money has been delivered," he said.

"You can't say that," Barbour interrupted.

"I can say that."

"You can if you want to have something that you don't know to be accurate to end up in the paper."

"I can say that money has been exchanged."

Most of the interview went on like that, the two men bickering like an old married couple, talking over each other, each holding up a hand to try to hush the other.

I'd learned not to try to follow along too closely. The best thing when talking with Francis was to sit back and listen. Take notes when possible but try to keep a wall up against the barrage of often jumbled information coming in.

Francis' mood went from jittery to resigned. He'd stand and fidget, then drop back into his seat and put his face in his hands. When he wasn't focused on one thing, he was all over the board. He might stop a train of thought on a dime, then charge off in a different direction in a flash.

I'm much too Southern in my thought processing. I like a smooth, quiet stream of information, not the splashing, thunderous waterfall that was Joe Francis. But, I very much felt like I was sitting in an imaginary rocking chair on an imaginary wooden porch and watching two bumper cars bang into each other, repeatedly, at high speeds. It was pretty entertaining, so I just sipped my imaginary bourbon and tried to take it all in.

Barbour was in the middle of talking about the settlement when Francis interrupted.

"You comfortable?" he asked me.

If nothing else, the question jarred me off the porch.

"I'm fine."

"You want a corn dog?"

I stopped for a beat and I can honestly say my mind went blank trying to figure out the question. Then I laughed; a good heartfelt laugh that Francis the entertainer seemed to really appreciate.

"How about a Jello-O? I think they got a few cups of Jello-O around somewhere," he pressed on, smiling.

"No thanks," I said, still laughing. "I'm fine."

He tried to cross his left leg over his right, but kicked the desk again. This time the leg stayed, perched ankle-on-knee-cap. The desk made a rhythmic, hollow thud as Francis repeatedly tapped it with his toe.

He uncrossed the leg and leaned forward.

"I think Bay County needs to be done with Joe Francis," he said. "I'd like to come back sometime on vacation. Maybe buy a couple condos. I hear there's plenty available."

Panama City Beach's dream of ousting Spring Breakers in exchange for year-round, wealthy residents who enjoyed living in high-rise condominiums, wasn't moving as quickly as planned. The high-rises were there, but they were practically empty.

Francis turned serious and pointed at my note pad.

"You need to do something for me."

I leaned back, put my hand over the pad and looked at him. This was dangerous territory; I didn't like having to do anything for anyone.

"You spoke to Ronn Torossian and quoted him saying that I had no intention of honoring the judge's order. That quote is the reason I'm here."

"That's not the only reason," Barbour said, laughing in a way to show me that Francis didn't mean to offend. Francis held up his hand.

"I didn't mean that was the only reason. It's just that I would never not honor a judge's order."

He said the only reason he didn't fly out the Thursday he was supposed to turn himself in was because he couldn't find a pilot. And because it was Easter weekend, he couldn't line up a commercial flight.

He wanted to make sure I noted that. I scribbled it into my notebook.

I asked him if this was a particularly difficult case for him to settle. He'd been sued before, several times since starting Girls Gone Wild, and had settled those cases without much incident.

He'd also taken a lawsuit to trial in Texas in 2006 and won in an area that was more conservative than Bay County. Jurors weren't overly sympathetic to girls who willingly exposed themselves to a clearly marked Girls Gone Wild camera and then sued for emotional damages.

"Absolutely," he said, "this case destroyed my life. I was a guy, who, in 2003, I was a cocky 29-year-old, I was on top of the world.

Prior to these incidents I was happy. This case has caused me to lose friends, family, a large part of my business. It’s caused me the most pain and suffering of anything in my life.”

He put his hands over his face.

“Before this happened, I’d often thought about faking my own demise,” he muttered through his hands. “Not faking my own death, but my own demise. Just to see who my real friends were. But I didn’t have to fake it. This case did that for me. It made me realize who my friends were and what my life was all about.

“Now I know who has the real power in this world: the judges, the police, the press.”

He wouldn’t talk about the money that had ended this case. The settlement had a provision to keep the girls’ identities secret along with the amount they received.

“It was a lot,” Francis said. “It hurt me a lot and it was hard to get, I can say that.”

Barbour spoke up, saying it would put a dent in Mantra’s operating funds for some time to come. That’s big money for a company that made $43 million – $29 million in profit – in 2005.

“It was not an inconsequential amount in any shape or form,” he said. “But it was a fair resolution to this case.”

“Let’s not say fair,” Francis broke in. “Let’s just say it was a resolution.”

• • •

Hours after my interview with Joe Francis at the Bay County Jail, guards returned him to cell pod B, which had been cleared of all other inmates.

Some time in the evening, Francis asked a guard for a bottled water. The guard refused. Francis offered to buy the water for $100, then made it $500 and showed the guard the money.

It is against the law for inmates to possess cash in the jail. It is considered contraband. Having it was a felony.

When the guard reported Francis to his superiors, they searched Francis' cell and found sixteen prescription pills. They were Francis' anti-anxiety medicine and sleeping pills.

The search resulted in two felony charges, a maximum of 10 years in prison if he was convicted as charged. The State Attorney's Office immediately drew up a motion to have Francis' bond in the still-pending 2003 criminal case revoked upon his release from federal custody.

Francis, who was truly suffering in jail and had settled the civil case hoping it would facilitate his release, had done the unthinkable. He had bought himself weeks, months or years behind bars.

Chapter 13

Insanity

On April 12, the day after the pills were found, Francis returned to federal court for what was supposed to be a bond hearing in the criminal contempt case. Record producer Quincy Jones was in the audience, ready to testify as a character witness. Francis' parents, Ray and Maria Francis, also came to support their son.

Francis walked in looking haggard, bags under his eyes, hair disheveled. He scanned the crowd as he shuffled in with chains jingling from his wrists and ankles.

Mantra President Scott Barbour, numerous lawyers, court personnel who'd taken a break to watch the proceedings, three state prosecutors including Mark Graham who was spearheading the 2003 case, and three Bay County Sheriff's Office investigators had turned out to watch.

State prosecutor Larry Basford sat near the back of the room with a file folder containing the contraband warrants on his lap and the motion to revoke bond. If U.S. Magistrate Larry Bodiford gave Francis a bond, Basford would file the paperwork to keep him in jail.

Francis blew a kiss to his mother as she entered the room. Maria Francis, a tiny woman with wavy blonde hair and nervous, fluttering hands, blew back two quick kisses. Francis sat with his back to the audience and his mother sat nearby. She changed seats, moving in a crouch between pews, trying to get a look at his face. She sat next to Jones, then moved closer to me and got up again to find another seat.

Bodiford entered the room and attorneys Jan Handzlik and Jim White asked him for a short recess before starting the hearing. They took Francis aside. When they returned, they waived the hearing. Handzlik said later that considering the new charges, there was no point in going forward.

Francis stood and with Marshals reaching to take him back into custody he turned to his mother. He was crying.

"I didn't do anything," he said in a high, strained voice. "You know I didn't do anything."

When officers led him out the courthouse's back door, he couldn't face the cameras as he'd done so many times before. The last time he'd gone in the courthouse by these stairs, he'd done a stiff-legged hop for the cameras' benefit. He'd once danced down the federal courthouse stairs.

This time he hid his face behind an empty file folder.

Francis returned to a different situation at the jail. He was now without his medication, which made sleep and a quiet mind hard enough. But he'd broken jail rules, and that meant 30 days in solitary confinement, what jail personnel call "segregated population."

He was in a small, bare cell with concrete walls and floor. The bed was a rectangle of cold steel mounted on the wall. Francis was given a towel and a blanket.

Within the cell block's walls were the worst of Bay County's offenders, including Robert Bailey, who'd just been convicted of gunning down a police officer. Bailey, a lifelong gang member from Wisconsin, kept chanting "Joe Francis! Girls Gone Wild! Whoo!" He said it over and over and over, sometimes late into the night.

Francis says he was shackled constantly when he was outside his cell, including showers. He would tell people afterwards that guards paraded him naked and chained to and from his showers.

Sleep was impossible.

He was allowed visitors, but kept separated from them by a thick glass window.

Francis called his girlfriend, Christina McLarty, his first day in solitary. McLarty was a TV reporter in Los Angeles, and when Francis called she was on assignment. When she answered the phone she was all business, while Francis was weeping.

"Hello."

"Oh my god, thank you." Francis sobbed into the phone.

"Hi hon." McLarty said, calmly.

"I don't know what to do."

"What's wrong?"

"They put me in the solitary thing. They put me in a solitary cell."

McLarty told him that attorney Chris Rudd was awaiting approval from Michael Burke to fly to Panama City to offer his help. McLarty, who was clearly frustrated with Burke, said Rudd had been sitting in an airport for hours waiting for the call.

"I'm OKing it," Francis said, the whine dropping from his voice.

"Can I be rude to Michael? Is that OK?" McLarty asked. "I think I'm gonna be rude to him because he won't listen to me."

Francis wanted to know why Burke hadn't come to see him in jail.

"I'm gonna die. There's no way I can spend 10 days in solitary confinement."

"OK. You're supposed to be there for 21 days," McLarty responded, not sounding the least bit sympathetic.

Francis wanted to know if that meant he was going to be in jail for 21 days, or in solitary confinement for 21 days.

"If I'm here for 21 days, I'll die."

"I know."

Francis believed he was scheduled to be released from jail the day the pills were found. He asked McLarty what he was supposed to do about that situation.

"You're supposed to turn it around and say they were trying to extort money," McLarty told him, repeating what she thought she'd heard from a lawyer.

"This call's being recorded, so you're my attorney," Francis said, believing that just saying she was an attorney would make their conversation confidential.

"Keep a stiff upper lip," McLarty told him. She was still working and talking to someone else while juggling the call with Francis. "Can you call me back?"

"I only get one phone call a day," Francis said.

"Can you call me back in like 20 minutes?"

"I'll try."

"Keep the faith hon," McLarty said before ending the call.

Aaron Dyer, the lawyer who had stood with Francis from the beginning of the 2003 criminal case, was sick at home in Los Angeles when Francis flew out for the March 30 hearing. He was still in California on April 12 when Francis got the new charges.

He flew out the next day.

He called me on my cell phone around 10:30 that night.

"For four years I was able to keep him away from you," Dyer said. "The one time I get sick and you get the interview."

He wanted to know if I was up for a beer.

"What are you doing in town?" I asked.

"I had to come over and work on some of this stuff. Where you at?"

"I'm playing poker. Come on over, we've got plenty of beer. You can finally get in on the game."

"I'll come by, but I'll just watch."

Burke dropped him off 10 minutes later and I met him at the back gate. We walked to the pool house where the game had been underway for a good two hours.

Dyer sat in a recliner and drank a beer while the game went on. Tacked to the wall on his left was a poster of celebrity arrest photos.

"How much do you have sitting in front of you?" he asked me after an hour.

"Ninety-five dollars."

"I thought you said this was a low-stakes game."

"It is," I said, indicating the rows of chips. "These are all quarters."

Between hands we talked about the case.

"This is really penny-ante stuff," he said of the contraband charges. "He asks for a bottle of water so he can take the pills that have been prescribed for him."

But, I said, the jail didn't prescribe them and he hid the pills under a mattress and towel, indicating he knew he shouldn't have had them.

"Don't forget them arresting Scott Barbour for smuggling them in," I added.

"I don't think that happened. I think Joe had them with him."

"I don't know. When I went to visit him he had unlimited, private access to Barbour. I think that's one reason why they're coming down so hard on him. They gave him all this freedom and he smuggled pills in."

"Maybe. Do you think they're intentionally trying to goad him into doing something? I mean, are they making it so bad that he takes a swing at someone?"

"I don't think so. But they're definitely enjoying it."

"The one thing that gets me is this $500 for a bottled water. I know Joe Francis. I could get all the charges dismissed and he wouldn't pay me $500."

• • •

On April 23, 2007, Joe Francis came into the small, now-familiar courtroom on the federal courthouse's second floor and, as was his custom, scanned the onlookers in the three rows of wooden pews. He grinned and looked down before looking up again. He seemed torn between acknowledging his audience and embarrassment.

He was dressed in a clean, green jumpsuit with the words "Segregated inmate Bay County Jail" in white letters across the back.

For the first time in his two weeks of incarceration at the jail, he looked rested.

He turned his back to the small crowd of media, courthouse personnel and spectators, and sat. He faced forward for barely a moment before glancing back again.

Francis smiled at the two young, brunette television reporters from Panama City's competing stations who could have passed for sisters.

He kept his head down as he looked from face to face, until Aaron Dyer walked in. He sat up instantly and motioned for Dyer to join him at the defendant's table.

Dyer, taller than the 6-foot-2 Francis, carried a file folder pressed to his chest with his left hand and pushed open the swinging gate at his knees with the other. Francis clapped him on the shoulder as soon as Dyer sat down and leaned forward to talk to him.

The clap on the shoulder seemed to be a mixture of greeting and a desperate cling. Dyer, who stood by him through four years of legal problems, had been Francis' lifeline throughout the last 10 days of his incarceration, when Francis had found himself in solitary confinement, shackled and cut off from the human contact he craved. Dyer had visited him every day.

Dyer stood and took a seat on the first pew. He wouldn't be representing Francis at this hearing. That was for Jan Handzlick and Jim White, who were in the judge's chambers negotiating a plea deal.

Francis asked a Marshal for a Kleenex, wiped his eyes, blew his nose and waited.

Gone was Francis' usual cocky body language. He had an unfortunate habit of putting his hands in his pockets when he stood before the judge, but the green prison garb didn't have pockets and he wouldn't have been able to use them with his wrists shackled.

Francis believed for a long time that Smoak considered him to be "the devil." On this day, Francis was scheduled for a hearing so the prosecution could convince the judge that Francis had committed the crime of criminal contempt of court. What it came down to was that Smoak had issued a complaint against Francis charging him with contempt of his court and then ordered him to show why he shouldn't be incarcerated for it. Smoak said the prosecution was going to have to prove the charge beyond a reasonable doubt, but that was hard to believe since the judge was the one who filed the complaint in the first place.

Francis was guilty until proven innocent.

Before the hearing had started, Francis' Panama City lawyer, Jim White, had come out of some whispered discussions and stood off to the side by himself.

He had his hands in the pants pockets of his gray suit and the tip of his tongue protruded from between his teeth; his eyes were looking off into the distance, lost in thought. He was a respected Bay County lawyer with a brilliant legal mind. That day, he looked like an excited school boy.

"Interesting," he said when I caught his eye. After the hearing, he explained that comment. "I was thinking about the dynamics of this case. This has never been seen before."

He meant it was rare, if not unheard of, for someone to be jailed for criminal contempt of court in a civil lawsuit.

Francis did what was expected of him that day: he pleaded guilty to one count of criminal contempt of court. He admitted that he did not turn himself in to authorities on April 5 when ordered to do so. Instead, he flew in to Panama City five days later and was arrested by airport police.

In the two weeks since, Francis had gone from a cocky 34-year-old millionaire to a thoroughly beaten man.

"He stands before you transformed," Handzlik, who was seeking a lenient sentence, told Judge Smoak.

Francis also was charged with contempt for supposedly lying to the judge in a hearing on March 30. As a part of the deal, the prosecutor agreed to drop that charge, but Smoak went through the allegation anyway before explaining why he would dismiss it.

Smoak said even though Francis had said attorney Rachael Pontikes had called him an "a-hole" during mediation, and Pontikes said she hadn't, Smoak couldn't prove beyond a reasonable doubt that Francis had lied.

The charge of criminal contempt for not turning himself in on time, however, was better defined.

Smoak sentenced him to 35 days in jail. The judge made it clear that the sentence was for more than a year of aggravation Francis had caused him.

Smoak wouldn't come off the sentence, either. Thirty-five days – seven days for every one that Francis was a fugitive in violation of the judge's order to surrender himself.

Aaron Dyer said privately that Francis didn't immediately turn himself in because he had a meeting with a probation officer during that time that he was afraid to miss. Dyer said Francis' lawyers were in daily contact with the U.S. Marshal's Office in Los Angeles during this time and there was always a plan for Francis to voluntarily surrender.

Francis cried quietly throughout the 30-minute hearing and blew his nose a half-dozen times. Nearly every time Francis blew his nose, Smoak would have to stop what he was saying. The judge, though, continued on as Joe wiped his nose.

Thirty-five days was a lot. Handzlik begged the judge for no more than 30 days, saying anything more than that would elevate Francis' criminal history and make him eligible for up to a year in prison if he goes before a federal judge again.

Apparently, Handzlik had alerted Judge Smoak to that two days before and the judge was aware of the consequences, but still refused to back off the sentence. He said it would be improper for him to consider the ramifications of the sentence on other cases.

Smoak knew that Francis had been indicted in Nevada on April 11 for tax fraud and was facing up to 10 years in prison.

He stuck with his sentence.

• • •

State Prosecutor Mark Graham sat in a cushioned leather seat in a courtroom of Bay County's new courthouse. The chairs were comfortable, the room distinguished with its dark wood accents, a contrast to the bland federal courtrooms where Joe Francis had been spending much of his time.

Despite the comfortable surroundings, Circuit Judge Dedee Costello had put Graham on the spot by questioning his ability to count to 35. Graham had asked for an emergency hearing on Tuesday, May 8 for Costello to enforce her order that Joe Francis be placed in her custody once he completed his federal contempt of court sentence.

Graham had asked to have the hearing on May 8, believing it was the last day of Francis' sentence. Federal Judge Richard Smoak, however, put the sentence's last day as Sunday, May 6. When the sentence had run, Smoak allowed the Department of Justice to remove Francis from the Bay County Jail.

Now Francis was in Marianna, a town 50 miles north of Panama City, waiting for transfer to Atlanta where he would be bussed to Reno, Nevada.

"We believe our math was correct," Graham insisted. "We didn't expect the federal marshals to spirit Mr. Francis away in the middle of the night."

Now, Costello was scrambling to stop his transfer so she and the state prosecutors could finally put to rest his 2003 charges and possibly resolve the new contraband case at the same time. She asked Francis' lawyer, Larry Simpson, if he could be ready for trial by mid-July.

Simpson was reluctant to commit. He said he had more discovery to collect and witnesses to interview.

"I think I've been more than patient with allowing this case to proceed slowly," Costello told him. "I would have expected your discovery to be completed by now."

Simpson said Francis' settlement of the lawsuit meant he could now question the four girls – the alleged victims – in the case about things that were off limits while the lawsuit was pending.

Costello scheduled the trial for July, hoping to convince federal authorities that they could get these cases resolved without any inconvenience to them.

It made no difference.

Smoak denied Assistant State Attorney Bill Lewis' request for a hearing on the matter and ordered Francis' transfer.

Francis' lawyers, too had worked to get him out of the Bay County Jail, where they believed the guards were trying to spur him into some kind of violent outburst so they could put more charges on him.

There was probably little truth to that. If jailers treated him uncaringly or rudely, it was because he was a number to them, an inmate. They insisted then, and in interviews years later, that Francis was actually treated better than most inmates in solitary confinement.

Francis, however, claimed he was virtually tortured.

Now Francis was on his way to Reno to resolve the second of three cases that had fallen on him in the span of one extraordinary week in April. After being jailed for contempt of court, Francis was charged with new state crimes of smuggling pills into the Bay County Jail and trying to bribe a guard. Then came the federal tax indictment in Reno. Then he was charged with misdemeanor sexual assault in California, for allegedly touching a girl against her wishes.

When he reached Reno, his lawyers asked for bail. The judge granted him a $1.5 million bond but said he had to resolve his bond issues in Bay County before being turned loose.

As a part of his bond request, Dyer included a report from a psychologist who had interviewed Francis in jail.

Dr. Ronald Markman wrote in his report that he'd met with Francis for two hours and during that time, Francis told him he was isolated in a small cell with the light burning 24 hours a day.

"All murderers in my section," Francis said. "I started freaking out and screaming. I couldn't breathe. I don't think I can handle this on a long-term thing. I'm not a criminal."

Dyer said Francis had been kept in the same area as two of Bay County's most notorious killers – Robert Bailey and Blake Collier.

Collier had decapitated his wife and taken a bite out of her ovary because he thought she was carrying another man's child, or to fulfill a Biblical prophesy or because she had refused to give him a blowjob. All three were reasons he'd given to police. Collier was bugshit crazy.

Dyer said Bailey did his best to drive Francis insane with his constant taunting.

Markman agreed that the situation was not conducive to Francis' mental stability.

Francis had been denying some mental problems since he was a teen. Diagnosed at age 6 with attention deficit hyperactivity disorder, Francis was prescribed meditation but refused to take it. That led to so many problems that a teacher once told his parents: "If all children were like Joe, no one would have children."

At a boarding school in Connecticut, the teachers found him angry and uncooperative. His parents finally sent him on to a military academy in California.

In all, Francis was diagnosed with ADHD, bipolar with adjustment disorder with anxiety, anxiety disorder, personality disorder and deemed immature with narcissistic tendencies.

Dr. Markham met with Francis twice during his incarceration: April 20, 2007, in Bay County and again three months later in Washoe County, Nev. The first time they spoke, Francis was in control of himself even though he was frazzled.

The next time, though:

"The once clinically stable defendant was repeatedly screaming invectives and demonstrating little emotional control, likely due to the cessation of his medications and the constant stress he was experiencing while in custody."

Dr. Earl Nielsen met with Francis as well after his transfer from Bay County to the county jail in Reno, Nev.

"Francis' thinking has turned to the bizarre," Nielsen wrote. "Mr. Francis has lost confidence in his counsel. He frequently flies into rages or fits of frustration and has outbursts that are no longer rational or reflective of his immediate reality."

Francis' lawyer wrote in a motion that Francis was locked up in a small cell in solitary confinement 23 hours a day. The lights were constantly burning. The concrete cell was always cold and Francis had little more than a towel to keep him warm.

The motion said jailers would put his food outside his door and just past arm's reach, so on many occasions Francis went hungry.

When he was transported to Reno, his lawyers said Francis wasn't given his anxiety medication during the trip, even though the meds were on the bus, because no one was "authorized" to administer medications.

Once in Reno, his living conditions improved, but Francis' mental condition continued to deteriorate. He became increasingly suspicious of his long-time lawyer Aaron Dyer when Dyer was unable to convince Judge Dedee Costello to reinstate Francis' bond.

Dyer once said to me that Francis had been able to channel his hyperactivity, attention deficit and bipolar disorders into short bursts of formidable marketing drive.

Francis drove Girls Gone Wild into an empire that was reaching $1 billion in sales by the end of 2007.

Francis decided not to treat his disorders, only taking medication to stave off stress and panic attacks, so he could maintain the high-energy or manic phases in his bipolar disorder. During those times, Francis was intense, even brilliant, Dyer said.

He respected the Joe Francis that walked into Smoak's courtroom in early April 2007, but didn't recognize the man who cried in Smoak's court a few days later.

"You've seen Joe Francis breakdown in court," Dyer said. "That's not Joe Francis.

Chapter 14

Heat wave

"She says she can say good morning and talk about the weather if you want to come in," bailiff Brian Gilchrist said.

"Sure, I'd love to talk about the weather," I said, squeezing past the landmass that was Gilchrist and into Circuit Judge Dedee Costello's chambers.

The judge was seated at the head of a large rectangular table with an arched window behind her. The window looked out at a yellow brick wall and the glass was honeycombed with a black bulletproof web.

Costello smiled and launched in to the prior week's heat wave.

"You been walking in this?" I asked. Costello and a friend walked for exercise every evening through the mossy, oak shaded Cove neighborhood that she shared with Federal Judge Richard Smoak and Federal Magistrate Larry Bodiford.

The summer of 2007 was late in coming on, not turning hot until very late in June. But by July, the temperatures were consistently in the 90s with enough humidity to make it feel like 100 degrees or worse.

"Yes. I walked last night and went to the gym this morning," she said.

"The gym," I said, my voice full of distaste.

"The gym is fun," Costello said.

The small talk continued for a few minutes, both of us testing the patience of the other. Using pleasantries to gain an advantage or dictate the pace of a business conversation is a revered but often overlooked Southern trait.

I knew the conversation had to be a short one. The judge was indulging me, but I'd been bugging her for three weeks as I waited for a ruling on three motions to dismiss the remaining state charges against Joe Francis.

In March 2007, Aaron Dyer and Larry Simpson had filed three motions to dismiss the last felonies Francis was facing: two counts each of using and conspiring to use minors in a sexual performance.

The first two charges were second-degree felonies, carrying 15-year prison sentences. The second two were five-year felonies. Francis was still looking at 40 years in prison despite having almost 40 felonies thrown out.

The case, which once encompassed everything from racketeering to giving alcohol to minors, now boiled down to "the shower scene."

Christina and Darlene were 17 when they'd climbed into a shower together while cameraman Mark Schmitz filmed them.

Francis was in another room, trying to talk two other underage girls into jerking him off. He ultimately paid them $50 each, and he still faced misdemeanor prostitution charges for that.

Dyer and Simpson argued that Francis had to know Christina's and Darlene's ages to be guilty of using a minor in a sexual performance. Criminal intent, they said, was an essential part of all Florida laws unless otherwise specified. There were certainly some charges where knowledge of age didn't apply – for instance, what was once called statutory rape.

The same standard applied to the conspiracy charges – you can't argue there was a conspiracy between Schmitz and Francis to videotape underage girls having sex unless they both knew the girls were underage. Otherwise, Dyer said, all Francis was guilty of was filming two girls naked like he'd legally done on hundreds of occasions. The only difference was this time the girls had lied about being 18.

Prosecutor Mark Graham countered with several motions, saying the law made exceptions to criminal intent to protect children. He also said if the judge found that intent was necessary, he'd be able to prove knowledge on two fronts: Francis knew or should have known the girls' ages because he'd gotten in trouble before for filming underage girls and because he was talking to Christina's and Darlene's friends in the other room and they had surely confessed their ages.

The argument was set to be decided in June, but Graham filed a last minute reply and Judge Costello gave Simpson a week to respond in writing.

Then, for three weeks, Costello did nothing on the case.

Instead, she enjoyed some time off for Independence Day, had her granddaughter visit and did a little traveling.

Meanwhile, Francis was calling his lawyers endlessly trying to find out what was going on. This was a huge issue for him. If Costello dismissed the 2003 charges it would put in motion a series of events that would get him out of jail for the first time in months. He wanted that badly.

If the 2003 charges were gone, Costello would lift a detainer she'd placed on Francis holding him for transport back to Panama City if he made bond in Nevada. Costello would then issue a monetary bond for Francis on the contraband charges. Francis could then pay his bonds in Panama City and Nevada and be free.

How did I know that he was calling his lawyers? Because they were calling me almost every day asking if I'd heard anything.

"My client wants to talk to you," Dyer said as soon as I answered the phone the afternoon of July 16.

"Well put him on," I said cheerfully.

"I said no."

"How come?"

"He thinks something's going on between you and me because we're talking so much. Not, you know, something sexual. Just that he thinks something's up."

This was a big change from the Joe Francis of the first five years of his criminal case. Dyer said in 2004 that Francis trusted him and allowed him to do his work.

"Well put him on. I'll explain it to him."

"Have you heard anything?"

"I talked to the judge this morning and she said she wasn't going to rule. She said to check with her tomorrow, or maybe she'll wait until Wednesday."

"What's your take on this? Why's she taking so long?"

"General consensus around here is she's going to rule for you guys and is in no rush to do it."

I was working on another story – a third lawsuit in three weeks had just been filed against Girls Gone Wild and I wanted to ask him a few questions.

"Let me get Joe off the other line and I'll call you back."

My desk phone had been ringing and the newsroom's business secretary Melissa Clemmons answered it. She sent Francis' corporate lawyer Michael Burke to me as soon as I hung up with Dyer.

We talked about the wave of lawsuits.

Once U.S. District Judge Richard Smoak issued his now-famous "settle or jail" ultimatum in March, which ultimately led to both Francis' incarceration and a settlement of a 2003 lawsuit, lawyers across the country started smelling blood in the water.

Two girls in Orlando, who say Girls Gone Wild cameramen got them drunk even though they weren't 21, then filmed them in sexual situations in the GGW tour bus, sued the company in Panama City. They didn't have any legal standing to file in Panama City because the incident happened in Orlando, but they thought they had a sympathetic judge in Smoak.

Burke said the company had never seen this many lawsuits in such a short period of time. Girls were no longer asking the company to leave them out of videos because they'd changed their minds. Instead, they were filing lawsuits in Panama City.

"Everybody's waiting to see what Judge Smoak is going to do, whether he'll wash his hands of all this," Burke said.

"Are you kidding? Smoak's already got the soap out and ready," I said.

Smoak was a very serious judge who had no interest in tying his name that closely with Girls Gone Wild. He'd made his rulings and wanted nothing more to do with Francis, I reasoned. I turned out to be wrong.

Dyer and Francis were waiting impatiently to see what Costello would do.

The next day they got their answer.

I'd picked up two small stories in the morning and was happily working on something other than GGW when Dyer sent my cell phone a text message.

"Heard anything yet?"

I hadn't. It was a little past one in the afternoon and Costello would be back from lunch at any time. I decided to drive up to the courthouse to check on a ruling.

I breathed in the heat as I left the cool of the newsroom. So few people appreciated the summer heat, but I was a Florida boy and this was refreshing. I'd spent three winters in St. Louis and had my fill of cold.

The sky was a brilliant blue with towering white clouds. It was too dry for rain today, but over the next few days the humidity would build until those white clouds turned to thunder boomers.

The drive to the courthouse was a short one, about a mile. When I walked into the judge's chambers, a secretary told me the judge was in a meeting but had left something for me.

Three rulings.

I texted Dyer back.

"She ruled. Denied all three. I need a quote."

"My quote is 'Mother-effer,'" he said a few minutes later over the phone. "But that would be inappropriate."

Costello had decided that the charges were strict liability offenses, criminal intent and knowledge of age were not issues. The charges would stand and Francis would have to stand trial.

It also meant Aaron Dyer was no longer Francis' lawyer, but I didn't find that out until August. Dyer wasn't going to be the last lawyer fired as Francis became increasingly desperate and lost faith in his legal team.

• • •

The windows were down in my 11-year-old Pathfinder as I drove home across the Tarpon Dock drawbridge after work on Thursday August 23, 2007. I was talking on my cell phone to my girlfriend, Angela Seaton, when the other line beeped in. The 310 area code told me it was Girls Gone Wild business.

"Hey David. It's Joe Francis." He sounded the same, his voice rising at the end of each name, despite four months of incarceration in two county jails.

"And Michael Burke on the other line," Francis' corporate lawyer said, breaking in.

"Well, Michael Burke, Joe Francis, how you guys doin?" I said, smiling at both the embarrassed tone of Burke's voice and the exaggerated enthusiasm of Francis.

Burke was a good lawyer and a smart man, but every time I'd seen him he was spending his time trying to keep Joe Francis from doing something impulsive. It was like watching an overworked nanny chasing a spoiled child. He was also friendly and funny, but keeping track of the manic Francis drove his sense of humor into hiding.

"How's it going in Panama City? What's news out there?" Francis asked.

"Stayin' busy, you know."

He wanted to talk off the record. He was calling to give me a heads up about something "huge" and "groundbreaking" that was going to be filed the next day.

He got into that a little, then his time ran out on the jail phone he was using. A recording of a woman's voice came on the line telling him his three minutes were up. All I heard was Francis yelling at someone down the hall to help him with his phone and then silence.

I was home by then, but since my cell phone didn't get reception inside the house I stayed out on the lawn waiting for a call back. It was obvious that Francis hadn't gotten to the real reason for the call.

I walked across the patchwork of grass and sand that I called a lawn to my oleander bushes. They were growing fast, already taller than me even though I'd planted them just two years before. A Chinese fan palm in the corner of the lawn was a strange yellow color, which didn't look natural, and it seemed to be struggling with the sandy soil.

It took about a minute for the phone to ring again.

"I heard you gave an interview to VH-1," Francis said, forcing nonchalance into his voice. "I heard you said I was getting screwed out there."

"I said that? I might have said that public sympathy was coming around to your side and more people might think that you were not treated properly out here. I think I said something along those lines."

He changed the subject and told me to call his new publicist the next day after the big event broke.

Burke hadn't been able to tell me what was going on, so I called Aaron Dyer. Dyer didn't answer. Nor did he respond to a text message.

So I waited.

The next day nothing happened. I finally got a hold of Burke in the afternoon.

"It's not going to happen today," he said. "If it gets filed it will be the week of Labor Day."

It ended up happening the next Tuesday.

Francis fired Dyer and Tallahassee lawyer Larry Simpson and brought in Roy Black, the powerful celebrity lawyer from Miami.

I finally found Dyer on his cell phone that afternoon.

"You might be right about it being a relief," he said, not sounding relieved. He sounded disappointed. He'd been with Francis from the beginning and was a staunch defender.

"He's been sitting in jail for four months," Dyer said. "People are asking him what his lawyers are doing with him sitting in jail all this time."

So Francis decided to shake things up.

He said he had other projects that he was trying to get done and thought he'd be off all the Girls Gone Wild cases by the end of the week. Then we talked college football. His Trojans were getting ready for "Idaho or Idaho State or something like that" and were favored by 45 points.

"I don't care if you are playing Idaho, 45 points is a lot," he said.

I told him my Gators were getting ready for Western Kentucky.

"We're all on the edge of our seats."

"You know, my first three pointer came against Western Kentucky," Dyer said. He'd played college basketball for USC. He described the shot in detail. "It's really tough to bank in a three."

"I'm surprised you remember it, being so long ago."

"You never forget your first three."

I invited him to come fishing some time – the same thing I told him at the end of every conversation – and we promised to stay in touch.

• • •

Soon after leaving this case, Dyer, the devote Catholic and family man told me he had "the opportunity to take on clients that were similarly situated" as Joe Francis. "I wasn't willing to take on those kinds of cases."

It took me a second to figure out what he was talking about. But then it hit me: "You poor man. Are you saying, you became the porn lawyer?"

"No!" Dyer shot back. "What I'm saying is I declined to become the porn lawyer."

He said he would never have taken Francis' case if it wasn't for the First Amendment issues, as well as what seemed to him to be heavy handed tactics on the part of Bay County law enforcement.

I talked to Larry Simpson shortly after finishing my conversation with Dyer. We talked about his time on the case.

"Four years, you make it sound like a lifetime," he said.

"Didn't it seem like one?"

"I'll let you answer that."

Chapter 15

Misconduct

Joe Francis is usually fully charged, but this time he couldn't contain himself.

"What would you say if I told you Steve Meadows' career was over? On a scale of one to ten, how likely would you be to believe me?"

Tough question, especially since I had no idea what he was talking about. No need to worry though, Francis plowed ahead with the answer.

"Steve Meadows is fucked! His career is over. By this time next year, he's going to be in jail," Francis said, practically squealing the last line.

A soft female voice interrupted the conversation, The Washoe County Jail's recording system, telling Francis that the call was being recorded and he had three minutes left.

When the recording abruptly ended, Francis picked right back up again. He wouldn't tell me what was going to be Panama City State Attorney Steve Meadows' undoing. All he would say was something big was going to be filed the next day.

It turned out to be a motion to dismiss the charges for prosecutorial misconduct as well as letters to the governor, attorney general and Florida Bar asking for criminal investigations.

Francis was accusing Meadows of disseminating child pornography.

"It's incredible. The same fucking thing he's accused me of," Francis said.

In September, Meadows gave Nightline reporter Martin Bashir an interview, during which Meadows and prosecutor Mark Graham showed Bashir the tape of the shower scene. The story aired on November 9 and showed Bashir standing with Meadows while the two looked up at a monitor. Both men were trying to look professional and serious in a decidedly awkward situation.

Audio from a segment of the tape played in the background.

Roy Black wrote in his motion that it was incredible for Meadows to show another person something he had labeled as child pornography. Francis had always maintained that he didn't know how old the girls were when the video was shot, mainly because the girls had lied about their ages.

But Meadows knew they were underage and he still played the tape for Bashir. Black sounded convincingly shocked.

Black asked Circuit Judge Dedee Costello for a range of remedies. If she wasn't inclined to dismiss the charges, Black wanted her to take the case away from Meadows' office and give it to another prosecutor. He also asked her to take custody of the evidence since Meadows seemed incapable of maintaining it properly.

Meadows, who hadn't spoken to me in more than a year, again refused to answer the charges directly. He sent out a bland email complaining that Black took his allegations to the press before they went to the judge.

The motion made some ripples in the community, but nobody thought the allegations would take off. It was unimaginable that a State Attorney could be charged with crimes. No one thought that a judge would even justify the motion by granting any part of it.

Roy Black finally accepted a phone call from me. We talked like people who shared a common ailment, the Joe Francis flu.

"Joe anxious to get out of jail?" It was an obvious, easy question, but I wanted to set an easy tone.

"You figured that out?" He asked back. I could deal with a smartass.

What I wanted to know, and knew he wouldn't answer is how risky was it to file motions accusing Meadows of prosecutorial misconduct, while at the same time Francis' other lawyers were asking for criminal investigations.

"I'm not involved in that," Black insisted. "I don't have any part in the requests for criminal investigations."

His job, he said, was to point out problems in the process as they occur, even if it meant accusing the prosecutor of committing a crime.

He admitted that there wasn't much of a chance that Meadows would be charged, but he did hope that the case would go to another prosecutor – one that wasn't invested in the case and wasn't up for reelection.

Costello scheduled a hearing for January, then changed it to February. She gave Meadows until January to file a written response, which didn't sit well with Francis because it meant he would stay in jail through the holidays.

The State Attorney's Office missed the January 4 deadline. Prosecutor Joe Grammer filed a request for 10 more days, which Costello granted.

Black also moved for Costello to enforce an interstate compact and require Bashir to testify at the hearing. The motion sat on Costello's desk for more than a week. I ran into her in the courthouse parking lot on January 11 and asked her if it was something she needed to rule on before the February 8 hearing. She said it was, but it wasn't anything that needed her immediate attention.

Other defense attorneys sometimes complained of the same treatment from Costello. One lawyer said Costello likes it when a defendant is in jail, especially in jail outside the county so the local taxpayers don't have to pay.

If a defendant is incarcerated, Costello routinely took her time making rulings, he said. If they're out on bond, she'd crack the whip and get the case moving as quickly as possible.

Meadows, meanwhile, was under pressure from several directions. Sitting Circuit Judge Glenn Hess took his first step on January 2 to begin his campaign for Meadows' seat. He wouldn't admit on the record that he would challenge Meadows, but it was the worst kept secret in Bay County.

Hess would be a candidate and Meadows knew it. Meadows called the News Herald several times the week of Hess's resignation, complaining about how many stories there were on the judge.

On January 17, Meadows filed his written response to Black's allegations, denying any misconduct, and signed it himself. It was the only remarkable issue in the document – that Meadows hadn't had another attorney file it which would have insulated him from perjury.

My phone rang shortly after 4 p.m.

"You ready?" Joe Francis asked.

"Sure," I said. I was walking my dog. Francis wanted to give me a quote.

I had my laptop in a messenger bag over my shoulder, which in Panama City meant I was carrying a man purse, and my German shepherd Hiaasen was straining his leash. I was ready.

"It's interesting," he began in a slow tone, "that Steve Meadows and Mark Graham have decided to add perjury to their list of offenses in this case."

"Perjury? In what way?"

"What Meadows doesn't know, because we intentionally kept it out of the motion, was that we have a videotape of Martin Bashir describing, in detail, everything he saw on that tape including a tattoo on one of the girl's asses. We left it out because we knew Meadows would deny it. We set the trap and he walked right in."

I let him talk. He went on for several minutes, growing more excited, his voice getting higher and the words coming faster.

"I'm curious to see if they leave the hearing in handcuffs," he finished, breathlessly. "Now I want to talk off the record. Can we go off the record?"

"Sure," I said. Hiaasen had paused at a particularly appealing spot on the ground. My 95-pound German shepherd doesn't just sniff, he sets his paws and dares you to pull him away. I was distracted, so he gained a few extra seconds before I dragged him on. He still craned his neck back for as long as possible to catch every nuance.

"He's so screwed!" Francis squealed into the phone. "He," of course, was Steve Meadows.

I finished walking to my girlfriend's house and called Will Glover, one of my editors, to pass along the quotes. Will chuckled a few times as he typed Francis' words. Sitting on the back patio, I lit a cigar as I finished talking, and now sat back and took a draw. It was one of my favorites, a La Gloria Cubana.

I let the smoke drift out of my mouth and swirl around my nose before blowing it away. I let myself contemplate for a minute what I'd heard.

I'd spent the morning writing about State Meadows' response, naturally focusing on the child porn allegations.

When the allegations first came out, Meadows put out a press release saying he'd given an edited version of the tape to ABC in response to a public records request. He said nothing about the private viewing Bashir had shown in his story.

In his written motion, Meadows "categorically" denied showing child pornography to Bashir, but he hedged the wording to make it somewhat unclear as to what he was saying. He said Black had referred to the full video in his motion, "not the abridged version as shown."

Meadows wrote that the video he gave to ABC News in November 2007 was edited to remove the visual portion as the girls began to undress, leaving only the audio.

"The attempted bargaining on the part of the camera crew may also be heard, but not seen," he wrote.

He doesn't go into specifics about what he showed Bashir on the day of the interview. That was the issue, not what his office had given ABC as a part of a public records request.

Meadows said that the media has special access, even to view child pornography during court cases, and emphasized that the press had even seen the whole tape in court. Essentially, his argument was that he didn't show Bashir pornography, but if he did it would have been perfectly fine.

Meadows concentrated most of his argument on the allegations that his media interviews were intended to taint the jury pool. He wrote, basically, that Francis started the media war and all Meadows was doing was trying to set the record straight.

Meadows said he gave two interviews, compared to dozens that Francis had given.

Meadows wrote that Francis started it all with his website, meetjoefrancis.com, and advertising in newspapers across the region that readers could get the real story there. Francis took out a big ad with The News Herald and paid for a banner to run across the paper's website with a link. When the bill came in, more than $100,000, Francis refused to pay and The News Herald had to sue.

Meadows said he was well within his rights to refute claims that he felt could influence potential jurors.

Michael Burke was amazed that Meadows had signed it.

"You never write the response yourself. You always have another lawyer in your office write it so you have some insulation from it."

Meadows had left himself exposed. If Bashir came forward and disputed any part of the response, Meadows could be in trouble.

I believed Francis, to a point, about having Bashir on video describing what he'd seen. And it was that point that was starting to worry me. I texted Burke, seeking confirmation. A few minutes later, he called me.

"So, does he have a video?"

"Yes."

"Of Bashir describing sexual activity that he saw in the video that Meadows showed him?"

"To be completely factual, I would take the words 'sexual activity' out of any report you might be writing."

"He didn't see sexual activity?"

"He didn't describe sexual activity."

"Joe says Bashir described the girls' bodies, even a tattoo on one of their backsides."

"That's right. He described nudity, not sexual activity."

"But as soon as there's nudity there's sexual activity."

"I'm not saying he didn't see sexual activity. I'm saying to be completely accurate in any story that you're putting out you would be better served by leaving the words 'sexual activity' out of anything pertaining to what Martin Bashir described."

I found out later that the real issue had been what Meadows *said* in his interviews with Bashir and on VH-1, not necessarily what he *showed* Bashir.

Meadows had talked a lot about the evidence that Judge Costello had thrown out and a jury would never see. He also misstated the girls' ages, saying they were 16. Black argued that all these things that would never get to a jury in court were getting to a jury panel through the interviews.

Meadows might have lost the evidence, but that didn't stop him from trying to inform potential jurors. Even the tape was no longer evidence in Francis' case.

"That was the real winner," Burke said months later. "There wasn't going to be any argument over what was shown to Bashir and what he saw and didn't see. All we had to do was play the interviews."

Judge Costello had responded to Meadows' interviews by issuing an order reminding the attorneys on both sides that they had a legal and ethical obligation to limit their comments in the press. Burke saw that order as another attempt to salvage the case by warning Meadows that he was talking too much.

Three weeks later I got a copy of "The Bashir tape." It was about 30 minutes long and never once was Bashir in the video. It was clearly his voice from off camera, but Brooke Keats, with the Washoe County, Nev., Sheriff's Department, said the videos are shot of the defendants, and so the camera stayed trained on Francis and attorney David Houston.

Much of what was on the tape was Francis fidgeting and arguing with Bashir. But Bashir did say some interesting things and described enough to make it certain that he'd seen sexual activity.

He staunchly refused, however, to say who showed him the shower scene. He only said that when the story aired there would be no doubt where he got it.

The defense had asked Costello to order Bashir's appearance at a hearing on the prosecutorial misconduct. It was a complicated issue because Bashir lived out of state. Costello would have to issue an order, then it would have to go to a judge in Bashir's home state for consideration and a ruling there. Costello, however, put off her order for some time, even with the hearing fast approaching.

Meadows requested a continuance of the hearing so they could better prepare. He also asked Costello to quash the subpoena requiring his testimony, and that of three of his prosecutors. In exchange, prosecutors said, they wouldn't fight an order compelling Bashir's appearance.

It was another puzzling move. Meadows wouldn't fight the one guy who could bury them with his testimony, but didn't want the three guys who were on his side to testify.

The defense didn't hesitate to sign off on that deal.

"Here's a quote for your next story," Francis said to me. "My lawyers and I often sit around asking ourselves if Mike Nifong is personally advising Steve Meadows in this case."

Nifong was the notorious prosecutor of the Duke Lacrosse team, who finally resigned after a series of public blunders and terrible interviews.

Francis said Meadows was desperate to avoid the hearing and was making plea offers to settle the case.

"I'm not kidding, they call me every other day asking me to take a plea. The day before Meadows filed his response, they called me 12 times. Twelve times. I literally told my lawyers to tell him to go fuck himself. I told him, 'I'm going to bury your fat, fucking piggly ass."

He said the offer was to a single felony count of child abuse, time served, no probation to follow.

"Are you sure you don't want to take that plea?" I asked. "You'd be out of jail today. It would be done."

"I'll be out of jail very soon," he said. "I'm only sitting here on principal. I'm only staying in jail to give you a better ending for your book."

• • •

Joe Francis filed six requests for bond in the 11 months he was incarcerated. His pleas were so desperate that Reality TV star Dog the Bounty Hunter gave Costello his personal guarantee that if she released Francis from jail on bond he would track him down and bring him back if he absconded.

"The guy with the hair?" Costello asked when I told her about it. I wanted a comment for my story, which she wouldn't give me. She just smiled and walked away.

Francis asked for bond on account of his deteriorating mental condition.

"You can tell just by watching him that he's not the same," Aaron Dyer said months after he was off the case.

Francis hired a New York attorney to file a single motion saying Costello's refusal to allow him to post bond was unconstitutional, based on the offense and her reasons for holding him. She reminded the lawyer that her ruling had been upheld on appeal.

Francis was stubborn, but the denials wore on him. He got his hopes up every time a bond motion was filed.

His last bond request was in federal court. His newest lawyer, Fred Atcheson of Nevada, asked a judge to find that Panama City federal Judge Richard Smoak had effectively placed Francis in federal hands when he ordered his removal from Panama City despite Costello's objections.

Atcheson argued that the Nevada court had the authority to override Costello's detainer and release Francis from custody on a bail. Francis even promised to hire a retired FBI agent to follow him and assure his return to court.

It was a good argument, but it was denied just the same. The order was designed to leave the matter with the appeals court and Francis' lawyers said they felt confident it would be overturned and Francis would finally make bail.

Francis, however, was going to have to sit in jail for another few months. He was crushed. Despite his bravado in interviews with Martin Bashir and Greta Van Susteren, Francis was desperate to get out of custody.

Finally, he agreed to Meadows' plea offer.

• • •

Prosecutor Joe Grammer confirmed the plea deal on March 10. He wouldn't talk about it too much, saying the plea was for a felony, but he wouldn't talk terms. Negotiations were ongoing and he'd know by the end of the day whether Francis would resolve his case.

"If Judge Costello signs an order lifting her detainer, that should tell you that the deal is done," Grammer said.

"That would be the only reason?"

"I can't think of any other reason," he said.

Costello had put a detainer on Francis in May 2007, saying he'd have to return to Bay County to face his charges is he was released from the Nevada jail.

A U.S. District Judge in Reno had issued a $1.5 million bond on the federal cases, which Francis could easily pay. But Francis' greatest fear was returning to the Bay County Jail where he believed the guards had tortured him.

So instead of making bond, Francis stayed in the Washoe County Jail in Reno until March 10, 2008, when Atcheson handed a clerk a cashier's check for $1.5 million and Francis jogged out the front door to a waiting car.

Costello had lifted the detainer. Francis was free and due to be in Costello's court in two days.

The next day, a Tuesday, rumors were persistent that the State Attorney's Office was trying to convince Francis to fly to Bay County a day early – without fanfare – and enter his plea quietly.

There was no chance of that. Francis spent most of Tuesday at a spa getting coifed and tanned. He decided not to shave or cut his hair.

On Wednesday, Lt. Bob Willoughby stood at the Bay County Courthouse entrance with three or four other bailiffs. They watched a foreign assortment of reporters, cameramen and gawkers roaming around the covered ramp and steps leading to the door.

Bailiffs in general don't like disruptions to their routine, but Willoughby looked amused and relaxed. He didn't anticipate trouble with anything he was seeing, so he didn't worry.

When I walked in, he asked me the same question everyone else had since Monday afternoon: "What do you think he's getting?"

I didn't get a chance to answer, he was too quick with his own guess. He'd seen a notation on a docket for the day indicating that Francis was pleading only to misdemeanor prostitution charges and no felonies. He sent me to the clerk's office to see if I could find what he'd seen.

I couldn't. Clerk Brittany Hutchison complained that she didn't know there was going to be a plea until she read it the day before in the paper. She didn't really believe it was going to happen.

There wasn't an empty courtroom that day, so Costello had asked the other judges if she could borrow a room during lunch. Circuit Judge Michael Overstreet was conducting a trial that day on a man charged with seven counts of lewd and lascivious battery – molesting a child.

Overstreet had agreed to vacate the courtroom at noon and even moved a hearing he'd had for the lunch break to his chambers. But Overstreet was adamant that no one was to enter the courtroom until the jurors had left.

For once, Joe Francis was early.

I'd gone inside to say hello to Roy Black and missed the big entrance, but the other reporters followed him like baby ducks. They deposited their cameras – everything from digital camcorders to full-sized television cameras that rested on shoulders like bazookas – on the conveyor belt and stood in line for the metal detector. The first ones that cleared snatched up their cameras and circled Francis and Black like mosquitos.

When Overstreet's jurors walked out, they ran into the swarm of reporters, who parted reluctantly to let them pass. They looked around a little nervously, hoping that their trial hadn't gained some unwelcome notoriety that would put them on TV.

Overstreet was still on the bench when I walked in. He glanced up at the crowd pouring in, then went back to gathering his papers. Prosecutor Al Sauline hurried to clear his table and pack up his file box. He would say later that seeing every seat filled with spectators for Joe Francis' plea was unsettling, considering his trial went unnoticed.

"Here's a guy charged with seven counts of molesting kids, a really bad guy, and no one cares. Then I look out and see courthouse employees skipping their lunch breaks to watch Joe Francis and I think, 'What does this say about our society?'"

I took a seat in the jury box, out of camera range. Bob Pell, the lawyer representing Mantra Films President Scott Barbour, took the seat beside me. Barbour was charged with smuggling in the pills Francis was found with back in April. Pell hoped that once Francis' case was out of the way he could resolve Barbour's.

Francis walked in, the engine to his lawyer train, in a navy blue pinstriped suit and white shirt opened at the collar. He had a week-old beard and, as usual, he looked at the crowd as he made his way in. He smiled at a few, his hands in his pockets.

He approached the table that Sauline had just vacated and pulled out one of the rolling, padded black chairs. He stood for a minute, looking from the chair to the crowd, uncertain of whether to sit with his back to the audience or stay standing.

Black called him to a table in front of the judge's bench, saying this wouldn't take long enough for him to need to sit.

He buried his hands back in his pockets, the bottom of his suit coat bunched up around his forearms. He smiled and glanced around the room.

Bailiff Brian Gilbert led Costello into the room with a gruff "All rise."

Costello stepped quickly up to her seat. Her hair, usually kept short, was higher off the collar than Francis'. She wore her usual bright red lipstick.

"Are we ready to proceed? Is there an announcement at this time?" she asked.

Roy Black told her Francis was prepared to plead no contest to two amended informations for a sentence of time served – a total of 336 days in jail.

The comprehensive plea was to one felony count of child abuse and four misdemeanors – two soliciting prostitution charges and two violations of posted jail rules for having a water bottle and currency in his jail cell.

The court costs and fines would total more than $70,000. The State Attorney's Office would received $12,600 for its nearly five years of prosecution. The county would get $38,500 – even though Sheriff Frank McKeithen refused to endorse the plea or even give the prosecutors a dollar amount as to his office's cost in investigating the case.

"There is no amount of money Joe Francis could pay that would begin to offset the past five years of flagrant and repeated disrespect for the citizens of Bay County," he wrote in a letter to prosecutor Bill Lewis. "I will not give Mr. Francis the pleasure of thinking he can buy or pay for the services of the Bay County Sheriff's Office. It is our day-to-day job to protect the citizens of our county from such criminal elements as Joe Francis. This is one segment of his life he will not be able to buy his way out of. There is no price for justice."

Francis would get his Ferrari back, but he'd have to promise not to sue the sheriff's office over costs of deterioration. He'd have to take it back "as is."

The first issue that came up was discrepancy over the amount Francis would have to pay to the Victims' Compensation Trust Fund. Shapiro thought the amount was $1,600, but prosecutor Mark Graham told him the amount was actually $1,650. That got Shapiro and Black searching their wallets for cash.

"We are out of checks this morning so we will have to ..." Shapiro said, flipping the cash in his wallet with his thumb.

"Dig in your pockets," Costello joked.

"I might have $20 in cash on me, that's about it," Shapiro said.

"Mr. Black has got it," Costello said, smiling.

"Let him cover it," Francis laughed, slapping Black on the shoulder.

Costello went through the usual questions with Francis that a judge asks a defendant who is entering a plea. She asked if he was on medication or taking drugs, what his education level was and whether he'd been treated for a mental illness.

When Francis said no to the last question, Costello stopped.

"At one point you were claiming you were having some emotional problems while you were being held in jail in Nevada. Are those problems resolved?" she asked. Francis' lawyers had asked for bond while he was in Nevada, claiming incarceration was making him crazy and would ultimately make him unfit for trial.

"Ah, yes, for the most part," Francis answered.

"Your honor," Black said, "Mr. Francis is a very high energy person and is an excellent business man, he does have some various matters that came to him while he was in custody, that's why we filed that motion. It was directed at the terms of his incarceration, which were causing that problem. However, there is nothing that interferes with his competency here today to enter this plea."

"It's my obligation to make sure that you know what you're doing," Costello told Francis. "That you understand all its consequences and that you're in full control of your faculties. I want to make sure for your best interest as well as everyone else's, we don't want to go through this twice."

"I can assure you that Mr. Francis doesn't want to go through this twice," Black said.

"Do you think this is in your best interest, primarily because you're getting out of jail today?" Costello asked Francis.

"Ah, yes," he said, struggling to keep the sarcasm down.

Costello read to him the part of the plea that said Francis and his companies had to stay out of the Florida Panhandle for three years. From Pensacola to Marianna, Girls Gone Wild couldn't even advertise in the area.

"Your honor, I'm happy not to come back. I'm done with Bay County," Francis said.

There were two telling things about the plea. First, Shapiro told the judge that a condition of the arrangement was that Francis had to drop his prosecutorial misconduct motion. That stipulation jumped out to me because it was a part of a motion to dismiss the charges. Francis, through his plea, was resolving his charges. There should have been no reason to stipulate that he had to drop the motion to dismiss.

The second item was something that Costello caught. She read from the plea form that all the tapes collected as evidence in the 2003 case were to be destroyed. Costello said, instead, they were going to be turned over to the sheriff's office for safekeeping until she issued another order.

The tapes weren't evidence in Francis case, but they still were in the case against Mark Schmitz, the cameraman charged along with Francis in the "shower scene" episode. The State Attorney's Office had just asked for evidence to be destroyed – including the shower scene that was at the heart of the prosecutorial misconduct motion. That was that tape that Meadows showed to Martin Bashir.

Finally, Costello named Francis a convicted felon. First offenders usually get this label withheld, but Francis didn't seem surprised.

As Francis was being fingerprinted, several cameramen ducked out of the courtroom and took up station in a semi-circle around the door. I waited a few minutes longer, but still left ahead of Francis.

I walked out with attorney Bob Pell. We went down the first flight of stairs and I stopped.

"What do you think? Is that going to help your case?" I asked him.

He sputtered for a minute, trying to find the words. Finally he said, "I'm going to go home and take a shower."

• • •

I was leaning against a bike rack at the end of the ramp leading to the courthouse door when Francis came out, followed by his lawyers and entourage. We shook hands and he moved to a shaded spot on the grass under a tree where the gaggle of reporters who had followed him out of the courthouse formed a half-circle in front of him.

In usual fashion, he got right to it.

"I'm 100-percent innocent of anything I just pled to. Everything I pled to, I pled, like the judge said, to get out of jail. I have been held by this county for 11 months of what I deem illegal incarceration. I have done nothing wrong. I am not guilty of a single thing," he said.

"This plea negotiation has been going on for quite some time. The state attorney, Steve Meadows, upon Roy Black's filing of a prosecutorial misconduct motion, has been begging, calling every single day almost in tears for us to make a deal with him.

"I chose to finally plea to a felony just to get out of jail. That was the only reason I pled here to something I did not do. I have never committed a crime and it is just absurd.

"This is embarrassing to the entire criminal justice system. The fact that a few corrupt individuals in Bay County, Panama City, Florida, were able to pull this off and successfully keep an innocent man incarcerated for 11 months."

A reporter asked him who the corrupt individuals were.

"You've got State Attorney Steve Meadows is definitely corrupt. I feel bad for the people of Bay County who have to deal with it. This is not fair, this is not fair to you. The fact that this town and these corrupt individuals in this small town were able to do this to me, railroad me like this, keep me incarcerated for 11 months, seize my plane illegally, say there was cocaine on my plane, which all turned out to be false, the fact that they were able to railroad me like this in the United States of America and keep me incarcerated for that long when they knew I did no wrong, it hurts us all guys because you're next. If people get away with this then you're next.

"If I didn't have money, if I didn't have notoriety I would have had a very different result. If I didn't have Roy Black I probably would have had a very different result than I had in that courtroom today. Guys, no time, no probation, this was a total victory for us.

"I'm gonna go back to my life. I'm gonna go back to making great 'Girls Gone Wild' videos – not here."

Black had been standing to the side, mainly looking at the grass and trying not to smile or cringe, depending on the statement. Francis waved him forward so he could say a few words.

"The reason Joe is particularly upset is that because of the type of charges and the ruling by the court that it was strict liability, that he didn't have to have the intent to commit a crime, is what I really think has caused this anguish here. He always thought that the young ladies involved were over 18, they said they were over 18, they signed forms saying they were over 18 and they were on videotape saying they were over 18, but they were only 17.

"Because of the way the law's written in Florida, the court ruled that it makes no difference that they lied and you believe them you're still guilty of a crime. I will say I think the judge handled this very professionally, I think the actual prosecutors that we dealt with in court like Mark Graham and Joe Grammer were professional and of course I don't want to characterize anyone else in this case like Joe has."

"Steve Meadows," Francis said, smiling.

"I understand why Joe was so upset," Black continued. "He has a right to be upset because, just think in his business how dangerous this is – expressing your First Amendment rights and the next thing you know they put you in jail for 11 months when none of it was your fault."

Francis cut back in.

"Yes, I asserted my First Amendment right and all of us have been told just how many rights we have by Bay County, Florida, and it just sucks because this sets us all back. Yeah, I'm walking free but we're all less free because of what happened in this town and this courtroom today," he said.

News Herald Managing Editor Mike Cazalas, who had come to the proceedings out of curiosity, asked Francis if it was difficult to plead to a felony.

"I could have taken this exact same deal three months ago when Roy was performing, what I like to call defense sodomy on Steve Meadows and he was …"

"I'd rather not characterize it that way if possible," Black interrupted.

"He was begging for me to take a felony and that was a sticking point for me. I did not want to plead to a felony but at the end of the day no one was going to believe that two 17 year old girls lie about their age, I wasn't even present, they show fake ID, falsify a release form and I'm somehow a child abuser? It's ridiculous. It's absurd and no one would believe it. So who cares," Francis said.

Meadows held a press conference a few minutes later. News Herald reporter Ed Offley covered it for me so I could work another angle.

"This case has drawn on now for way too long," Meadows started. "We have seen the evidence in this case, all the films, suppressed because of some misstatements by law enforcement. We've seen a nationwide media blitz in which Mr. Francis attempted to gain favor with the public and to discredit the prosecution through media outlets from coast to coast.

"We've seen outrageous claims filed in defense motions attempting to smear and color the prosecution. We've seen Mr. Francis personally threaten to fund a political opponent in the upcoming state attorneys race in opposition to me.

"Throughout all of these attacks we have stood strong. We have stood strong in the belief that Mr. Francis should be held accountable for what he did. Wherever he goes from this day forward for the remainder of his life, he will be a convicted child abuser. He will always have to acknowledge that he is a convicted felon."

Meadows classified Francis' allegations as "rantings," but said since Francis was attacking him along with Costello, Smoak and the "people of this community," Meadows felt like he was in good company.

He talked about the condition that Francis and Mantra stay out of the Panhandle for three years – an entirely unenforceable caveat that meant next to nothing. Even the advertising condition didn't apply to the late night national ads that Francis had built his empire on.

"Mr. Francis has made his living exploiting young women throughout this country but thanks to this agreement he will not, for at least the next three years, make his living from Pensacola to Tallahassee. Girls Gone Wild cannot operate filming girls within this community for the next three years," Meadows said.

He said he wanted the video tapes destroyed so the "people who were captured will not ever have to be concerned about their images having to appear in future Girls Gone Wild productions."

He gave a different take on the plea negotiations. He said he would not accept anything less than a felony plea and Francis had been unwilling to "come forward and admit his felonious conduct."

There's no doubt that this plea came about through a combination of things. The prosecutorial misconduct motion and upcoming election were factors for Meadows.

For Francis, his most recent bond motion before U.S. District Judge Robert McQuaid, Jr. had gone badly. McQuaid denied the motion, saying only that Francis' lawyers had raised some excellent points and the decision had been a close one.

The lawyers felt confident that the circuit court of appeals would look favorably on the argument and overturn McQuaid's ruling. But that meant months more time in jail awaiting the appeal.

Francis had run out of patience with incarceration.

Meadows ended his speech saying he felt the sentence was appropriate.

"I feel that we can now move forward in this community with the self assurance that in spite of continued rantings of Mr. Francis that he cannot change the fact that he is a convicted child abuser," he said.

Offley asked him if the prosecutorial misconduct motion played a part in the plea negotiations.

"Absolutely not," Meadows answered. "I felt for sure it was meritless. In fact, the defense, in their subsequent filings, have now withdrawn any suggestion of inappropriate display."

That last statement went unchallenged. What "subsequent filings" was he talking about?

"Anytime we have somebody like Mr. Francis, who has never before in the history of this country been prosecuted for this type of conduct, to come to this area and know that we take these crimes seriously, and it didn't matter how long it took, we were willing to stay with it and stand strong and that his money and his rantings and that his smear campaign were not going to deter us. We've continued to stand strong today.

"We have taken a year of his life, almost."

Meadows also said the re-election had nothing to do with resolution of the case, but he was the one who talked about Francis' threat to fund a political opponent in the upcoming race. He wasn't asked to explain that either.

The questions ended and the event was over.

When Offley and online editor Tony Simmons left the room they were talking about the striking difference in Meadows' body language compared to Francis. Simmons said Meadows had positioned himself in front of a wall and looked trapped.

The press conferences were over and it was time for lunch.

Coincidentally, both Meadows and Francis picked the same restaurant – Smitty's Barbecue. It had great chicken salad and Texas toast sandwiches and it was the place for the movers and shakers in the community.

"Can you believe that Meadows came in and had lunch in the next booth?" Francis asked a day later. "It was freakin' hilarious."

"Let me ask you something, do you think the judge was flirting with me?" he asked. "I'm serious. She seemed smiley and flirty and joking with me."

• • •

"Portions of the tape that we were shown included passages in which two naked 17-year-olds were engaged in mutual masturbation," Martin Bashir told his audience in a March 2008 broadcast.

He'd promised to put to rest the question of whether Steve Meadows had shown him child pornography at the end of the night's show and he delivered. If Bashir had seen the girls masturbating, he'd seen everything else. That segment is at the end of the tape.

Bashir's crew had recorded him and Meadows leaning against a desk and looking toward something off camera. In the background can be heard a shower running and some of the conversation that was going on between the girls and cameraman Mark Schmitz during the shower scene.

In his November 8 broadcast, Bashir had shown a similar scene but in his last story on the subject, he showed another part.

They're leaning against the desk and Bashir looks embarrassed. His arms are crossed over his chest and his head is down while Meadows is watching the video closely.

"We get it," Bashir says, pushing himself off the desk and turning toward the door.

"You haven't seen the most offensive part," Meadows says.

Meadows had insisted in his filing that he hadn't shown Bashir pornography. His court filing, while it didn't specifically address what Bashir was shown, categorically denied the allegation that he'd given Bashir a private viewing of the shower scene.

But after Bashir's broadcast, Meadows had to admit that Bashir had seen nudity.

"He saw no sexual contact," Meadows told reporter Ed Offley. "He did see nudity. Simple nudity is not child pornography."

The tape, however, has only a few seconds in which the girls are nude and not pornographic and it's well before the masturbation scene. Meadows told Offley that the reason Bashir was shown the tape at all was to disprove Francis' claim that he wasn't in the motel room and didn't know about the filming.

But the only segment of the tape that shows Francis and the girls together is when they're walking into the room. There's nothing in the shower scene that indicates Francis was in the room or watching. He can't be heard giving direction or making comments and is never shown.

Francis crowed over Bashir's revelation.

"We finally caught State Attorney Steve Meadows," he said. "He showed child pornography to Martin Bashir. That's what ultimately led to the resolution of this case."

• • •

Francis' 11 months in jail were a fairly tumultuous time for Steve Meadows as well. He was preparing for his re-election campaign, and the words "prosecutorial misconduct" were a poor way to start.

On March 3, 2008, a supervisor in Meadows' office filed a sexual harassment complaint against him with the state Commission on Human Relations. Two more complaints followed and Meadows was looking at the very real possibility that on the eve of the election the reports would become public and he would be painted as a miscreant.

The commission investigated for a year and released its report in March 2009. But reports of the investigation and interviews with people involved, had leaked well in advance and in the midst of the campaign.

Office manager Randy Berling, the man responsible for investigating sexual harassment complaints at the State Attorney's Office, summed up Meadows' actions in one complainant by saying, "The boy just can't help himself."

The state investigators found convincing evidence to support both the main claims. In their report, they said the State Attorney's Office was divided into two "factions." The first, all management within the office, believed that Meadows was a great guy whose only fault was he treated all his employees like family.

The other side were the secretaries, not all the secretaries, but more than a few who suffered the brunt of Meadows' harassment who described the work atmosphere as constantly tense.

The investigators even validated one claim from a secretary who said Meadows had sex with her on his office couch that she described as "practically a rape."

Meadows didn't deny having sex with the woman, only declining to tell investigators where they'd had sex.

Meadows' primary concern during this investigation, according to the report, was when it was going to be made public. The investigators noted instances when Meadows or his attorney asked to delay the report's release until after the November 4 election.

Meadows was certain the sexual harassment claims and the investigation were part of a political plot to get him out of office that went "as far up the food chain" as the governor's office.

I was able to do two stories based on information from those employees who had been interviewed and a Tallahassee attorney, Marie Mattox, who was preparing a lawsuit and was only waiting for the investigation to be completed. For the next six weeks after the stories broke and before the November 4 election, Meadows spent considerable time at public forums fending off questions about sexual harassment in his office. He lost the election by 10,000 votes.

On January 9, 2009, Meadows left office

Chapter 16

Last lawsuit

In March 2008, not long after Francis entered his plea and was released from jail, a new lawsuit was filed in federal court in Panama City. It included the last one of the four girls who were at the Chateau Motel room on March 31, 2003.

Plaintiff V was three days from her 17th birthday when she and three friends met up with Francis and his film crew. They went to room 320 of the Chateau where two of V's friends were filmed in the "shower scene." Francis took V and another girl into the bedroom and tried to get them both to jerk him off.

V didn't sign on to the first lawsuit and missed out on filing for damages three years later when she was interviewed as a victim in Mantra's federal criminal case. Her statement was the one that Francis was forced to read out loud when Mantra was sentenced to probation in that case.

Now she and three other girls had their own lawsuit and they'd gone with the same attorneys who won the 2003 lawsuit, D. Ross McCloy, Larry Selander, Thomas Dent and Rachael Pontikes. These were the lawyers who Francis cussed during mediation in 2007, ultimately leading to his contempt of court sentence. Francis signed a settlement in that lawsuit from a jail cell.

Besides V, there were two girls, Plaintiff J, 13, and her sister, Plaintiff S, 15, who flashed their breasts for GGW cameras in March 2000. They were passengers in a car that was riding the strip during the height of Spring Break. Traffic was stop and go, mostly stop, and at one pause an independent cameraman came up to the car and asked them to flash. The footage, which was sold to GGW, ended up in two videos.

Plaintiff B was 17 when she came down from Charlotte, North Carolina, to Panama City Beach for Spring Break in 2002. At a party, a cameraman invited her and her friends up to a hotel room, where she was offered alcohol, which she claimed was spiked with drugs that "impaired her judgment and made her susceptible to coercion." She signed a release, saying she was 18 and wrote down a fake birth date. She then went into a bedroom and had sex with a female friend, which was videotaped and included in two GGW DVDs.

A month after their initial filing, McCloy, Selander, Dent and Pontikes amended the lawsuit as a class-action suit. They claimed there were potentially hundreds of girls who had been victimized by Girls Gone Wild over the years, but the only way they'd be able to say how many there were was to search all of Mantra's records.

The classes were all minor girls in the nation who GGW had used in its videos; Florida minor girls who were filmed flashing; and Florida minor girls who'd been filmed having some kind of sexual encounter.

Almost as soon as the lawsuit had been filed, Francis filed motions asking Federal Judge Richard Smoak to take himself off the case. Attorney Robert Barnes said Smoak was undeniably biased against Francis because of comments he'd made in Francis' hearings. Smoak's friendship with McCloy was also cited as a reason for Smoak to remove himself.

But Smoak insisted his rulings had been justified and his comments harmless. He said his friendship with McCloy, while going back some years, was a disappointingly distant one. He denied all three motions for recusal that Francis filed, but he also denied the motion to certify the lawsuit as class-action and motions to summarily award damages to the plaintiffs because Francis wasn't providing discovery to the plaintiff's lawyers.

Francis hired and fired two sets of lawyers in the first 10 months of the lawsuit. He was driving those lawyers, and attorneys in another Panama City lawsuit, to file dangerously aggressive motions accusing Smoak of bias in his case and for the most part his lawyers did what they could to argue for Smoak's recusal without risking contempt charges themselves.

Shortly after Joe Francis signed the settlement from a jail cell in 2003, a rash of lawsuits were filed against him in federal Judge Richard Smoak's court.

One was from two girls in Orlando who said they were plied with alcohol and filmed in a sexual situation in a GGW van, even though the cameraman assured them that the film would never be used. Those girls would eventually walk away from this lawsuit when Francis' lawyers showed them their entire, unedited video and threatened them with a counter suit.

Another was from former cheerleader, who said she was 16 when a GGW cameraman filmed her flashing. Topless pictures of her made it to the cover of a Girls Gone Wild video.

Jean Marie Downing, a Panama City lawyer, filed a motion asking Smoak to recuse himself from the cheerleader's case because the public might view him as having lost his impartiality when it came to Joe Francis. After all, Downing wrote, he is the judge who gave Francis the "settle or jail" ultimatum.

Smoak was not amused.

"In my more than 34-year history as a trial attorney and judge, the pending motion to disqualify is the first time that anyone represented by counsel has ever filed a motion questioning my ethics or moved to disqualify me from presiding over a case," he wrote in his order denying Downing's motion.

"I have never had, nor do I currently harbor, any animosity, bias or prejudice toward Joe Francis or Girls Gone Wild that would cause me to question my ability to fairly and impartially preside over this case."

Smoak's order was extraordinary not only in its length and detail, but in the fact that he first notes that GGW itself doesn't question his impartiality, but only says the public might. He says there's really no need to go any further because GGW lacks standing, that's on Page 4 of a 49-page order.

On Page 5, he says the motion ignores the fact that Francis was always represented by good lawyers who didn't object to what was going on and Smoak's rulings have all been affirmed on appeal. That should have been all that needed to be said.

But Smoak pressed on with a history of the GGW federal case, the rationale for his actions and the inaccuracies in press reports: "The pending motion is not the first time that Girls Gone Wild and its attorneys have made charges of unethical conduct against members of the bar and sought their disqualification," Smoak wrote, referencing the 2006 motion from Miami attorney Tom Julin asking Smoak to remove Tom Dent and Ross McCloy from representing the plaintiffs in the 2003 lawsuit.

Smoak said he exposed "the motion in Doe v. Francis for what it was – a 'below-the-belt" cheap shot at plaintiffs and their attorneys."

In his recusal order, he said "a reasonable person could well perceive the motion requesting my disqualification as simply an attempt by Joe Francis, Girls Gone Wild and their counsel to broaden the campaign of ethical assaults on members of the bar to now include a member of the judiciary."

He said in his order that Downing distorted the legal question of recusal – whether a well-informed bystander would see the judge's actions as biased – to whether "public opinion" would see them so.

"Even if I were to assume that 'public perception' is a relevant consideration in assessing the merits of the pending motion," Smoak wrote, "defendants have failed to submit evidence that the public does indeed perceive me as biased against Joe Francis."

Then Smoak addressed "settle or jail," The News Herald's headline on the day that Smoak found Francis to be in civil contempt of court.

"Simply stated, my order did not require that Joe Francis settle the lawsuit; rather, it unambiguously required that Joe Francis mediate his case in good faith after I found him in civil contempt for exploiting a court-ordered mediation. I can only assume that Angier, a non-attorney, misunderstood the difference between requiring a party to settle a case and requiring a party to mediate a case in good faith when he wrote the 'settle or jail' article."

What Smoak left out of this explanation was his exchange in the civil contempt hearing with Michael Burke. Smoak had ordered Francis to jail for contempt until such time that the parties could convene for "meaningful mediation." Smoak said in the hearing that it would probably take a few days for a mediator to be lined up and the parties put into place, during that time Francis would be in jail.

"I had no inclination to punish Francis or to cause him to 'lose' the civil lawsuit," Smoak wrote. "That sanction imposed was simply intended to force Joe Francis to obey an order of this Court – my order to mediate."

Next item, the judge's comment on Francis' language during mediation. Smoak had commented in the hearing that Francis' behavior was the worst he's seen in his career. Smoak scoffed at Francis' lawyer's characterization of the behavior as "colorful."

"Perhaps the next time any of us are at our mother's dinner table and we talk like Mr. Francis, we can simply tell our mother that we're just 'being colorful' and see how that flies," Smoak said.

He defended those statements as the truth, not bias.

He went through Francis' actions during that belated mediation point-by-point, from the bare feet and profanity laced tirade to the only proposal Francis made that day – "suck my dick!"

"How defense counsel can reasonably question my characterization of these events is astounding," Smoak wrote. "Not only had I never witnessed or experienced such vile behavior by a litigant at a court-ordered function in my long career as an attorney and mediator, but plaintiffs' counsel all testified that neither had they.

"Simply put, Francis' behavior was not mediation. It was not posturing. It was violent. Anyone attending that mediation, including Joe Francis himself, could have been injured. I will not permit a litigant in this federal court to exploit an order issued by me for the sole purpose of abusing and threatening another party."

Smoak wrote that his order to incarcerate Francis had been the right one. His mistake, he said, was in delaying that order because Francis' attorneys told him a settlement offer had been made.

Then Smoak gets into the dicey part of the negotiations. On March 31, 2007, Francis made an unconditional offer to the plaintiffs. As the negotiations continued, he added conditions that "substantially and materially decreased the dollar amount of the offer.

"In other words, even under a threat of incarceration, Francis had unlawfully revoked his unconditional offer after it had already been accepted," Smoak wrote. "Francis had also fled."

Actually, he left Panama City to spend his birthday with his girlfriend in Miami.

Smoak never mentioned why the plaintiffs' lawyers would break the silence of mediation to complain about the conditions that Francis had attached to the offer.

• • •

The cheerleader withdrew her lawsuit in late 2008 when Francis threatened her with a countersuit. The lawyers and judges called it a "settlement," but when I wrote that in the newspaper, Francis called to complain. The next day we ran another story under the headline "Don't call it a settlement." Francis wanted everyone to know that this case was an unequivocal victory.

Less than a month after Downing filed her motion to recuse in Pitts' case, a similar motion was filed in the Plaintiff B case. This one didn't hint that Smoak might be perceived as biased based on popular opinion. Attorney Ross Babbitt wrote that the strongest evidence that Smoak was biased was the fact that Plaintiff B's lawyers were the same ones who had manipulated Smoak into forcing a settlement out of Francis in the 2003 lawsuit.

"The touchstone for this Court's determination of this motion is the overwhelming appearance of bias that lawyers from all over this country clearly perceive to be in their favor in this court," Babbitt wrote. "The evidence of that perception is further manifested in the hundreds upon hundreds of hours of attorney time the plaintiff's lawyers claim to have invested in this case. It is clear that those lawyers are hoping to maneuver the defendants into an unfair bargaining position to extract an extortionate settlement from the defendants (as they have in the past), irrespective of the merits of their case. And those lawyers can only hope to do that with the help of this Court, which they perceive to be biased in their favor."

Babbitt said a recent ruling by Smoak denying a defense motion that was clearly supported by law was evidence of bias.

"That two-page Order from this federal court, which addresses none of the legal arguments Defendants raised in their Motion For Judgment on the Pleadings, is predicated on the incorrect legal standard, and even contains misspellings and typographical errors, is further evidence which would tend to support an impartial observer's perception that this Court is biased against these defendants."

That's about as disrespectful as a lawyer gets in addressing a federal judge. But Smoak's ruling did not rise to the bait. He kept his composure and denied the motion.

His reasons for wanting to stay on the case were not expressed, but he was determined to prove that he had not been biased and was not going to be anything but fair in dealing with Francis.

And the Plaintiff B case was not going anywhere. Smoak had already denied a motion to dismiss the case. Francis' lawyers, who were struggling to keep him happy while working both the lawsuit and the tax evasion case, weren't providing the plaintiffs with the materials they'd demanded, despite three warnings from a magistrate judge to turn over the paperwork.

On March 18, 2009, Francis' third attorney, Rick Bateman of Tallahassee, went before Smoak after just a few weeks on the case.

Bateman, who propped his reading glasses up on his brow when he wanted them out of the way then dropped them into place with a quick nod of his head, was constantly in motion during the hearing. When Selander or Dent were making their arguments, Bateman would shoot to his feet, sit back down, stand up and walk to the podium next to the other attorney and stand with his hands on his hips sighing or grumbling, seemingly incapable of containing his outrage at what he was hearing.

His mannerisms aside, he was thoroughly prepared for the hearing and Smoak was satisfied that Bateman had righted the ship.

Bateman assured Smoak that he could and would control Francis and get the case to trial in July. He said the discovery in question was waiting for the plaintiffs, but he argued that there were certain documents that shouldn't be provided because Francis, who was going to trial in the early part of July on federal tax evasion charges, had a right against incriminating himself by turning over financial documents to the plaintiffs that could end up in the government's hands.

In May, the sides were scheduled to go before recently retired Florida Supreme Court Justice Kenneth Bell for mediation.

Chapter 17

"War"

"They fucked with the wrong guy!"

It's the same old Joe.

"Whatcha doin?" I'd asked when I got connected to Francis on August 19, 2008. He'd just filed letters of intent to sue Bay County officials and a separate lawsuit seeking to rescind the 2003 lawsuit settlement.

"What do you think I'm doing?" Francis answered.

"I think you're sitting around having a drink and a smoking a cigar."

"I'm getting ready to go to war."

The Francis camp had been throwing the word "war" around for days. On this day, Francis had opened three fronts: he'd filed a lavishly written lawsuit to rescind the settlement; two complaints to Bay County officials putting them on notice that they were in line for a lawsuit; and started a Web campaign to impeach U.S. District Judge Richard Smoak.

Francis didn't wait long to get to the point of his call – the same point he always came to in our conversations.

"People are gonna hate me out there, aren't they?" he asked, nearly giggling. "What are they saying?"

"I don't know, nobody's returning my calls."

I was on deadline and wanted to ask him a few questions on the record.

"The one thing everybody is gonna ask me," I started, "is why can't Joe Francis let this go?"

"Let it go?" he spat it out like sour milk. "They took millions of dollars from me. They damaged my business and my reputation and they're going to pay. It's disgusting what they did to me."

Earlier in the day, former Panama City Beach mayor and now conservative talk show host Lee Sullivan snorted when I told him Joe Francis accused him of damaging his reputation.

"You run an empire that's built off selling videos of little girls, or young women if you want to press the point, exposing their private parts, and I've done what?" he laughed in a series of short, deep bursts. "I guess I'll just have to deal with that."

Sullivan took a deep breath and started, very slowly, to lay out a quote for me. He started by facetiously praising Joe Francis "as the champion of American morality and virtue." He said he hoped Joe would be able to find the time to continue to "fight for truth, justice and the American way when he's not busy filming various women in states of undress."

Sullivan was still laughing when he hung up the phone.

• • •

Every change in this case began with changes in the lawyers, usually because the lawyers wouldn't risk their careers by doing exactly what Francis wanted them to do.

Michael Burke and Lisa Shulman were with Mantra Films Inc. for years, but both left abruptly in August 2008. Shulman wrote in a motion to withdraw from a federal case "that there comes a time when a lawyer and client no longer see things the same."

Burke said something similar a few days later over the phone. He said the lawsuit to rescind the settlement had been around for more than a year, since Francis signed the settlement. It was first drafted by Francis' longtime criminal defense lawyer, Aaron Dyer.

The one filed in August, however, was significantly different. Francis' federal tax case hadn't resolved itself with a favorable plea the way he'd said it would in March.

The case was instead moving slowly toward trial. Everything that happened before and after the charges were filed could have some impact on a potential sentence. Insulting a federal judge in one venue while facing a federal judge in another was not wise.

And Francis' filings were insulting. They were also ludicrous:

"In duplicitous treachery only the dogmatic and rigid can embrace, the local powers that be publicly threaten to arrest and imprison the young Californian if he steps foot in their town to simply observe and capture for the world the very spring break behavior that Panama City uses to stuff its pockets and placate the tax concerned locals," attorney Robert Barnes wrote in the lawsuit to rescind. "Southern injustice, sadly symbolic for centuries as a land without law, where guns and gavels too easily replaced law and logic, where the robe and the tree too often substituted for the rule of law and the Bill of Rights, reared again."

It goes on and on, claiming at one point that Ross McCloy and his co-counsel in Chicago somehow knew years in advance that President Bush would appoint Smoak as Panama City's federal judge.

"Since Southern injustice is never concluded without a friendly judge," Barnes wrote, "the lawyers file, dismiss, then re-file their civil claim in federal court on behalf of the women and their parents, then affirm a stay, while secretly awaiting a new federal judicial appointment. After that appointment they move to lift the stay. Who was this new judge they waited on? Their long time friend and decade-long former law partner Richard Smoak, with a visceral bias against Francis' business, likely known to them."

The language of the lawsuit was so outrageous, so laughable, and the timing so bad it seemed just crazy. Francis had always had his own perspective and selective memory about events in his case, but the lawsuit was filled with outright misrepresentations about the facts, plus incredible accusations and scenarios.

During Francis' incarceration, his lawyers privately discussed Francis' deteriorating mental condition. They filed motions asking for his release because confinement was exacerbating his bipolar and attention deficit disorders.

Now, Francis seemed to be losing touch with reality and becoming increasingly self-destructive.

When the lawsuit was filed, Francis recorded a message that was posted on his Web site. He sat in front of an American flag, sporting a new bowl-cut hair style, and said he was fighting for the rights of all Americans.

"This can happen to you," flashed on the screen before Francis appeared.

"Free speech is what I want to talk to you about today," Francis said, his hands clasped in front of him. "I learned the hard way that you can't take your free speech rights for granted. In 2003, I was falsely accused of illegal activity and wrongfully imprisoned by a small town courthouse gang, including Federal Judge Richard Smoak."

He complained about his 11-month incarceration without bail and declared it another violation of his civil rights.

"They shackled me and threw me in solitary confinement. I realized, if this can happen to me it can happen to anyone. What happened to me in Panama City is not what we expect in America. When a person is jailed without bail for 11 months in a civil lawsuit it violates the U.S. Constitution and our basic freedoms and liberties.

"I will never stop fighting for free speech, free expression and our right to read or view whatever we choose. As for the clique of conspirators in Panama City, Florida, you can run but you can't hide from justice."

He encouraged those viewing the tape to click on an accompanying link that would allow them to email the head of the U.S. House of Representatives Judiciary Committee to urge impeachment action be taken against Smoak.

It didn't have the desired effect because Smoak remained on the bench, and even continued to preside over Francis' remaining lawsuit in Panama City for another two years.

Chapter 18

Taxing

On April 6, 2009, Francis' brand new team of lawyers filed a motion to have the federal tax case thrown out because the prosecutors had been listening in on Joe's phone calls.

While Francis was locked up in the Washoe County Jail in Reno, Nevada, from June 2007 to March 2008, he'd called his lawyers, and anybody else he could talk to. All of the phone calls – all 6,000 – were recorded.

Francis knew the calls were recorded and in an effort to retain some privacy when talking with his lawyers he would say the words "attorney-client privilege" during those conversations. The federal prosecutors got all those recordings and listened to more than a few of them, even the ones in which Francis was talking strategy with his attorneys.

"Here's the thing, and this is attorney-client privilege," Francis said in a call to Miami attorney Roy Black on August 3, 2007, "but where you're going to be able to slaughter that case, you're going to be able to slaughter their star witness, slaughter. I've done a lot of legal research and every single case, murder, whatever it is, always comes down to just slaughtering that person."

Francis' attorney, Brad Brian wrote in the motion that Francis was talking to Black about Black taking over the tax case.

Brian said the prosecutors quoted Francis from this conversation, but edited out the part where Francis said the words "attorney-client privilege." Brian said the prosecutors also misquoted Francis as saying he wanted the trial postponed for two or three years, as long as he didn't have to wait in jail that whole time.

Brian said neither Francis nor Black says that. Instead, Francis said he wouldn't mind the trial being postponed until Black could get up to speed.

Brian said the prosecutors couldn't argue that they hadn't listened to the conversations because they'd quoted one of them in a motion to the court. He said if the prosecutors had listened to one privileged conversation, who was to say they didn't listen to all of them, including the ones in which trial strategy was discussed.

Brian argued to California federal Judge S. James Otero that there was no way to remove that stain from the case, that Francis was hopelessly prejudiced by this intentional invasion of privacy.

Assistant U.S. Attorney Caryn Mark wrote in her response that Francis shouldn't have been talking strategy with his attorneys on a line he knew to be recorded. She said Francis waived his attorney-client privilege by talking on a recorded line. She said he "double waived" this privilege on those times when he placed the call through his office.

Francis would very often call his office and have an assistant find the number he needed and place the three-way call. Mark said that meant that a third person, Francis' assistant, was listening in to the conversation. Any call that Francis made to his office from the jail, Mark said, was fair game.

But, she said, even though they believed that Francis didn't have an attorney-client privilege any time he called his lawyer on a recorded line, if he called his lawyers directly, instead of going through his office, the prosecutors would treat that call as private and didn't listen.

The tax case shaped up like this:

On April 11, 2007, a federal grand jury handed down an indictment against Joe Francis on charges of tax evasion. The Department of Justice sent out a press release saying Francis was accused of deducting $20 million in false business expenses from his companies' 2002 and 2003 corporate income tax returns.

Mantra Films Inc., which was headquartered in Santa Monica, Calif., didn't pay income tax. Instead, Mantra's income or losses were given to its lone shareholder, Joe Francis, who would then report the income on his individual income tax return.

Sands Media Inc., which did Mantra's marketing and promotional services and was headquartered in Nevada, was another corporation that didn't pay income tax and passed everything along to its sole shareholder, Joe Francis, who then had to report the income on his tax return.

In July 2001, according to the indictment:

Francis opened an account with Morgan Stanley in the name of Rothwell Limited, utilizing nominee signatories to conceal his beneficial ownership of this brokerage account.

Francis then had Rothwell Limited open a bank account at the Bermuda Commercial Bank Limited in Hamilton, Bermuda, again using "nominee signatories" to hide his ownership of the account.

Francis then allegedly overstated millions of dollars in deductions on his 2002 and 2003 tax forms.

He was facing 10 years in prison and a $500,000 fine, plus the delinquent taxes.

His defense was simple: he blamed his former accountant, Michael Barrett, the guy who prepared all the tax forms. Francis said Barrett took advantage of a federal whistleblower program in which the whistleblower could get up to 30 percent of the tax money. It was called an IRS informant bounty and in this case, that would bring the accountant about $6-10 million.

Francis sued Barrett, saying among other things he failed in his duties to protect his client.

Aaron Dyer said shortly after the indictment came down that the tax case shouldn't be a problem. According to federal law, the prosecutors would have to show that Francis knew about the fraudulent activity and did it on purpose. Dyer said the feds were also claiming that the Punta Mita property wasn't a business expense, but a private residence.

"That's the Girls Gone Wild mansion," he said. They do a lot of filming there.

The tax case, which lasted from 2007 to 2009, was where Francis' paranoia really became a problem. He went through five sets of lawyers. His divorce from the last firm, Bob Bernhoft and Bob Barnes, was nasty and very public.

Barnes and Bernhoft, known simply as "The Bobs," were trying to move their Minnesota practice into the Los Angeles market. Francis made it clear that he wouldn't be recommending them.

"As for a practice in LA," Francis wrote in an email to the Bobs, "it is highly unlikely if you piss me off. I KNOW EVERYONE AND THEY WILL DO WHAT I SAY!"

Francis told the press on January 22, 2009, that he planned to sue the Bobs because the Bobs wouldn't "perform certain acts."

It was a pattern. He'd hired several lawyers over the last year for the sole purpose of filing a single motion attacking Smoak and seeking his recusal from the case. Barnes had filed one and argued it in court. Smoak denied it, as he did two others.

Francis fired his entire corporate legal staff in 2008, including longtime counsel Michael Burke.

The revolving door of lawyers began in jail when Francis couldn't make bond. He went through a string of lawyers then, who would file a motion for bond as soon as they were hired. As often as not, they were gone the day the motions were denied.

• • •

Joe Francis' rage was caught on tape on August 28, 2009, as he was walking through a West Hollywoood nightclub called Guys & Dolls.

He was inching through the crowd near the bar when Jayde Nicole, a Playboy playmate, reached a long arm past two other men and poured a drink down Francis' neck. He jerked away, then turned toward the bar, trying to figure out what happened. Then instantly, he snapped. He pushed through the two men between him and Nicole, reached out and jerked her off a barstool by her long black hair. He threw her to the ground, but before anything else could happen several men charged him, surging through the crowd.

Francis ran, pushing hands off him as he bulled through those ahead of him who had no idea of what was going on, while a tide of men followed in his wake, many of whom stepped on Nicole as she was struggling to get off the bar floor.

She got back to her stool and sobbed uncontrollably while her friends held her.

Joe Francis claimed he acted in self-defense, saying the 115-pound girl had threatened to kill him and he yanked her from the bar stool as she was reaching for a bottle to hit him with.

Nicole filed suit, and said she was standing up to Francis for all the women he'd abused through the years who didn't have the resources to fight back.

Francis countersued.

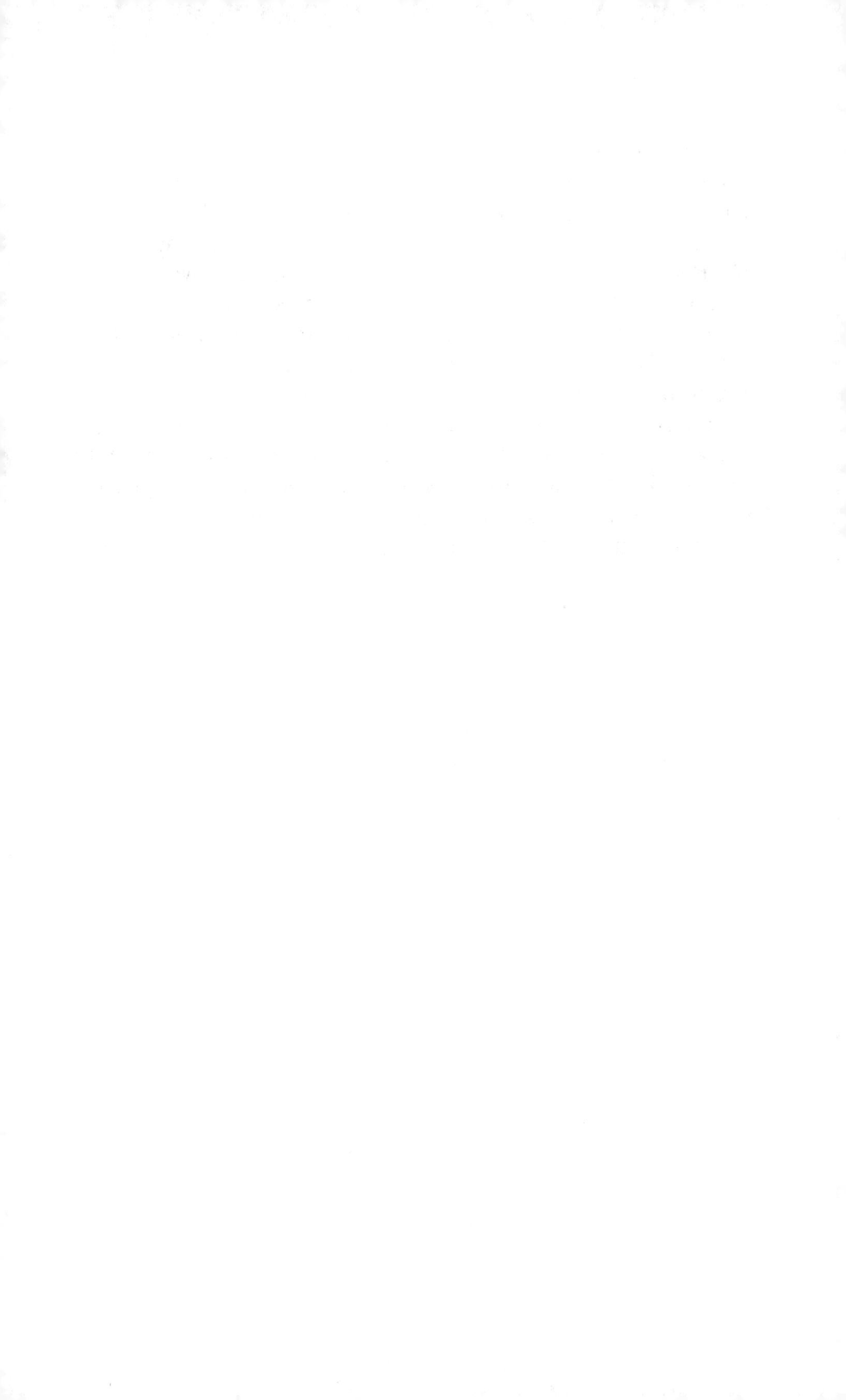

Chapter 19

Contemptuous

Joe Francis was full of contempt. It was something the lawyers in the Plaintiff B lawsuit were counting on.

On Wednesday, April 22, 2009, 10:27 a.m. in Los Angeles, Ross McCloy and Rachel Pontikes were questioning Joe Francis with his attorney Rick Bateman present while Larry Selander and Tom Dent listened in by phone. For the most part, McCloy was asking the questions:

"Do you sell the DVDs?" McCloy asked.

"I don't understand the question as to 'you,'" Francis answered.

"Does Mantra Films Inc. sell these DVDs? What does Mantra Films do with these DVDs?"

"We sell the DVDs."

"And do you sell them internationally as well as nationally?"

"Sir, once again, as to 'you,' I don't understand the question. What do you mean by 'you'?"

"Does Mantra Films Inc. sell these nationally and internationally?"

"I'm not going to answer ..."

Bateman interrupted, "Excuse me."

"Wait just a minute. I …" McCloy said.

"Excuse me. Let me … Mr. Francis' concern is simply that when you're asking if you sell the films, he is here as Joe Francis. Mantra sells the films. Could you clarify that for us? And I think it's a valid concern," Bateman persisted.

"Well, let me ask you just some basic questions then," McCloy said.

"I'm not Mantra Films," Francis said. "So if you're going to ask me a question you're going to have to specifically state a plaintiff."

"What is your relationship to MRA, LLC?"

"I don't have one. I don't know."

"Is there an entity known as that anymore?"

"I don't know. I'm not aware."

"You're not president or an officer or director or member of MRA LLC?"

"I don't know."

"You do know that's the defendant in this case don't you? Have you ever had any relationship or ownership interest in Aero Falcons LLC?"

"I don't quite understand the structure."

"There's not a structure. It's just, I'm asking you a question as to whether you have any ownership interest."

Bateman interrupted, "He has answered the question."

"Is that an objection?" McCloy asked.

"You may answer," Bateman said to Francis. "Ask it again. Are you asking it again?"

"I'm trying to get …" McCloy started.

"You can repeat the question," Bateman repeated.

"I'm trying to get an answer to the question and I'd appreciate it if you would not coach the witness by holding your hand out and things of that nature."

"I'm not coaching the witness at all. It's on videotape, Mr. McCloy. The judge asked that we conduct this deposition with straightforward questions and straightforward answers. You asked the question regarding the corporate makeup of a particular company. Mr. Francis replied that he did not know, he did not understand the structure. You're welcome to ask a question over and over if you want to, that's appropriate until we get to the point of harassment. But he has answered the question.

"OK," McCloy began again. "From here on out, Mr. Bateman, if you have an objection, I would ask that you simply object to the form, as the rules provide and that you don't give Mr. Francis any type of assistance in giving an answer to a question."

"I have not done so. And I will take your suggestion in stride. But I do know the rules and I do know how to conduct myself. And we are being recorded and we are being taken down in the transcript. So I know how to conduct myself appropriately. I've never been chastised for not, I've never been censured for not, I've never been sanctioned for not. So you are an attorney, you need to operate by the rules and I will do so as well. Please proceed."

"What does a CEO of Mantra Films Inc. do?"

"Just oversee the general corporate activities just from a macro scale."

"And what are the general corporate activities of Mantra Films Inc?"

"You know, I don't know the day-to-day job. I'm a figurehead. Go out there and promote the brand."

"Are you the sole shareholder of Mantra Films, Inc?"

"I don't know how things are structured."

"Are you the owner of Girls Gone Wild? Are you the president of Mantra Films Inc?"

"I don't know what that means."

"You don't know what being a president of a company means?"

"If you can explain it to me, I'll be happy to answer it sir. I'm here to answer your questions and participate in any way I can to answer your questions. I'm here to ... I'm here to answer all your questions sir, so to ..."

"Let's start from scratch Mr. Francis. You're 36 years old?"

"That's true."

"Did you go to kindergarten?"

"No."

"Did you go to elementary school?"

"Yes."

"Did you graduate?"

"I don't remember."

"Did you go to junior high school?"

"No."

"Or middle school, whatever they call it wherever you went?"

"I went to middle school, yes."

"Did you graduate?"

"I don't remember."

"Can you read and write English?"

"Fairly well."

"Have you ever been diagnosed as having any type of mental disorder?"

"Object to that," a lawyer said, "and instruct him not to answer that question based on his fifth amendment rights."

"If he doesn't know what a president of a corporation is, I just want to make sure I understand that he has capable mental faculties.

When you gave a deposition, the last time you gave a deposition, did you get into arguments with counsel like this?"

"I haven't gotten into any argument whatsoever. This entire deposition is on video. And as I said before, I'm here. I'm just waiting here, just waiting for your questions sir. And I'm here to answer them."

"Have you been sued?"

"Have I been sued? Yes."

"Are you currently being sued?"

"Probably. I don't pay any attention."

"Were you physically arrested when the charges were levied against you?"

"I don't remember."

"You don't remember if you were arrested and taken down to a jail?"

"Nope."

"Has that happened to you on more than one occasion?"

"No."

"So the only time you've ever been physically arrested was in Panama City?"

"Uh-huh."

"How many times were you physically arrested in Panama City?"

"Six probably."

"Are you a convicted felon?"

"Fifth," Francis said, as in his Fifth Amendment right to stay silent instead of saying something that would incriminate him.

"Mr. Francis, did you enter a plea in the circuit court in and for Bay County individually to no contest to one count of child abuse, which is a third-degree felony?"

"I'm not sure. I'm a hundred percent … I didn't do anything wrong here. I only entered this as I told the judge, Dedee Costello, in court was to get out of jail. I did nothing wrong and none of this is true."

"Regardless of that, did you enter the plea?"

"No. I merely agreed to get out of jail in exchange for .. it was an extortion situation."

"Do you understand that you have been adjudicated guilty of this crime?"

"It's a joke. It doesn't mean …"

"Mr. Francis, are you refusing to answer the question as to whether you have ever been convicted of a felony?"

"I'm not a felon."

"The question is, have you ever been convicted of a felony?"

"I don't understand what that means."

"You don't understand what being a convicted felon is?"

"No. Can you explain it to me?"

"Did you serve any time in jail?"

"What do you mean 'serve'?"

"Were you behind bars?"

Bateman interrupted, "I want to go on the record and say, Joe, I don't want you … if you don't understand the question …"

"I don't understand," Francis said. "You asked if I was ever behind bars. Was I illegally incarcerated? Yes, I was illegally incarcerated."

"That wasn't the question," McCloy said. "The question I'm trying to get to, to make it as simple as I can so that you can understand and follow with me, do you know what a felon is?"

"No."

"Do you know what a prisoner is?"

"No."

"Do you know what a cellmate is in a jail?"

"No."

"Do you know what a jail is?"

"Sort of."

"Have you lived in jail?"

"No."

"Mr. Francis, didn't you serve time in the Bay County Jail and a jail in Nevada that totaled almost a year?"

"I was illegally incarcerated. I didn't serve any time."

"But that's where you took your meals and that's where you slept wasn't it?"

"Depends when they gave you food."

"Mr. Francis, let's go back to the plea agreement here. Did you sign Page 3 of this plea agreement? Is that your signature?"

"It could be. I don't know. Do you have an original document?"

"So you don't know whether that is your signature?"

"No."

"Relative to these criminal charges, Mr. Francis, were you masturbated by PV and BW in the Chateau Motel in March 2003?" PV was Plaintiff V and BW was the other girl in the room, who was not a plaintiff in the lawsuit.

"I don't know who those people are."

"Were you masturbated by anyone in March of 2003 while on Spring Break in Panama City Beach?"

"I don't remember. I doubt it."

"Did you pay anyone to masturbate you in late March of 2003?"

"No."

"You have no recall at all of ever being in a motel room where you were masturbated by two minors?"

"No. Never."

"You have no recall at all of ever being masturbated by two minors by grabbing their hands and placing them on your penis and moving it – and moving them up and down?"

"Sir, I'm offended by ..."

Bateman interrupted, "Just answer the question."

"... that's absolutely ..." Francis continued.

"But just answer the question," Bateman said.

"I would never ... that's disgusting. I'm offended sir. And you know what? If you're going to make these allegations ..."

"No, no, no. We'll take a break if ..." Bateman said, trying to head off a meltdown.

"... That's gone too far. I mean ..."

"Just answer the questions."

"That's – to allege conduct like that, sir, that's just disgusting. You are disgusting sir. Disgusting."

"Mr. Francis, did you pay two minors in March of 2003 to masturbate you?" McCloy asked again, possibly seeing an opening.

"Absolutely not, sir."

"Did you admit in the prior lawsuit that you did?"

"No."

"Did you admit in the prior lawsuit that you paid $50 to PV and BW?"

"Are you joking? No. That's disgusting. I don't know who those people are."

"Did you tell others after the masturbation had taken place that you were, quote, 'Busy getting a hand job' in that bedroom?"

"I never said anything of the sort."

"Have you ever told anyone that you got a hand job or you were masturbated or you were jerked off, or whatever you want to call it, by two teenagers in Panama City Beach?"

"Never. And it's not true."

"Do you have any witnesses who can confirm that you did not – that you were not masturbated by PV and BW?"

"I read a police report preparing for my deposition where PV clearly states that no one ever masturbated me and it was a complete lie. So I guess the two witnesses would be your two clients."

Francis couldn't keep up the act, or maybe he thought he'd scored big with that last line, but it made him laugh.

"What is so funny?" McCloy asked.

Bateman spoke up, "Object to the form of the question. You don't have to answer that."

"Well, I'd like to know what is so funny," McCloy said.

"It doesn't matter Ross," Bateman said. "You're going too far with, 'What is so funny?' That has no rational basis or nexus to anything that has to do with the facts of this case. You're sitting here, which you've got the right to do, to push the client and that's fine. But let's ask questions about the case, at least remotely, not what does he think is funny. If you want to take that up with the judge, that I take offense to 'Is that funny', then that's fine."

McCloy got back on track, "Mr. Francis do you think that the allegations that have been levied against you in this case, including the allegation that you paid PV $50 to masturbate you with another person is something that we ought to joke about?"

"I think the absurdity of the allegations here is disgusting and laughable that you would be accusing a man like me of such disgusting allegations. Just the mere fact, yes, it's laughable that you would sit me in a room, and with a straight face, a man of my integrity, try to sit here and say that. Yes, it's laughable and it's funny because I'm not that person. And that is absolutely disgusting and laughable and disgusting on the part of you, sir, that you would try to do that to get money and make up some ridiculous story and try to exploit some girls to try to ..."

Bateman jumped in, "Be quiet, be quiet. You've answered the question."

"It's disgusting. It's horrible. Horrible."

"Now, do you usually have to pay minor teenage girls to have sex with you?" McCloy asked.

"Absolutely not. And I never have."

"You have never paid minor girls to have sex with you?" McCloy asked, then said: "To make absolutely, positively sure I know what your answer is, Mr. Francis, before I move on to another area, you completely deny ever masturbating, ever having paid PV to masturbate you on March 31, or thereabouts, 2003?"

"I don't know who PV is sir. But I don't pay girls to masturbate me."

"And that's a blanket rule for you? You don't ever pay girls to masturbate you?"

"Do you?"

Bateman spoke up quickly, "Joe, this is what the judge asked you not to do. Just answer the question."

"Do I have a blanket rule, sir? I just think the ... what you're describing is disgusting and I don't partake in it."

"So your answer is no, you do not do that."

"No, I like to masturbate myself but I've never paid myself to masturbate myself. Actually, I love to masturbate myself since I was like 14."

Chapter 20

Gateway porn

My computer locked up trying to reformat a file. I stood and watched a small color wheel spin on the screen and saw my day whirling around with it.

I picked up my keys and cell phone, walked to my truck and drove to the federal courthouse to read a transcript out of the Girls Gone Wild civil case. Cell phones aren't allowed inside the courthouse, so I set it in the center console before crunching across the gravel parking lot to the coral encrusted building.

A white haired man was using the lone computer in the clerk's office, so I sat on a sofa near the window and watched the wind draw lines and push spray off the gray bay water. The beginning of 2010 in Panama City was unbearably cold, with nights sliding into the 20s and days barely reaching 40, even with the sun shining. After six straight nights of subfreezing temperatures I could feel the cold seeping through my hardwood floors. My feet were miserable. I was miserable and I had very little patience with white-haired guys using the computer when I needed it, regardless of how nice the view.

I crunched back across the parking lot to my truck and checked my cell phone: two missed calls and a text message from Joe Francis. The text message and voice mail said pretty much the same thing: "Call me."

Joe added a little extra on the voice mail, "I got something interesting to tell ya."

"Can I call you right back?" Joe said almost immediately after answering the phone. "Forty seconds. Oh, they're going through the safety drill. I'll call you right back. Just give me forty seconds."

Forty seconds later, the phone rang.

"Real quick," he started. "Did you hear?"

One or two of the girls suing him in Panama City for damages they suffered by being filmed by Girls Gone Wild had done additional pornographic films. Rick Bateman had filed a motion demanding the plaintiffs either turn over these films to the defense, or give them a lot more detail about what these girls had done in the movies.

One of the girls, Plaintiff B, moved to California after her Girls Gone Wild experience and had roles, as an extra, on Spider-Man 2 and Starsky and Hutch. Her participation in two pornographic movies, however, was not detailed. All she'd told Bateman was she'd been filmed nude. She wouldn't describe in what way, where or how it came about.

All she would say was she "believes she was videotaped on two separate occasions at two studios in Los Angeles, California, sometime in 2003. She believes this included sexually explicit conduct. She does not know the name or location of the studios or who created the videos. She does not have a copy of any such video and does not know who does have a copy."

Bateman asked Judge Allan Kornblum to order the plaintiffs to reveal these pornographic films, or give them more details.

Kornblum denied Bateman's motion on January 19, 2010, the day before the girl was to be deposed again.

"At this late date," Kornblum wrote in his order, "even were the court to grant defendant's motion, insufficient time remains for the films to be obtained and reviewed prior to the deposition tomorrow. However, Plaintiff B and her attorneys should be prepared to be questioned exhaustively about the circumstances surrounding the making of these films, much like Defendant Francis was grilled about the financial information he claimed to know little about. The court cannot strongarm a witness into providing information they adamantly claim they do not have, but the party seeking the information is entitled to ask as much as they can to aid them in obtaining the information by other means, or to build a record to show the jury that they tried."

Around the same time, Judge Smoak was reviewing the Girls Gone Wild footage of the four girls in order to resolve a motion from Bateman to dismiss the case. Bateman argued that at least one count of all four girls' claims should be dismissed because there was no sexual conduct in the footage.

"The entire video footage of Plaintiffs J and S lasts a mere twenty-one seconds, and the actual exposure of their breasts lasts only seconds for each girl," Smoak wrote in his order. "Throughout the footage the Plaintiffs are seated in a vehicle driving past the camera. With them in the car are two other females, including the older sister of one of the Plaintiffs. Plaintiffs J and S and one of the other females in the vehicle quickly lift up their bathing suit tops once each for mere seconds."

Smoak then wrote the most interesting line of any order in the Girls Gone Wild case: "There is no sign of coercion and everyone is all smiles in the footage."

This was the same judge who told Francis, "Doesn't take a real brave man to go out and corner some young female who has had four or five beers in the middle of Spring Break and convince them to do something dumb."

Smoak dismissed the counts plaintiffs J and S brought, saying there was no sexual content. He also dismissed this count when it came to plaintiff V, the girl Joe had paid to masturbate him. She's flashed for the camera in a parking lot.

"Although she exposes her breasts several times in the footage, each time it is only seconds. This is in stark contrast to the extremely lengthy video footage of Plaintiff B."

Smoak allowed the lawsuit to stand on a number of other counts, including the unfilmed interaction, the masturbation, between Joe and plaintiff V.

Joe, however, took this as a major victory. He called me from a commercial flight out of Las Vegas, which was on the tarmac preparing to take off. He said he expected the rest of the lawsuit to fall like dominoes after this ruling.

That didn't come true. Bateman asked the judge a week later if he could file another motion to dismiss, but the judge denied that. Smoak said the deadline for those motions had passed. They were on track for trial.

"How's the book coming?" Joe asked at the end of the telephone conversation.

"Real good. It's moving right along," I lied.

Joe started to say something, then stopped. He clearly wasn't expecting the book to be moving right along. He started to say something else, but stopped again.

Finally, he got out what he wanted to say, "You better make me look good, you bastard."

Chapter 21

Beginning of the end.

Rick Bateman flopped into his seat with the same frustration and indignation that propelled him out of the cushioned chair to begin with. He sighed, groaned, buried his face in his hands, rubbed his palms roughly across his face, sat forward, launched backward, stood again, held out his arms, pushed his glasses to his forehead, dropped them back again onto the bridge of his nose and then sat back down as if some unseen hand had forced him.

"I apologize for my twitching," Bateman told Federal Judge Richard Smoak. "It's a bad habit I have and it's not professional. But when I hear some of the things that are given to this court as a foundation, as a factual basis for you to make your ruling, and they're wrong, just completely wrong, it bothers me."

Smoak had called this hearing to address a motion for default judgment filed by the plaintiffs in a lawsuit claiming that Girls Gone Wild had filmed three underage girls in sex scenes, or at least flashing, and then included them in videos that were sold worldwide. Another girl was on the lawsuit, although she'd never been filmed, because Joe Francis had paid her $50 to masturbate him in a Panama City Beach motel room. According to her complaint, Joe did most of the work.

Attorneys Ross McCloy, Rachael Pontikes and Tom Dent had every reason to expect a favorable outcome to their motion for default judgment against Joe Francis. He hadn't been the most cooperative witness during his deposition, and that behavior had worked in their favor in the past. McCloy, Pontikes and Dent had scored a multi-million dollar settlement in 2007 when Smoak had ordered Francis to jail for bad behavior during mediation.

After a mostly worthless deposition in April, Smoak had ordered Francis to give a second deposition to McCloy and Pontikes, this time to be held with a magistrate in the room to keep Francis in line. Smoak commented on Joe's evasiveness.

"He seemed to claim a total ignorance about the business of which he's the sole owner," Smoak told the lawyers before Francis' second deposition. "If he pulls that stunt again, we'll decide, but it's not going to work to his advantage. I mean, that was an exercise, I think I can only characterize it, is silliness.

"But he needs to be very clear that there is not to be any evasion or parsing. And I suggest that he show up this time prepared to talk about his business activity, of which he's the sole owner and in total control, as if he was meeting with his most important investment broker."

What Dent, McCloy and Pontikes were complaining about, and what they felt like they should be paid for was "gamesmanship" on Joe Francis' part. Dent claimed Francis had frustrated the process of discovery to the point of making a mockery of the court.

It was theater and both Dent and Bateman were playing their roles with flair. It's unlikely that Joe would have enjoyed the show, but he wasn't there. He was sick in a Mexican hospital with an ear infection that was preventing him from flying.

"When I talked to him," Bateman told Smoak, "he was delirious. I'm not trying to be funny."

Bateman produced a letter from a doctor.

"Mr. Francis was not, in any way, trying to avoid this hearing," Bateman said. He assured the court that Francis' ailment, "is not anything scandalous."

The issue to be resolved in this hearing was not a simple one: whether Francis should be stripped of his defenses because he'd been intentionally frustrating the plaintiffs' efforts to prepare for trial. If Smoak ruled in their favor, a trial would only be necessary to determine how much the girls should be paid for their suffering. Joe would be unable to say that he didn't damage them, that he wasn't guilty.

This was the fifth time that Dent, McCloy and Pontikes had moved for default judgment in this case. It was sound strategy, based on history.

Judge Smoak started, as he often had in 2009 by cutting out the chaff the lawyers were expected to present and telling them what he wanted to focus on. Numerous times in his court, witnesses would be left sitting in the audience for hours, called by a lawyer to testify, only to find out the judge wasn't interested in what they had to say.

Smoak wanted this hearing to focus solely on the discovery issues and the first thing he wanted to know was why, if they were having problems with Francis, the lawyers hadn't brought it up with the magistrate at the time of the deposition. That had been one of Bateman's arguments in his reply brief and his head rose and fell in exaggerated nods as the judge made that announcement.

Pontikes said even though Magistrate Allan Kornblum was supposed to be overseeing the deposition he was rarely in the room. A law clerk, she said, was there in Kornblum's place and, a few times, they did call the magistrate in to settle some issue.

"Did you all at any point during these days stop the deposition, ask to talk to Judge Kornblum and ask, 'Judge we're having this problem, would you please rule so we can continue?'" Smoak asked Pontikes.

"Well, a lot of the objectionable material..."

"Did you all ever do that?"

"Well, your honor, we didn't because a lot of the objectionable material came at the end of the deposition."

"I didn't order Francis to come from California just to get a pep talk. I mean, it was (in Gainesville) so that if there was misbehavior you all could seek the intervention of the magistrate judge. You all understood that didn't you?"

"Yes we did, your honor, that process was not effective for Mr. Francis. We are here before you again, your honor, because Judge Kornblum couldn't resolve this situation."

"Did you all ever say, 'Judge Kornblum we are getting unresponsive answers from Francis. Would you please rule and direct him to respond?'"

"During the middle of the first day, we called in Judge Kornblum and that's when he gave the speech that defendants have excerpted into the second part of the motion."

"The question was, did you specifically ask him to intervene and order that there be responsive answers?"

"We did not ask him to order anything, your honor. We did ask for assistance and the assistance we got was the law clerk coming in."

Bateman, however, noted numerous comments from Kornblum that showed he thought Francis was cooperating with the attorneys and it was McCloy who was asking bad questions and not getting to the heart of the matter. Reading the deposition from that perspective, it looked as if McCloy was simply asking the questions he knew would anger Joe, make him lash out.

"I'm going to direct most of my remarks to Mr. McCloy," Kornblum had said during the deposition. "You've got Mr. Francis here and I'm pleased to say that Mr. Francis is not being evasive; he's not playing Mortimus Snerd. He's paying attention, he's into it and he's answering questions. But I think you're missing the opportunity to get to the heart of the case."

Kornblum told McCoy that he was wasting time asking Francis about things that were already on record, like whether he was a convicted felon. And Francis was avoiding those questions. He kept insisting that he didn't know what it meant to be a convicted felon and he didn't think of himself as a felon.

"Mr. McCloy, it's not my job to prevent lawyers from wasting their clients' money and you can ask any questions you want," Kornblum said. "What I am suggesting is you defer and get to Panama City and get that on the record while Mr. Francis is here;

and then, if you wish to go back and spend the time and money to ask about the plea agreements, you're perfectly free to do so. You're free to do whatever you wish. I am not here to micromanage. But as an objective observer, and that's what I am here; I really am the neutral, detached magistrate. And from an objective observer, my point is, I think at this point in time, you're on the wrong track."

Kornblum noted that Francis, who started his deposition in his normal combative mode, was far more cooperative as the two-day questioning continued. What Ponitkes cited in her motion were his answers from the first morning session. And, that morning, Joe left little doubt about his dislike of the lawyers questioning him.

"Do you make money with these videos?" McCloy asked Francis during the October 6, 2009 deposition.

"Do I make money selling DVDs and videos? Yes."

"And you make a lot of money with it, don't you? Do you make millions of dollars selling these DVDs?"

"Other than some you stole from me, I'm going to come back for."

"Do you make millions of dollars off the sale ..."

"Coming, coming."

"Answer the question, Joe, please," Bateman said.

"Do you make millions of dollars off the sale ..."

"Coming."

Dent complained to Smoak in the hearing that Joe wouldn't even tell them how much money the DVDs had made for his company. He wouldn't even say how much he was charging for the DVDs.

Smoak smiled as Bateman launched himself out of his seat and hovered in a crouch between sitting and standing. He teetered for a minute, wanting to say something, then sat back down.

"Don't you know from late-night TV," Smoak said, "that (the DVDs) are 19.95?"

Bateman nodded in such an exaggerated way he looked like he would hit his head off the table.

"They're $19.95," he said.

Dent said not all tapes are sold at the same price and it should be a matter of finding the right business record to say how many of the tapes were sold at what amount.

The point of questioning Francis, McCloy and Dent explained, was to ascertain his involvement in what they believed to be a conspiracy, a company policy, to record underage girls for inclusion in Girls Gone Wild videos. That involvement, and the conspiracy, were spelled out in court documents that Francis had signed.

"Mr. Francis and these companies knowingly and consistently, as a business practice, violate federal law for profit in producing pornography, including child pornography," Dent told Smoak. "We need to show that. This wasn't inadvertence. This was the business plan and we're entitled to talk to Mr. Francis. He ran this company. He owns it. He founded it. He developed it. He's the CEO and we're entitled to truthful answers from him regarding that company's operation.

"I think it is very relevant, the operation of the company, whether the girls were included inadvertently or whether this was part of the business plan. All of those things are relevant to the jury's consideration, both in terms of actual liability, but also in terms of punitive damages. So, it is the details of the process, the details of Mantra's operation and Joe Francis' involvement in that operation that go to the very core of the evidence for us."

The federal plea agreement that Francis signed in 2007 and the state criminal plea in 2008, McCloy said, were the proof of Girls Gone Wild's sinister plan. Now, however, Francis was saying that he didn't read the plea agreements and was even contesting that he signed them.

"I've got the court records," McCloy told Smoak. "And I'm going to use the court records. I'm going to ram those right down Mr. Francis' throat at trial.

"But for Mr. Francis now to get up and say, 'You know those are all lies. I never saw those. I never read those. I sure wish I had and I'm doing a better job of listening to what my lawyers have to say.' That puts the burden on us to refute what Mr. Francis is obviously intending on saying at the time of trial."

Bateman said Francis was not playing games when he blamed his lawyers.

"In his heart and mind, and what he'll testify to every time, is that he signed those documents to get out of jail, period. That he didn't know it, that he didn't believe it, that he doesn't believe they violated the law. That he signed those because he wanted to get out of jail. He had been in jail and that was how to get out."

Smoak recognized the importance of Francis' plea agreements and told the lawyers on January 19, 2010, that he was inclined to grant a motion that would strip Francis of his defenses when it came to Plaintiffs B and V, because he'd already admitted to the illegal conduct in the pleas. Smoak held off on issuing that ruling until February.

During the November hearing, McCloy continued to ask for all of Francis' defenses to be done away with because Francis was being evasive in answering questions about his personal wealth. The lawyers needed to know how much money Francis made so they could show that to the jury, which would decide how much money they should take from him in punishment. The jury couldn't award more in punitive damages than Francis was able to pay.

But Francis kept saying he had no idea what his assets were or how much he was worth. McCloy said Francis refused to give them the simple financial documents they needed to show his net worth.

Bateman told the judge that Francis had disclosed all of that in his income tax returns and Mantra's financial documents. McCloy said he had those documents, but surely that wasn't everything that Francis had.

Bateman said Francis had never had to apply for a business loan after launching Girls Gone Wild and therefore had never had to prepare the type of documents that McCloy wanted.

"Is he the unusual person that has so much money coming in that he's never had to prepare any kind of documentation for his net worth?" Smoak asked.

"That is what I understand," Bateman said. He said Francis has simply lived off the profits from the DVDs ever since 1998.

He hired people to run the business and when he said he oversees things from "30,000 feet," he's not kidding. Francis simply flies around the world, going to spring break destinations, parties, exotic locations and appearing in and promoting "Girls Gone Wild" videos.

Bateman told the judge that while McCloy and Dent were complaining about Francis being evasive, they hadn't hired a forensic accountant to go over the financial records that had been supplied. With six weeks left until trial, Smoak said he was concerned that the plaintiffs had been too focused on Francis and not in getting prepared to argue their case.

"You have all been so obsessed with Francis that you couldn't see anything else," Smoak said. "You've had all these witness who you have not deposed. Had you started with any of them, even the most insignificant, you might have developed a picture and closed in on Francis so that by the time you took his deposition he would have nowhere to run. That just seems to be a common investigative technique.

"You all really have been obsessed with Francis. And for whatever flaws he has, Mr. Bateman's explanation of his unstructured way of doing things is plausible. He's just had more money than he ever needed to keep track of."

"It's easy to get obsessed with a personality like his that does everything he can to thwart the discovery process," McCloy insisted.

Bateman pleaded for the judge to keep the case on track for trial in January.

"There's been no evidence, not one person, not one, not one line, not Joe's enemy, not the guy that told me he would be the first one to give him KY if he went to jail, has testified there was any policy of filming girls under the age of 18," Bateman said. "Nobody. Not a scintilla of all the enemies he's made that they've taken depositions of, not one has said that was a policy. And in fact, everybody that's testified has said they were told not to do it. They didn't want to tape young girls.

"Let's go try this case, your honor, on January 4. Enough's enough. They've gotten enough here that a forensic accountant can throw whatever number they want at a jury and let the jury determine whether or not Mr. Francis, who wasn't even here for two of the instances, or Mantra or Girls Gone Wild has some liability.

"Let's let the jury decide it and do it and let people appeal and stop playing the default game. That's the game we're playing."

Dent and Ponikes insisted that Francis was dolling out the names of employees who could help them. This launched Bateman into another round of standing, sitting, sighing and gesturing. Smoak didn't need Bateman's help. He asked Pontikes for a list of the employees they'd been provided and how long they knew about them. Most had been disclosed early on, but Pontikes admitted that few had been deposed.

"Surely you recognize now that trying to depose Francis is an exercise in futility," Smoak said. "Surely you could find some honest souls within that organization who would tell you what's really going on and you could use that to close the noose (around Francis).

Smoak denied the motion for default judgment. He allowed for a short continuance of the trial, an extra month so the plaintiffs could prepare their case.

"I'm determined that we're going to get this case tried," Smoak said. "I want there to be as few grounds for appeal as possible."

Bateman also told Smoak that the IRS had placed liens against Joe's assets and cash holdings, nearly $140 million worth, and Francis might have to file bankruptcy.

"Of the several years of this saga, what else can happen Mr. Bateman?" Smoak asked.

"I told my secretary I could probably make more money by just getting a reality TV camera to follow this case around, rather than practicing law. I'm flabbergasted, but I guess there are no surprises anymore."

• • •

With three weeks left until the start of Francis' trial in Panama City, Rick Bateman asked Smoak to divide the case and hold two separate trials. He asked that Plaintiffs B and V be tried later and not with the other two girls.

He had a good reason for wanting to delay Plaintiff B's trial: he needed more time to explore her recent admission that she'd been in two more pornographic movies since her Girls Gone Wild shoot.

Bateman had gotten to question Plaintiff B about those movies on January 20, and the questioning got a little heated, and a little childish, at times.

"I just remembered something, I think I told my aunt what I had done, that I had been in videos," the girl said. "I didn't think she believed the fact that I did ... I was trying so hard to tell someone about it, but I couldn't. I was so embarrassed and humiliated and ashamed of myself."

"You were so embarrassed and ashamed of yourself you went right out and filmed two pornographic movies, voluntarily and for money; that's how ashamed you were?"

"Yes."

Bateman asked her why she didn't tell the psychologist, the one hired by her lawyers who had interviewed her to ascertain how psychologically damaged she was, about these other movies.

"If I spoke to her now and told her about it, she wouldn't be shocked. It's part of the damages."

"Why didn't you tell her then? You're here trying to get money for damages. Why didn't you tell her then?"

"I wasn't ready to talk to anybody about it."

"You're ready to come to this court and sue these defendants and talk about just what you're ready to talk about, but not really what really happened?"

Dent objected, saying Bateman wasn't letting the girl finish her answers.

"You're talking over her answers."

"I'm not talking over her answers, she said, 'that's it.'"

"Because you talked over her answer, so I'm making sure she's finished ..."

"I'm not going to listen to that."

There's some talk that the court reporter didn't pick up, but apparently Dent asked Bateman if he was getting upset.

"I'm not mad a bit. I'm perfectly fine. I just want an answer to my question."

"And all I want you to do is to allow her to answer the question. If you don't like the answer, then you interrupt."

"No, I got the answer."

"Be quiet."

"You be quiet."

"You be quiet while she's answering, that's your obligation."

By this time, no one remembered what the question was. It was read back for the girl.

"Do you understand the question?" Dent asked the girl.

"No, I don't."

"Then re-ask it," he said to Bateman.

"Wait a minute, you're not through answering the question or you don't understand it?" Bateman said.

"Please repeat the question," the girl said.

"Why didn't you tell Dr. Lebowitz? You're here trying to get money, you said it would be part of the damages, she probably ..."

"I wasn't ready ..."

"Can I finish, please?"

"That was at a time I wasn't ready ..."

"Can I finish, please?"

"... to talk about it."

"Can I finish, please? Why didn't you tell her about it?"

"I wasn't ready to talk about it."

"You were ready to talk about Girls Gone Wild and that so you could get money, but you weren't ready to talk about what you did as an adult voluntarily?"

He then asked her why she didn't tell him about the films during their first deposition.

"I asked you and you ..."

"I left it out."

"... said, 'No.'"

"There's a difference."

"Was that a lie when you told me, 'No.'?"

"I wasn't ready to ..."

"She said she was sorry," Dent said.

"When I asked you if there were any similar incidents to this, have you ever been filmed before and you said, 'No', was that a lie or not?"

"It was a lie."

Chapter 22

Default

On February 5, 2010, Smoak issued his order stripping Joe Francis of his defenses in three counts of the lawsuit pertaining to two girls. Joe Francis had pleaded out to criminal charges involving the same conduct he was being sued for, which Smoak deemed as pretty reliable proof of guilt.

Smoak found that Francis and Mantra had no defense as to sexual exploitation of Plaintiff B because they'd pleaded guilty in federal court to videotaping B, and couldn't dispute that she was a minor at the time she was filmed. He did, however, order that a jury would decide whether Mantra actually sold the video, whether B was damaged and by how much.

Smoak found that Francis couldn't defend himself against the count involving Plaintiff V in which he was accused of soliciting her for prostitution by offering her $50 to jerk him off. Francis had already pleaded no contest to that charge in state court, so he couldn't now claim that he didn't do it. A jury was still going to have to decide damages, and decide the other two plaintiffs' cases in full.

A little while later, Smoak told Bateman that Francis wouldn't even be able to testify that he pleaded guilty but didn't actually commit the crimes. In a hearing on February 12, 2010, plaintiffs' attorney Larry Selander asked Smoak to rule ahead of trial that Francis wouldn't be allowed to claim innocence.

"You've ruled that the defendants are collaterally estopped (barred) from denying the material in their guilty pleas," Selander told Smoak.

"Your honor," Bateman interjected, "what he's talking about is that my client has said that 'I wasn't guilty.' As a matter of law you have ruled that once he pled guilty ... you've ruled that for summary judgment, but if he wants to get on the stand and say, 'I wasn't guilty,' then there's certainly nothing to prohibit him from doing that."

Francis hadn't just said he wasn't guilty, he'd repeated it like a mantra throughout numerous interviews and depositions since he'd entered the pleas. It was certain that he planned to tell jurors the same thing.

"If he wants to get on the stand and do what?" Smoak asked Bateman, seeking some clarification as to Francis' intentions.

"Say, 'I wasn't guilty. I pled guilty, but I wasn't guilty.'" Bateman said.

"I don't think he can do that," Smoak said.

"Then that will have to be your ruling."

"That's what collateral estoppel is."

Bateman said he thought collateral estoppel meant that the jury would be instructed sometime during the trial that they couldn't consider Francis' denials, not that he couldn't make them.

"Estoppel means estoppel," Smoak reiterated.

"I've made my argument, and that's fine," Bateman said, looking to move on.

"Means you can't do it," Smoak persisted.

"That's fine."

"He cannot deny that plea."

"He wouldn't be denying the plea, your honor."

"No, he can't deny that he had ... he can't say he had his fingers crossed when he said he was guilty. That's conclusive."

Smoak had also decided that the courtroom was to remain open to the public throughout the trial, denying a motion from the plaintiffs to keep the public out while the girls were testifying and to keep their identities secret even after the trial began. Pontikes had moved early on in the case to have the plaintiffs identified in court records only by an initial. The local media didn't really care, so the motion was not challenged until she asked Smoak to take steps to keep the girls' names out of the press indefinitely.

News Herald Editor Mike Cazalas said privately that it would be exciting to challenge the new motion, a "real First Amendment issue," but told me as I was preparing the story to not mention whether the paper would actually take any steps in that direction. He waited until Smoak, in a preliminary hearing, indicated that he was leaning toward keeping the courtroom open. The next morning, the paper splashed the headline that it would challenge the motion. With the judge leaning the paper's way even before its lawyer filed any motions, it looked like an easy win and good PR.

Shortly before the trial was to begin, Smoak formally ruled that there was a presumption of openness in all trials and ordered that the girls' names would be used throughout the trial and the courtroom would remain open.

"Any social stigma that might attach to the Plaintiffs in this case is no different than that in the sexual discrimination or sexual harassment cases common in this district, where the plaintiffs are always named," Smoak wrote in his order. "Furthermore, the mere filing of a civil action against a defendant may cause damage to their reputation and may also result in economic harm. Basic fairness dictates that those among a defendant's accusers who wish to participate in the suit as individual party plaintiffs must do so under their real names. Plaintiffs also emphasize the difficulty they have had and will have in testifying, but this too does not compel closure of the trial. Although the events Plaintiffs B and V will have to recount in presenting their case may well be painful to recall, unfortunately this is the nature of many civil cases: tough testimony must be given. For example, few things are more painful to imagine than the death of a child, and yet plaintiffs in wrongful death cases are frequently forced to testify in detail about their child's death. Furthermore, this is not a criminal case where my decision on anonymity might be different. The government is not pursuing this suit against Defendants. The Plaintiffs chose, as adults, to bring this suit. Plaintiffs' argument that discontinuing anonymity would lead to a "chilling effect" on reporting crimes and a lack of punishment for child pornographers would be more persuasive in a criminal context than in a civil suit. In the parallel criminal prosecutions based on the events at issue in this civil case, the identities of the victims, who did not choose to bring the suit, were kept anonymous. The Defendants have already been subject to full criminal sanctions for the events that are the subject of this case. Reaching a different result on anonymity in a civil suit will not cause a chilling effect on reporting crimes and punishing criminals in the criminal arena."

He did, however, order that witnesses who might have been victims of crimes in these cases, such as underage girls who were filmed by Girls Gone Wild, but aren't a part of the lawsuit would remain anonymous throughout the trial.

Pontikes responded by appealing the order and asking for a continuance of the trial, which Smoak reluctantly granted. In court, he told the lawyers that he feared this case would turn into the Flying Dutchman of the legal world – sailing the seas endlessly without finding a port. He ordered that the lawyers needed to be ready for trial within a month of the appeals court's ruling, whatever it might be.

Selander asked for some leeway in that ruling because Rachael Pontikes was planning to get married October 30. Smoak promised to keep that in mind if a decision came down from the appellate court in September.

And as far as "social stigma" attached to this case, the plaintiffs were claiming lots of it. In the February 25 hearing, Bateman alluded to a suggestion from the plaintiffs' lawyers that they might claim a diagnoses of "bipolarism" as damages to one of the girls.

Larry Selander didn't touch on that in his reply, but he did loosely address the damages that they might seek in trial.

"Plaintiff B was a straight-A student in high school and went to the University of Texas. This whole incident knocked her out of school. It changed her life drastically. She believes she killed her father as a result of it. How much is that worth? This is all about remediation of a horrifying situation that occurred to these women. But we can't put it on a piece of paper and multiply this by the other thing and come up with a profit margin and apply it."

He said Girls Gone Wild could. They made "multiple millions of dollars for the very tapes we're involved with here."

Bateman wanted to know if Selander was going to claim economic damages, not just emotional ones. If so, he said, he wanted those spelled out and calculated so he could challenge them at trial.

"There are economic damages,"Selander said, "but they aren't calculable. What is the economic damage to one not being able to get a job in their life? That is an economic loss."

"Do you have an economist that's going to talk about her work life expectancy?" Smoak asked. Bateman nodded along and voiced his agreement with the judge's question.

"We do not, judge," Selander answered.

"If we're talking about loss of ... economic damage I think would include loss of past earnings, loss of future earnings capacity and I think you ought to be able to disclose, you know, confirm are you seeking those?" Smoak asked.

"I haven't been able to determine any of those," Bateman chimed in, like a choir backing up a preacher.

"Are you claiming that there has been a physical type injury, or even psychic, that has required treatment or is going to need treatment in the future?"

"Exactly," Bateman added.

But despite the judge's questions and enthusiastic support Smoak was receiving from Bateman, Selander didn't answer.

"Are they not claiming any of those economic damages that you described?" Bateman asked the judge. "If so, I think they ought to give that information."

There was a standing order that the sides discuss issues, including damages, that would come up at trial. Bateman wanted a deadline on deciding the issue.

"Mr. Selander, can you get it in two weeks?" Smoak asked.

"Sure, judge, we will get it in two weeks."

But Selander also complained that he felt Bateman was intentionally trying to smear his clients by putting identifying information into his motions and supplying them to the press. Selander said Bateman also put in damaging, and false, information about additional pornographic movies that a plaintiff had done after Girls Gone Wild. There was no doubt that one girl had, but Bateman had written in a motion that he thought another of the four girls had as well. He'd been wrong.

"And you see the comments you get from, in, the daily Herald's comments section on its website. It's just unbelievable. And it's the very kind of thing that's damaging these people."

"Well," Smoak began, picking his words carefully, "I'm not sure ... one, we can't do anything about ... that darned thing on the internet. But I'm not sure you need to get too bothered up about it. My limited understanding, it's probably the same six, eight or ten people that are responsible for their willful ignorance and pig-headedness. I don't know any other way to describe it."

He was probably close to the truth. The News Herald's "Squall Line," a free-for-all anonymous comment section, and semi-anonymous commenters to stories (they only had to supply a pseudonym), were dominated by the same dozen or so people. They would often spend most of their time commenting on the idiotic comments made by other "Squallers," like an ugly family discussion at a Thanksgiving dinner.

Smoak obviously followed what was said about him online.

"Mr. Francis has a frequent rant that he spent a year in jail because a federal judge denied him bond," the judge said. "I didn't have anything to do with that."

"Judge," Bateman jumped in, "I didn't say it and I'm not going to vouch for anything my client has said or is purported to have said."

"Obviously," Smoak said, getting back to Selander's issue, "for a certain segment, anything that happens in this case is like throwing red meat to them."

He said he expected the jury pool in this case would be composed of better people. And the case seemed destined for trial, once the appeal was out of the way.

"Have you all just given up the idea that this case can get settled?" Smoak asked.

"Yes, sir," Bateman said.

During this same hearing, Bateman also foreshadowed a motion he would file about two weeks later.

"If this thing is going on in October, your honor, I may not be here myself. I may prefer the jail cell."

• • •

On February 24, Bateman asked Smoak to allow him to step away from the case. He said Francis hadn't paid him in more than seven months. Bateman told the judge that now was a good time for a lawyer change because a new attorney could get up to speed on the case during the delay. Smoak granted Bateman's request on March 10, officially ending Bateman's participation in the case. Smoak ordered Francis to have a new lawyer in place by April.

On April 15, Bateman sued Francis for nearly $500,000 in unpaid legal fees. He wrote that his firm was retained in February 2009, with an upfront, nonrefundable $200,000 payment, with the expectation that the case would go to trial as then-scheduled in July 2009.

As Bateman noted in his lawsuit, Smoak ordered a continuance on July 1, 2009, to a new trial date of October 13, 2009. On August 28, the trial was rescheduled for January 4, 2010. On November 20, the case was rescheduled for February 22. Of course, in February, the trial was postponed because of the appeal. No wonder Smoak worried about the case becoming a legal Flying Dutchman.

According to the contract between Bateman and Francis, they were to renegotiate a fee if the trial was continued. Bateman said Francis ignored any attempt to negotiate a new contract and the meter had been running since July 1.

Fees for the firm's lawyers and paralegals had reached $497,313. Bateman and the other lawyers in his firm charged $350 an hour. Expenses had topped $50,000, but Francis had made a payment in September for some fees and the total Bateman was suing for was $491,109.

Again, Francis' distrust of his attorneys led to him withholding money that he easily had, and sabotage his own case. Bateman had done an outstanding job to that point and his mannerisms, while sometimes distracting, would probably have appealed to a jury.

Francis's disregard for judicial orders, another persistent problem, also resulted in his losing $99,556 in a judgment on April 9 to Panama City attorney Jean Marie Downing. Downing had represented Francis in another Bay County lawsuit and sued him after he refused to pay her $77,558 bill.When Francis ignored Smoak's orders to help pay for an arbittor, Smoak granted a request from Downing for a default judgment, declaring her the winner. The additional $20,000 that Downing received over her fees was interest and other costs associated with the lawsuit.

Two weeks later, Downing talked to Mantra's corporate lawyer who told her they'd like to "work it out."

"She was surprised to hear there was a judgment," Downing laughed.

Chapter 23

All stop

For months in 2010, just about everything in the Bay County case came to a halt. Joe Francis had to explain why he hadn't hired a lawyer by April to replace Bateman. Francis, claiming financial problems because of the tax lien, asked for and was given more time.

And life went on.

In July, Francis got engaged to Christina McLarty, the entertainment reporter with CBS News in Los Angeles who he had called from solitary confinement in the Bay County Jail. He issued a press release saying the couple would wed in Mexico, in a civil ceremony, to protest U.S. prohibitions against gay marriage.

Tiger Woods got divorced in Panama City and President Obama vacationed here.

In St. Louis, Francis won a civil trial in July. He was sued by a woman who was partying in a nightclub in May 2004 when a Girls Gone Wild cameraman began filming her. She refused to expose her breasts, but someone in the crowd yanked down her top and the incident made it into a video. She didn't realize it until years later when a friend of her husband watched the video and recognized her. She sued for $5 million.

She argued at trial that she didn't give consent. Francis' attorneys argued that she implied consent by just dancing in front of the camera at the club. After a 90-minute deliberation, 11 of the 12 jurors sided with Girls Gone Wild.

"This is just one more example of someone trying to make a quick buck off Girls Gone Wild by making false accusations against our company," Francis said in a press release. "This is also another great example of someone who got their ass kicked in a court room by a smart judge and a smart jury who saw the truth. Girls Gone Wild will always vigorously defend ourselves against anyone who makes such outrageous and defamatory allegations. Girls Gone Wild has NEVER lost a jury trial."

Francis' record in court was pretty impressive and he had a straightforward approach to plaintiffs – he attacked.

In 2004, a woman on vacation in Miami Beach accused Francis of raping her. She told police that she met Francis in a nightclub and they began arguing over Girls Gone Wild's exploitation of women. Francis invited her up to his hotel room. She and a friend went with him and they resumed their discussion of Francis' treatment of women until Francis got up and went into the bedroom. According to the police report, "she followed him into the bedroom and the next thing the victim remembers is waking up naked in bed, (Francis) was also naked next to her."

A month after the report became public, Francis sued her for defamation. In his lawsuit he said they did have a discussion about Girls Gone Wild that went into the early morning hours when they decided together to go to bed. Francis' bodyguard had checked her ID earlier in the night to ensure that she was of age.

Francis said they had consensual sex, then fell asleep together. The next morning, he said, they snuggled and he asked her if she wanted to do it again. She refused, saying she was concerned about returning her rental car late. They went out to the living room, where her friend and Francis' bodyguard were, and Francis ordered the two girls hamburgers from room service. Before leaving, the woman left her phone number and asked Francis if he was going to call her.

Francis sued her for $25,000,036. The $36 was the cost of the burgers.

Chapter 24

False hope

On September 27, attorney Christopher Pantel, of a law firm located on Hope Street in Los Angeles, filed his notice of appearance in Francis' case. His first duty was to address a motion for default judgment filed by the plaintiffs in the lawsuit, claiming that Francis had missed a drop-dead cutoff for getting new representation for his companies. Individuals don't have to be represented by a lawyer, but companies do. Judge Smoak had threatened Francis with default judgment if he missed this deadline and the plaintiffs were trying to hold him to it.

Pantel didn't say in his filing what day he'd been hired, only that the delay had been caused by Francis' inability to line up local counsel to assist. Lawyers practicing in specific federal courts must be certified in that district. That usually means hiring a local lawyer to at least put his or her name on the case and allow Francis' out-of-state lawyer to work the case. But in this case, Pantel had to get the certification himself, which he did on September 24.

The law firm advertised itself as trial specialists, listing several notable trial victories and noteworthy clients on its website. It looked like Francis was gearing up to finally finish this case. The 11th Circuit Court of Appeals, however, hadn't issued its findings in the open court matter, so everything was still on hold.

Still. Trial specialists. That was a good sign.

I'd left the News Herald in December 2009 and opened a small public relations business. My main client was the State Attorney's Office, which was paying me enough to make my bills. In return, I wrote their press releases. I had really left because Francis was supposed to go to trial three months later and I wanted to free up time to finish the book. But with the postponements, I'd been feeling like an idiot. At least I had a lot of free time to think about how idiotic I was.

For a while, I tried to treat it like a well-deserved break. I started windsurfing again. I picked up the jogging and spent a lot of time with my girlfriend's family.

Unfortunately, I wasn't able to really pour myself into this semi-retirement. It's nice to be leisurely when you can afford it, and lazy when you don't care, but I couldn't afford to not care.

• • •

In late September, North Florida finally shook off the smothering heat of a long summer and began tingling with the cool evenings of approaching autumn. It was refreshing for body, mind and spirit.

Then came the man from Hope Street. It felt like things were going to start happening. That was a misleading feeling. Pantel and his law partners moved in December to be allowed to withdraw from the case.

Jonathan E. Meislin, on behalf of Bassi, Edlin, Huie & Blum LLP, wrote the motion and claimed in it that Francis was asking the firm to do illegal things. Of course, he never came right out and said that, but he cited as their reason for withdrawing numerous rules of professional conduct dealing with clients who ask lawyers to do illegal things.

This is how a lawyer tells a judge that: "the Florida Rules of Professional Conduct require a lawyer to terminate representation when "the representation will result in violation of the Rules of Professional Conduct or law," or "the client persists in a course of action involving the lawyer's services that the lawyer reasonably believes is criminal or fraudulent..." Withdrawal is allowed if a client seeks to pursue an illegal course of conduct. A lawyer also may seek permissive withdrawal from a court if the client "insists that the member pursue a course of conduct that is illegal or that is prohibited under these rules or the State Bar Act. . . ." A lawyer may seek permissive withdrawal from a court if the "continued employment is likely to result in violation of these rules or of the State Bar Act. . . ."

That was all in the first paragraph. Subtle.

Meislin went on to write that withdrawal can be granted if there is a breakdown in communication or a disagreement about strategy between the client and attorney.

"There has been a total breakdown in the communication between BEHB and its clients."

And, of course, what had now become the standard reason that Francis couldn't keep a lawyer: "Failure or refusal of a client to pay or secure proper fees or expenses of an attorney after being reasonably requested to do so will furnish grounds for the attorney to withdraw from the case."

"Mr. Francis and his companies owe BEHB over $90,000 in legal fees and advanced costs that they have failed to pay."

Meislin and Blum offered to tell Smoak what Francis was asking them to do, and not paying them to do it, but in private. They couldn't in the motions because it would violate attorney/client confidentiality.

On January 18, 2011, Smoak granted the motion to withdraw and asked no questions of Blum and company.

Francis was, once again, without a lawyer and in danger of violating Smoak's orders.

Chapter 25

Anonymity

On February 1, the 11th Circuit Court of Appeal reversed Smoak's ruling on the anonymity issue. The appeals panel took a surprisingly sensitive stance on the matter and seemed to chastise Smoak for being overly concerned with the law instead of these girls' fragility.

Chief Judge Dubina wrote the opinion and led off with an overview of Smoak's reasoning in denying the motion for anonymity. Dubina said Smoak weighed the presumption of openness that is inherent in all trials against the plaintiffs' reluctance to publicly disclose "information of the utmost intimacy."

"According to the district court, Plaintiffs S's and J's claims stemmed from an incident that lasted 'less than a minute' and did not involve 'sexual conduct as a matter of law.' The district court conceded that Plaintiffs B and V would have to disclose information that "may be embarrassing," but concluded that "casual and voluntary sexual activity is not the type of fundamentally personal issue that warrants the imposition of anonymity like abortion, birth control, or religion."

Smoak had also concluded that none of the plaintiffs would be forced to disclose "information of the utmost intimacy." The fact that they were minors at the time was not given much weight, Dubina wrote.

"Finally, the district court held that the Plaintiffs' claims that they would suffer violence and retaliation for filing the suit were not of a sufficient degree to warrant anonymity. In light of all this, the district court held that the Plaintiffs did not overcome the presumption of openness in court and denied their motion to remain anonymous."

Dubina wrote that the appeals panel's job was to determine if Smoak abused his discretion in coming to his decision. "A district court abuses its discretion in denying a motion to remain anonymous if it fails to actually consider the circumstances of the case and to weigh the relevant factors and instead follows a blanket rule in making its final decision."

What Dubina found troubling in Smoak's order was that he "incorrectly deemed some of the plaintiffs' conduct casual and voluntary."

The panel decided that Smoak had abused his discretion and vacated the order. The appeals court found that Smoak should allow plaintiffs B and V to remain anonymous and told Smoak to reconsider allowing plaintiffs J and S to proceed anonymously.

"The district court failed to take into account the actual allegations made by the plaintiffs – as evident in its mischaracterization of the plaintiffs' conduct as "casual and voluntary" – and failed to adequately consider the Plaintiffs' extensive evidence about the scope of harm they faced if they were forced to reveal their identities.

"First, the district court gave inadequate consideration to the degree of intimacy the plaintiffs' testimony would reach. The issues involved in this case could not be of a more sensitive and highly personal nature – they involve descriptions of the Plaintiffs in various stages of nudity and engaged in explicit sexual conduct while they were minors who were coerced by the defendants into those activities. Plaintiffs J and S alleged that they were filmed displaying their breasts and that this footage was used by the defendants in films marketed as pornography."

Dubina wrote that Smoak was mistaken in thinking that just because J's and S's flashing was not illegal, or classified as "sexual conduct," under Florida law that it wasn't a "disclosure of utmost intimacy.'"

"Even if their conduct does not fall under the typical classification of "sexual," the district court should consider whether it requires disclosing information of "utmost intimacy" in light of their ages at the time of the filming."

Dubina wrote that Smoak also mischaracterized plaintiffs B's and V's conduct as being casual and voluntary.

"Plaintiff B alleges in the complaint that her filmed behavior was the possible result of being drugged by the defendants – a fact that makes her conduct decisively not 'voluntary.' In any case, the extremely graphic sexual activity she engages in with the other female in the footage can by no means be deemed "casual." Her filmed conduct includes a lengthy and explicit session of homosexual intimacy involving fondling and oral and manual sex with another underage woman. Requiring her to be identified by name closely connects her graphic homosexual conduct with her widespread public reputation and thus constitutes a matter of 'the utmost intimacy.'

"As for Plaintiff V, there is no real dispute that her conduct was not casual and voluntary. Francis was convicted under a plea agreement of one count of child abuse under Florida Statutes and two counts of prostitution for his actions with Plaintiff V. There is nothing voluntary about the conduct giving rise to those charges."

Dubina said Smoak was too quick to discount the testimony he heard from the plaintiffs' experts as to the damage the girls would suffer if their names were made public. In addition, neither the defendants, who did not even argue against anonymity, nor Florida Freedom Newspapers could show how they'd be damaged or prejudiced if the plaintiffs continued to remain anonymous.

Chapter 26

Here We Go

On March 2, Smoak vacated his order from February 5, 2010, and, in compliance with the appeals court, allowed all four girls to proceed anonymously. He'd already set the trial date for March 28 and gave Francis until March 15 to have a lawyer in place for his companies or face default.

On March 11, Francis wrote a letter to Smoak asking for more time. He said he thought he had a lawyer lined up on March 1, but two days later he discovered the attorney had not been admitted to practice in the Northern District of Florida. That was a poor excuse, one that Smoak would focus on in his order. Getting admitted to the District Court was a matter of filling out a form.

"I sincerely believe that if the trial date were continued for a short period, I would be more successful in my ability to retain counsel," Francis wrote. He asked for at least 30 more days.

His first mistake was telling Smoak that he had lined up a lawyer on March 1, when Smoak had allowed his last attorneys to withdraw on January 18. Francis insisted he was talking to lawyers in California and Florida, but the six-week gap looked like he had done nothing until after the 11th Circuit released its opinion.

Smoak, as was his habit when annoyed, went through every detail in Francis' history with lawyers in this case. He reminded Francis that Bateman had withdrawn in March 2010 and at that time he'd ordered Francis to have a new lawyer representing his companies by April of that year. Francis asked for more time. Smoak gave it to him. Francis asked for more time again. Smoak gave it to him.

"I informed Defendants that this would be the final extension granted to Defendants as they had already had months to secure counsel and had already received two 30-day extensions. I again reminded Defendants that jury trial would be held during the third or fourth week of the first calendar month following the date a decision was rendered by the 11th Circuit on Plaintiff's appeal. I also advised Defendant Francis that if he chose to proceed (without a lawyer), trial would not be delayed if he acquired counsel after the September 10, 2010, deadline.

"Defendants have failed to demonstrate good cause to continue the trial. I warned Defendants five times over the past year that the trial would be scheduled the third or fourth week of the calendar month following the date a decision was rendered by the 11th Circuit.

"I granted three motions for extension of time by Defendants. Now, on the eve of trial and the pretrial conference, which is scheduled in two business days, Defendants request their fourth 30-day extension. Defendants have failed to show extenuating circumstances why one year has been insufficient time to retain counsel. A year is ample time for any corporation or individual to retain counsel and prepare for trial. Defendants had fair warning of the consequences of failing to cause counsel to appear and fair notice of when the trial would be scheduled. In addition, admittance of an attorney to the Northern District of Florida is perfunctory and could easily be accomplished in a very few days by any attorney before the March 28, 2011, trial date. Thus, this additional reason Defendants have offered for failing to secure counsel also fails to provide sufficient grounds for a continuance. Furthermore, this case was filed in March of 2008, almost exactly three years ago to the day. This is markedly longer than it takes the average civil case in the Northern District of Florida to reach trial.

"It is time for this case to be put before a jury."

When the News Herald ran the story about Francis' motion for continuance being denied, it posted the story on its website. As usual, it got a lot of comments:

bobsmith32405 took the unpopular position that "the best thing for us all would be for Francis to settle. Pick a large number, write the check. Save the taxpayers' money for the trial and the county the embarrassment."

pcb999 asked, "who's paying these wannabe amateur porn stars' legal fees? I hope they get a big judgment for getting naked on film by their own choice and never are able to collect.

"Someone should post these girls' Facebook pages. I'm sure that would blow their case."

bchphotographer wrote, "After it's done and said, Joe Francis should sue these so called innocent girls."

The News Herald's readers often complained about the paper's coverage of the Girls Gone Wild case and repeatedly claimed they were tired of it. But Joe Francis always got a lot of responses and, for the most part, the comments were on his side.

Chapter 27

A Spring Break trial

The morning of March 15, my first stop on the federal courthouse's second floor was the clerk's office to read up on the latest filings. There were quite a few. I printed off 28 pages and went to the window to pay. The feds only charged 10 cents per page for copies, which was the best price in town, but they made up the difference by not having a cash drawer.

"We don't have change," the girl told me when I handed her a five dollar bill. They never had change. They probably owed me $100 in change.

"That's OK," I said, my usual line. "I need the copies more than I need the change."

I took a seat in the second row of the courtroom and Chris Olwell, the new courts reporter for the News Herald, sat down beside me.

"I get the feeling this is going to be the end of the road for this case," Olwell said.

I had to agree. All morning I'd been nervous about this hearing. There was every possibility that Joe Francis was going to default, or worse settle, and that would be the end of the book.

Default would mean a dry, cursory hearing before the judge to determine damages.

Plaintiffs' lawyers Ross McCloy, Larry Selander, Rachael Pontikes, Tom Dent and two people I didn't know came in the room.

U.S District Judge Richard Smoak entered the courtroom from behind his bench and took a quick, meaningful look at the defense table. The table's glossy blond wood was uncluttered by file folders and loose papers. All five of the padded wooden chairs were unburdened by defendants, lawyers and, more specifically, Joe Francis.

It was two weeks before trial in Panama City and Joe Francis was a no-show to the last scheduled pretrial hearing. His request for a continuance had been denied. No lawyer had notified the court that he would be sitting in Francis' place. So, Joe Francis was expected to be in court.

Smoak let out his breath and placed several hard-bound files on his desk. He was dressed in a gray suit and bow tie.

On the other side of the room, Selander, Pontikes, Dent, and McCloy stood quietly by their seats waiting for Smoak.

"Please be seated," the judge said and there was a unified shuffling as everyone in the room took their seats.

"Mr. Selander, did everyone make it OK from Chicago? You didn't leave anyone behind?" Smoak asked. Selander, Dent and Pontikes were based in Chicago.

"No sir. We're all here," Selander replied with a laugh.

The main door to the courtroom opened and there was a pause as everyone glanced over. A U.S. Deputy Marshal took a long, quiet stride into the room and took a seat immediately by the door.

Francis had been ordered to appear, but Smoak didn't seem angry or even surprised at his absence.

Joe had given up. But that didn't signify to Smoak that he'd waived all his rights. He'd basically waived his defenses, but the trial that was scheduled for March 28 would go ahead as planned with or without Joe Francis.

"With a jury," Smoak emphasized.

Smoak said if Francis didn't have a lawyer file a notice of appearance by midnight on behalf of Mantra Films and the other corporations, he would issue an order finding them in default. He would also allow a week for Francis to explain why he shouldn't be in default. If Smoak issued an order of default judgment, it would strip the defendants of their defenses. The only issue then would be to decide how much the plaintiffs should receive in damages.

That didn't seem significant in this case. Francis had already admitted to most of the charges, there really wasn't a defense. But of more importance was Francis' absence from the courtroom.

At trial, even a trial for damages, Francis' side could still argue that the girls had not been harmed, or the harm was minimal. Also, without someone there to represent him, anything about the girls that Selander didn't want shown – like the additional pornographic movies one of the defendants had made – would never be seen by the jury.

Selander and the plaintiffs would also be able to handpick the most favorable jury without objection from the defense.

In theory, it would be a cakewalk.

Selander, however, didn't want a jury. He wanted Magistrate Jones to make a finding on damages.

"I'm not going to do this to Magistrate Jones," Smoak said. "First, he's not familiar with the case. Second, he'd never forgive me. I don't think I ought to do it, given the record through many years of this case; Mr. Francis has found significant inference in far less profound issues. I don't think it's worth opening that can of worms."

A jury verdict, he said, would be "beyond reproach."

For the next hour, Selander gently argued that a jury trial would be too complicated and take too much time. Complicating a jury trial, he said, was the issue of anonymity. Because they'd won that issue and the girls would go to trial under their pseudonyms, jury selection would then be a mess. The lawyers wouldn't be able to ask prospective jurors if they knew the girls, because they wouldn't be able to use their names.

"If somebody did recognize the plaintiffs," Selander said, "we would not want them to sit on the jury."

In other words, anyone knowing these girls might not feel they deserved money for their interaction with Girls Gone Wild.

Selander said he would probably have the girls show up for a portion of jury selection to see if anyone on the panel recognized them. But the issues with anonymity went well beyond jury selection. Selander wanted to close the courtroom to spectators, not the press, when anyone was testifying who had information that could lead to the identification of the girls. That would mean, essentially, closing the courtroom during the entire trial.

Selander argued that someone discovering, for example, where one of the girls went to school could lead them to discovering her name by scouring yearbooks from the time that she attended.

Smoak was vehemently opposed to closing the courtroom for any reason. He firmly believed in open trials. He told Selander that he would have extra work on his hands to prepare his witnesses and assure that there would be no slip ups in their testimony.

"You may have to make more of an effort than perhaps you want to before we clear the courtroom," Smoak said.

Selander assured the judge that he didn't want a secret trial, that they'd never asked that the media be excluded.

Smoak asked him what assurances the press had given him that they wouldn't reveal identifying information that came out by accident. Smoak also asked him if anyone had taken information in the court files and tried to identify the girls.

Selander said he didn't know of anyone actively searching for the girls' names and the only assurance he had from the press was that they "would abide by what you say."

No one in the local media really cared who these girls were and were unlikely to release their names and risk litigation. The story had never been about the girls. It had always been about Joe Francis.

But Selander didn't want spectators, especially at this time of year.

"With Spring Break going on in Panama City Beach at the same time Mr. Francis is on trial, what's going to happen? We don't know."

Smoak refused to make a blanket ruling and said they'd take it up on a witness-by-witness basis. He asked Selander how long he would need to present his case, considering he would not have opposing counsel cross-examining witnesses.

"Two weeks."

"What? Why?"

Selander said they had roughly 20 witnesses to call and some, especially the expert witnesses like the psychologists and forensic accountants, would need a long time on the stand.

In all fairness, Selander, Pontikes and the other lawyers had made good use of the year that the appeals court had taken to decide the anonymity issue. They had more than 100 witnesses and statements listed in evidence. They'd addressed the weaknesses that were so glaring in 2010. They listed several of Francis' former attorneys as their witnesses, including Aaron Dyer and Michael Burke. They even listed two attorneys' motions to withdraw from this case as evidence.

Smoak cautioned them to go easy on the jury, don't overload them with useless information. And don't drag this out any longer than needed, he said, "They'll bless you for it."

And as far as the jury issue was concerned:

"The conclusion of this long saga really needs to be with a finding by a jury."

Amen.

• • •

That afternoon I stopped at Subway to get lunch. Standing in line, watching the woman make my sandwich, I was either deep in thought or really hungry. Either way, I didn't realize attorneys Jim White and Mike Grabner were in line behind me until Grabner poked my shoulder.

"We've been saying terrible things about you back here. Didn't you hear us?" he said.

"Sorry. I'm really focussed on my sandwich."

I told them a little about that morning's hearing.

"Hey," I said, "I'm surprised he didn't contact you guys about representing him."

White had represented Francis during his contempt of court.

"He wouldn't hire us," White said. He was of the old school when it came to being a lawyer, he didn't like to coddle clients. And Francis required a lot of coddling, so much so that Grabner had been retained to simply sit with him at the Bay County Jail while Francis was in solitary. "He said later it was the best money he'd ever spent."

"I thought he already had a lawyer," White said.

"Nope. That's one of the issues in this whole thing. It looks like he's giving up. He's probably not even going to come to trial."

"He's an idiot. With just a small amount of lawyering those girls wouldn't get a thing from a jury."

"Actually, what I think would be funny is if a jury didn't give them anything even without any lawyering at all."

"That could happen."

Chapter 28

Ashley Dupre

If Joe Francis was going to give up, it wouldn't be the first time, or even the first time in 2011. Amber Arpaio won a $3 million judgment from District Judge Joel Pisano in federal court in New Jersey on March 3. Francis had failed to respond to Arpaio's lawsuit and Pisano ordered default judgment then heard the evidence himself and made the ruling.

Arpaio was dragged into one of the hottest news stories of 2008 – that of call-girl Ashley Dupre and New York Gov. Eliot Spitzer. Spitzer had to resign after his associations with, as Pisano put it, "the infamous prostitute" Dupre came to light.

When the scandal hit, Francis offered Dupre $1 million to do a film and work in promoting Girls Gone Wild. He withdrew the offer after his employees found that they already had footage of her from years before. Dupre sued him, saying she was 17 when she was filmed by GGW. Francis responded to the lawsuit by releasing on the internet footage of her smiling and giggling for the camera, claiming to be 18 and displaying Arpaio's driver's license. Francis didn't attempt to conceal the license or Arpaio's name, which quickly gained its own infamy. An expert at her trial said he found 130,000 hits on a search of her name, most of them leading to porn sites.

On July 11, 2008, Arpaio sued for invasion of privacy, injury to her reputation and misappropriation of her identity.

She immediately ran into problems even serving papers on both Francis and Dupre. GGW simply waived their right to respond to the lawsuit and was defaulted on in April 2010.

Dupre was apparently never served. On March 9, 2009, Arpaio's process server saw a woman leaving from Dupre's last known address in Wall, New Jersey. When the woman got into her Mercedes Benz, the process server followed her to a gym, but couldn't tell if it was Dupre or her mother, "who looks extremely youthful and similar to Ashley," Pisano wrote in his order. So the process server waited until the following day and went back to the residence where loud music was playing.

"Upon the process server's knocking on the front door, the music ceased," Pisano wrote. "After twenty seconds, the process server began to knock again, and the music restarted. Now the process server knocks on the door using a large brass knocker fastened to the door. It is an extremely loud and effective knocker, but the music continues and no one comes to the door."

The process server left, but also left a copy of the summons in the mailbox. Apparently, the summons went unclaimed.

• • •

The day after the hearing, as expected, Judge Smoak issued the order finding Mantra Films, Aero Falcon and MRA Holdings in default. He also ordered Joe Francis to tell him why he, too, shouldn't be stripped of his defenses. Smoak had said during the hearing that he expected that Francis wouldn't even respond and both he and the plaintiffs' attorneys just assumed that Francis wouldn't be represented, or wouldn't be present at all for the trial.

But Francis surprised everyone by actually responding to the order. He wrote to the judge saying he'd gotten late notice that his prior counsel had been allowed to withdraw from the case and had been scrambling ever since to hire a lawyer. He said one of the things complicating his efforts to defend himself was that Rick Bateman was refusing to turn over the case files.

Francis assured Smoak that even if he couldn't line up a lawyer, he'd be there himself. Francis would act as his own lawyer.

Selander pointed out that Francis never explained why he didn't make the hearing and a default judgment should be issued just because he wasn't there.

Smoak ordered a hearing to be held the morning of jury selection and said Francis and Bateman both had to be there. He wanted Bateman to explain why he wasn't releasing the files.

Bateman wrote his explanation to the judge a day later. He said he'd sent Francis an email offering whatever Francis needed to make a smooth transition.

Francis responded, and CC'd Dennis : "Dennis, please sue Rick for my money back." And nothing more.

Bateman said case files were legal property of the attorney and would be released when the former client paid for them to be copied. Francis still owed him money and had made no efforts to pay the cost of having the files copied.

Chapter 29

Trial

The day started off with a haze over the water that blended with the white and gray sky. The lawn and palm trees at the front of the federal courthouse were a startling green by comparison.

Mary Scott Speigner, a reporter for local Channel 13, was sitting on a garden border eating a banana, her camera on the sidewalk at her feet. She told me she'd gotten up 20 minutes before and hadn't had time to eat or put on makeup.

"I know absolutely nothing about this case. I tried to read last night but ..."

She'd worked until 11 and couldn't do much research. I tried to give her an overview, until her eyes glazed over and her chin hit her palm.

"I'm listening. A 13-year-old and a 15-year-old flashed. A 17-year-old had a sex scene. And Joe paid a 16-year-old to jerk him off, even though he claims he likes to jerk himself off. That's my favorite part," she said, laughing.

She halfheartedly lifted her camera and filmed Rick Bateman, Larry Selander, Rachael Pontikes and Bubsey entering the courthouse.

"I got video," she said, her chin back in her palm. "I got one lawyer, two lawyers, one lawyer. Exciting stuff."

Local television reporters hate federal court because cameras aren't allowed in the courtroom. Getting usable footage is usually a challenge.

A taxi pulled up and Speigner looked up, showing her first signs of interest.

"Is that him?"

It wasn't. A skinny young man with a stubble of hair on his head stepped out, paid the driver and approached the reporters. He introduced himself as Steph Watts, a blogger from New York.

He was supposed to have flown in with Francis that morning so he could interview him on the flight.

"I'm in contact with Mr. Francis, so I'll keep you informed."

Joe Francis was late. His 9 a.m. hearing was rescheduled to 10 to allow him time to fly in from Atlanta. He'd missed his early flight out of Los Angeles and had to wait until Monday morning to fly out.

"How can you be late for your own federal trial?" News Herald photographer Robert Cooper asked no one in particular as he waited with the local reporters for Francis to arrive.

Uptstairs in the courtroom, Selander, Pontikes, Ross McCloy and Tom Dent were patiently waiting for the day, the hearing and the trial to begin. Selander had a look on his face like he was in a doctor's office waiting room: trying to be patient as the minutes ticked away but not exactly excited about what was to come.

Bateman lounged in one of the chairs at the defendant's table.

Judge Smoak, however, decided to go ahead with the hearing in chambers. The issue was a simple one: was Bateman withholding the case file and confounding Francis' attempts to get a new lawyer?

Bateman answered that succinctly in chambers. He told the judge he was legally allowed to keep the files until someone paid for the cost of copying them. So far, he said, no one had offered to pay for copies.

The hearing ended soon after. Bateman loped out of the courtroom with his satchel in hand. I asked him what happened as he was waiting for the elevator. As usual, it was a succinct answer.

"I did everything right. OK, you can go."

Tallahassee attorney William Bubsey was talking to the court reporter inside the courtroom when I pushed through the door. He was Bateman's former law partner, which is how his name got mentioned to Francis. He'd never met Joe Francis and knew nothing about the case, but he'd agreed to help out as much as he could.

Bubsey hadn't been retained for the trial either, and there was little chance that he'd be able to take on the case. His father had just died of cancer. The viewing was Tuesday and the funeral was Wednesday. Smoak had made it clear again that day that he wouldn't grant a continuance.

Bubsey was conflicted though. He was excited by the competition and the challenge of going into a trial blind and maybe pulling it out. He was also looking at a potentially large payoff, but it was all happening at the wrong time.

Bubsey, a former marine, wasn't too concerned about keeping Francis in check during the trial.

He went outside to wait for Francis, who, by this time, had landed and was driving in from the airport.

Bubsey was talking with the bailiffs in the black-top parking lot when a taxi van pulled in. Francis stepped out of the van wearing a black suit, white shirt and no tie. His hair was cut short and he looked skinny to the verge of being gaunt. He jogged up the lot on his way to the door, nearly running right past Bubsey, who caught his arm as he passed. They walked over to the trunk of Bubsey's Cadillac and talked in person for the first time.

They walked inside together, and came out a together a few minutes later, but Bubsey stayed on the top step as Francis trotted over to the reporters. Bubsey disappeared quietly back into the building as Francis talked.

“I’m here to answer your questions,” Francis said as he walked up.

“How does it feel to be back in Panama City?”

“Ah, any other questions?” Francis answered, immediately charming the small crowd of reporters.

“I guess the big news is, I’ve just informed the judge of my intention to proceed pro se, meaning I’ll be representing myself at trial.”

He grinned and looked down, stuck his hands in his pockets and smiled again. He talked about Smoak’s decision to let Bateman out of the case “right before trial,” even though Francis paid him a flat fee of $288,000. Francis thought the appeals court would look unfavorably upon that decision if the verdict was to go against him.

“Joe Francis is gonna represent himself in court,” he said, trying out the sound of it.

“What do you think about this case?”

“This case is 100 percent bullshit,” Francis said, warming up to the interview. “I can’t wait to get these girls on the stand and let them have it. I’m not going to be accused of something I did not do. This will be a slaughter.”

Mary Scott asked him about the fact that he’s already admitted to doing everything they’d accused him of.

“That’s absolutely untrue. Read the case file. Go to meetjoefrancis.com and read the legal history of this case. They’re liars. The only victim here is me.”

He thought that even if he lost he’d win on appeal.

“In the meantime, we can have some fun. This is gonna be fun.”

He was asked why he hadn’t tried to hire a Panama City lawyer.

“I don’t trust a lot of lawyers down here. I think I’m pretty qualified to represent myself.”

He said he’d already spent $20-25 million defending himself in Panama City cases.

“Is that a blip on your radar? How much money do you have?” the reporters asked.

"Everything's a blip on my radar. Being here is a blip on my radar, that's why I'm willing to defend myself in court as an American citizen. And with that, I have to go prepare for a trial."

He left the reporters buzzing.

Mary Scott was finally and completely out of her funk.

"That's the most incredible thing I've ever seen. 'This is 100-percent bullshit'! I love that. I love this guy."

Chapter 30

A fool for a client

Francis got to work almost immediately. The judge called him, and Bubsey, into the courtroom to address some pretrial issues. These would be his first arguments as his own lawyer.

One issue was to define what a journalist was, so there would be no confusion when the plaintiffs asked to have the courtroom cleared. I'd expected this to come up. It wasn't a secret that I was no longer covering this case for the News Herald. I knew someone would want to know what my credentials were and why I should be allowed to remain.

I tried to head off problems the week before the trial. I was out walking my girlfriend's dog, Boudreaux, and granddaughter, Vivi, and we passed the judge's driveway. Twenty-three-month-old Vivi was riding on my shoulders, and Boudreaux was straining his leash as we came up on Smoak's house.

It was his usual exercise time. He'd been riding a mountain bike through the Cove recently, bent over the handlebars and pumping the pedals like he was crushing grapes.

He was in his driveway, fingerless gloves on his hands, preparing for his ride. I asked if I could talk to him and approached with child on shoulders and dog on leash. As expected, Vivi charmed him into a mushy grandfatherly mess.

"I expect that there's going to be some question as to whether I should be allowed to stay. I don't want there to be any confusion with you. You know I'm no longer writing for the News Herald."

"Someone told me that."

"Well, I'm freelancing now. I can tell you that I'm not going to be attending the trial as a spectator. I'm going to be there to work."

Smoak remembered that conversation when Pontikes brought me up by name and asked that I be treated as a spectator. He told her about the meeting and denied her request.

Francis told me he'd argued for 15 minutes to let me stay in the courtroom and that's what saved me.

The second item had to do with the plaintiffs' sexual history. Francis wanted to be allowed to get into other experiences, call witnesses to testify about their sexual encounters.

"This is a sex case," Francis said. "All we're gonna be talking about is sex."

But Smoak put his foot down. The trial would only be about the sexual encounters that were at issue in the complaint.

"If anybody brings up (sexual history) you'll probably go into custody," Smoak growled. "There won't be a fine, but you probably won't be spending the night at the motel."

Francis also wanted to keep out any mention of the default judgment against the corporations. He said if the jurors heard the corporations had no defense it would automatically prejudice him in their eyes.

"This is about Joe Francis versus A, B, C and D. If they hear that there's been a default judgment as to the corporations it will infer guilt against me."

That same issue had been argued more than a year ago and denied then. Smoak stayed consistent and denied it again. The trial would be about damages the corporations would have to pay, whether Francis was liable personally and how much, if anything, he would have to pay in damages.

Francis wouldn't let it go and would continue the same objection through jury selection.

"All we have to tell them is, 'it's Joe Francis verses these four plaintiffs.' At least that makes it fair, your honor. At least that starts us on even ground."

Smoak stayed patient with Francis through each argument, but also stayed with his ruling. Now he was ready for the trial to begin. He called a recess for lunch, then told the sides to be ready to go again at 1.

"Could I have a little more time to prepare?" Francis asked.

"All right, we'll reconvene at 1:15."

"1:50?" Francis asked, scribbling something on a notepad.

"1:15," came the answer in chorus from the plaintiffs lawyers.

• • •

Joe Francis burst out of the courtroom door. He was searching for Bubsey, who'd left the room ahead of him. He trotted into the hallway, hesitated and took a step to his right. He'd seen the three reporters who were talking on the couch in the hallway and he couldn't stop his feet from taking him there.

"This is gonna be funnnn."

"That's what we're all betting on." News Herald reporter Chris Olwell said.

"Joe Francis represents himself in federal court, that's a great headline for you guys."

He introduced himself to Olwell and Chad Mira from Channel 7, then suddenly recalled why he'd come out in the hallway in the first place.

"Where's my lawyer?"

Bailiff George Dobos told him that Bubsey was at his car. Bubsey had wasted no time in leaving the courtroom when dismissed and making a beeline for his car. His job here was done.

Francis turned and hit the button for the elevator.

"You have to go out this way," Dobos said, indicating the stairs behind him.

"I'm just going downstairs," Francis said, staying put by the elevator.

"I understand that, but you have to go out this way. This is the stairwell. It will take you outside and not through the lobby."

"I need to find my lawyer," Francis said, not quite grasping what Dobos was saying.

"I understand that," Dobos said, his voice taking on that sharp edge that he gets after the first 10 seconds of dealing with someone he considers to be an idiot. "You have to go out this way."

"But ..."

"This way."

"I'm just ..."

"This way."

Finally, Francis pried himself away from the elevator doors. He took two hesitant steps toward Dobos and stopped, a confused look refusing to leave his face.

"This way," Dobos said again, this time sounding more like he was coaxing a cat out from under a couch.

Francis trotted past him, pushed open the door to the stairs and disappeared.

Thirty seconds later, a chime indicated the elevator had reached the second floor and the doors opened slowly to reveal Francis standing with his hands behind his back and a huge grin on his face.

"One of the bailiffs told me I had to come up the elevator."

The stairwell had deposited him outside the courthouse. For him to get into a position where a bailiff would have told him to ride back up the elevator, Francis would have had to turn away from the parking lot, go back in the front door, past the metal detectors and into the lobby. All that in just seconds, but he hadn't located Bubsey, his reason for going downstairs in the first place.

He edged out of the elevator and looked at Dobos who said nothing. Francis wasn't supposed to be riding the elevator because the members of the jury pool were using it and the bailiffs didn't want them mingling.

Francis jogged back to the stairwell door and rushed back down to find Bubsey.

Chapter 31

"Hi, I'm Joe Francis"

Ross McCloy's knees bounced as he sat at the plaintiffs' table, giving away the only sign of his anxiety. His face, as always, was perfectly composed under his neatly combed wheat colored hair.

Across the aisle, Joe Francis was a twitching mass of energy. Even as he made notes on a legal pad, his eyebrows hitched up and down and his lips pursed and puckered. He was never entirely still, which did not go unnoticed by the people in the jury pool.

As the jury pool was led into the room, Francis would rise, turn to them with his hands behind his back and smile.

"How ya doin'?" he'd ask.

After the first group had been seated, Francis turned back to his table. He paused, smiled at the four reporters who'd been given seats next to the table. He straightened up, stood tall, grinned and shifted his shoulders. He looked like a confident 6-year-old boy preparing for his first recital, certain he was going to be smash.

Steph Watts, who had taken a seat with the reporters, said Francis had hired him as an assistant for the trial. He would do his best to take notes for Francis as he went about questioning the prospective jurors.

The rest of the pool, 50 people total, were brought in row-by-row. They were seated according to the chart that both sides had. The first 21 went into the jury box and a row of seven chairs on the floor in front of the box. The rest filled the gallery.

Smoak asked McCloy to introduce himself and his co-counsel. Then Francis got his turn.

"My name is Joe Francis. I actually started the Girls Gone Wild company. I'm representing myself today because my attorney's father died Friday. I'm pretty sure I can win this case in two seconds once you guys see the tapes."

"Mr. Francis," Smoak said gently.

The judge then told the members of the panel that this case would be a little different because all the plaintiffs would remain anonymous.

He told them that the girls in this case were all minors when they had their encounters with Girls Gone Wild.

That drew a long sigh from Joe Francis, but he didn't interrupt.

"The fact that they are proceeding anonymously should not weigh in favor of or against the plaintiffs."

He went into a brief summation of the allegations and finished by saying that Francis denies all the the claims against him.

The judge then turned it over to the plaintiffs' lawyers to begin their questioning.

McCloy walked to the podium and started with a story about his mother's experience the time that she'd been summoned for jury duty. Francis quickly objected: "relevance?" Smoak, who was not a fan of lawyers using jury selection to ingratiate themselves with jurors, paused for a beat before overruling the objection.

"Your honor, I think the attorney should ask the jury questions and not go into this story about his mother," Francis said.

"I think he's getting to it," Smoak replied.

"Yeah, but …"

"Overruled."

When McCloy started in on a story about his mother-in-law, Francis objected again and was quickly overruled.

McCloy asked how many of the 50 people in the pool had heard of the Girls Gone Wild case. All but two raised a hand.

Of the first 21 people in the box, the first who would be sorted through in search of a jury, nineteen were women.

McCloy asked if anyone objected to the girls proceeding anonymously. Smoak explained again that it was his decision to conceal the girls' identities because they were minors at the time of their interactions with Girls Gone Wild and that should not be held against the plaintiffs.

No one raised a hand, so no one had a problem with not knowing the plaintiffs' names.

McCloy told the judge now would be a good time to bring the plaintiffs in so the jury pool could see them. One of his assistants went into the hallway and a minute later a side door opened and four young women walked in.

I don't know what I expected, but I was disappointed. Three were slightly stocky and somewhat boyish looking. The fourth, the prettiest of the group, was slim, dark haired and olive skinned. She was the only one who'd worn a dress, the others were in T-shirts and pants.

McCloy stood behind the first girl and, in a gentle tone, identified her as Plaintiff J. He moved to the second, Plaintiff S, and the third, Plaintiff B and the fourth …

"What's the third one's name?" Francis interrupted, half standing and scribbling frantically on a notepad.

"B."

"V?"

"B. B as in boy."

"And the second?"

"S."

"And the first one?"

"J."

Francis sat back down.

The girls had looked over the juror list and identified four names they thought they knew. Pontikes had told the judge that they'd probably have to interview these four privately. But now, only two people raised a hand when asked if they knew the plaintiffs.

"You honor, I was told there were four." Francis said from his table.

"Come, come up here Mr. Francis," Smoak said, calling both attorneys to sidebar.

"Any communications, you do on the side, out of the hearing of the jury," Smoak said quietly to Francis at a corner of the judge's desk. "They don't have any need to know what we talk about."

"Sorry."

They talked softly for a minute, going over the procedure they wanted to use in questioning the prospective jurors about their relationship to the girls. Francis was hung up on these four names he'd been given, instead of the two who'd raised their hands.

"Those were mistakes by Miss Pontikes?" Francis asked loudly, dramatically raising his eyebrows and cocking his head. McCloy said something and Francis continued with the sarcastic tone. "You identified them as knowing them ..."

He snorted a laugh and glanced sideways at Smoak as if to include him in on the joke, but Smoak and McCloy continued talking and ignored him.

The sidebar was winding down, but not without a few last comments from Francis.

"I just think that if you make an order," he told Smoak, "they should follow it."

Smoak tried to smile, but it came out as a tight rectangle that just showed his teeth.

"Mr. Francis, you're like the old fella they talk about down here who learned to whisper in a sawmill." He ended the sidebar and Francis returned to his seat. McCloy paused at the podium.

"Let me regroup," he said. Francis had a talent for breaking his train of thought.

He sought out one of the women who'd raised her hand when the group was asked if they'd never heard of this case.

"Are you not from around here?" McCloy asked her.

"I'm from Wassau," the woman said. Wassau is a tiny community with a single stoplight, a grocery store, gas station and post office. It is most famous for hosting the annual Wassau Possum Fest, which is attended by every serious political candidate in the area.

Others in the room were far more familiar with the case. One woman worked at the Chateau Motel when the famous "shower scene" was shot in 2003, leading to Joe Francis' arrest. She remembered Francis, he tipped her $50 for cleaning the room and bringing in fresh towels.

But she didn't think she could be fair, saying she'd seen a lot of the things that had gone on in that room. She wasn't asked to elaborate.

One man, who identified himself as a tomato farmer, said he'd been "following this case for years." He also said he'd "been all over the world and had formed an opinion."

"I don't know what I'm supposed to say," the man continued. "To live that kind of life, you had to believe otherwise."

I didn't try to figure out what that meant. Luckily, others in the group were better at public speaking.

"I can't help but think about my 14-year-old daughter," a woman said. "I've already formed an opinion."

McCloy asked if anyone in the room enjoyed commenting on stories on the News Herald's website. Those comments were consistently anti-plaintiff. No one raised a hand.

McCloy walked over to an easel and was starting to write the plaintiffs' ages next to their initials.

"The ages of the plaintiffs …" he began, his marker headed toward the oversized pad of paper.

"Objection," Francis said. "Relevance."

"Overruled."

The marker, which had paused on its way, resumed its course.

"Objection. Objection," Francis said again, waving a hand at McCloy. "Before he writes anything … excuse me!"

"Come up here," Smoak said, one of the few times he sounded like he'd lost his patience.

Francis and McCloy went to sidebar and Francis launched into his argument.

"Wait, wait, wait," the court reporter said. "Could you slow down?" She held up her hand with her finger and thumb spaced slightly apart, to indicate that he didn't have to talk too much slower.

Francis was all motion: his shoulders shifting, eyebrows jerking. He gestured, bobbed and weaved through his argument. Smoak, when he wasn't looking down at his desk, sat perfectly still with his eyes tracking Francis as he weaved his way through his argument.

"You know what I'm sayin'?" he asked the judge.

Smoak tried to get him to understand that McCloy was allowed to talk about the ages, but Francis continued to argue until Smoak just told him, "This is the way it's going to be."

McCloy returned to the easel and wrote the plaintiffs' ages on the sheet.

He asked the panel if the girls' ages had an impact on anyone, one way or the other.

"There's going to be some films you'll have to watch, including nudity with all these girls."

"Personally," one woman said, "I don't want to watch. I've never watched an adult rated movie."

Anyone ever seen a "Girls Gone Wild" video? Two men raised their hands.

Anyone ever attended a Girls Gone Wild party? No one confessed to that.

McCloy started into another issue that Francis was sensitive to, the issue of liability.

"Basically, it's a case of sexual exploitation of minors."

Objection. Sidebar.

"This is argument, your honor," Francis began.

Smoak said something quietly to him and Francis asked that at least the jurors should be told that the reason the companies were defaulted on was because they couldn't afford an attorney.

Smoak tried to explain his ruling and occasionally glanced down at his desk as he sorted his thoughts. Francis bobbed and stooped each time Smoak looked down, trying to maintain eye contact and press his point.

When the sidebar broke, McCloy returned to his questions and started explaining the claims for damages. He asked if anyone knew what punitive damages meant.

"Mental problems, physical problems," one man said.

No, punitive damages were awarded in an effort to punish a defendant.

"That's why they're called punitive."

He explained that Francis had been found personally liable as to one count, sexually exploiting Plaintiff B. That was from a summary judgment ruling much earlier in the case. But jurors were going to have to find whether Francis was liable in the other three counts.

He told them that they would not be allowed to do any independent investigation of their own if they were chosen as a juror.

"All the plaintiffs are trying to do today is to find eight jurors who are willing to do what's right, whether that's to rule for Mr. Francis or for us."

He looked around the room one last time and sat down.

Francis popped up from his seat, gathered some notebooks and went to the podium.

"Good late afternoon everybody," he started. "It's not my reason that you're here. Its because these eight lawyers have sued me."

"Mr. Francis," Smoak interrupted him.

"I'm just saying hello, your honor, just like he did. But I'll cut to the chase."

"How many of you recognize me?" Francis asked, holding his hands out, palms up, and turning slowly from the jury box to the prospective jurors sitting in the gallery seats. Most hands were up. "A lot of you. I don't know if that's good or bad."

"How many of you have a negative view of Girls Gone Wild?" He looked around slowly. "There's a lot of hands here."

Francis looked at the tomato farmer, who had his hand raised. "You really don't want to be on jury duty," his laugh trailed off into a giggle. "You'll go for anything."

He looked at a woman with her hand raised: "What's your negative deal?"

"I just think it's morally wrong," she said.

"What is?"

"Nudity."

"Nudity is morally wrong?"

"Pubic. Public nudity is immoral."

She said she had two daughters and wouldn't want them flashing for Girls Gone Wild.

"So, are you biased against the women participating or against Girls Gone Wild?"

"I just don't think they should be doing it."

One woman said she wasn't interested in seeing a video that included nude minors. Francis turned to the group in the box and said that just because he was being sued didn't mean he'd done something wrong.

"Anybody can sue anybody for anything. I can sue somebody for murder …"

"Mr. Francis, come up here," Smoak called to him from the bench. He tried to keep his voice down as he told Francis, "Ask your questions in a dispassionate, professional manner. This is not like 'Let's Make a Deal, come on down.' You're not to get up there and debate with them. I want you to take this to heart."

Francis returned to his seat while Smoak gave the jurors a brief history of the jury trial system in America and how it had been a primary reason for the Revolutionary War.

"It's pretty important that we carry out what those men thought was worth starting a war over," he said.

When the judge was done, Francis stood and said, "What the judge is trying to say …" I'm sure Smoak loved that.

Francis resumed his questions about the jurors' feelings about him and Girls Gone Wild.

"You want the truth?" one woman asked him. "I'm not interested in any video with minor girls."

"I agree, child pornography is awful, it's disgusting, it's wrong," Francis spat out. He was on a roll. "Personally, I'm opposed to that. It's disgusting. That's me."

McCloy stood and said to the judge, "May I invite us up to the bench this time?"

Francis looked from McCloy to Smoak, "For what?"

Smoak again told him that jury selection was not the time for him to talk about his own feelings.

Francis resumed his questioning by asking who had seen his late night television commercials.

"What I see," one man said, voicing his opinion about the commercials, "is someone has gotten young women drunk and taken advantage of the situation."

He assured Francis that his opinion wouldn't influence him if he was chosen as a juror.

"There's a lot of things I don't like," he said, shrugging off the suggestion that he couldn't be fair.

"Do you not like me?" Francis asked.

"I don't even know you."

Does anyone have a positive opinion of Girls Gone Wild?

One man raised his hand.

"I like it."

"There's nothing wrong with that," Francis said, laughing. "It's a free country."

"Mr. Francis," Smoak said quietly.

Another man raised his hand.

"I've seen it. I have nothing against it."

Does anyone have a negative opinion of me? One woman raised her hand.

"Would that influence you as a juror?"

"Absolutely."

"So you're biased."

"Absolutely."

Another woman raised her hand.

"I agree. I think I would have a very biased opinion of this."

"This what?"

"Girls Gone Wild, and you too."

Francis moved back to the main panel and asked the question that Smoak had cautioned the plaintiffs' attorneys against:

"How many of you guys have watched adult entertainment, ever? By a show of hands."

More than half the panel raised a hand.

Does anyone have a negative opinion of adult entertainment in general?

"I'm a Catholic ..." one woman began.

"Me too," Francis interrupted. "Everybody that I know from my church watches adult entertainment."

That drew a big laugh from the crowd.

"It's morally wrong, all of it," said the same woman who'd first spoke up about not liking Francis and Girls Gone Wild.

Francis asked how many people would be upset if their daughter had used a fake identification to get on a Girls Gone Wild video.

"Would you hold her responsible or would you hold Girls Gone Wild responsible?"

"Both," one woman said.

"Why?"

"For one, she knows better," the woman said.

"So you'd hold her responsible, not Girls Gone Wild?"

"I said both."

"Why would you hold Girls Gone Wild responsible?"

"Because it invites that kind of stuff."

Smoak called a sidebar and cautioned Francis not to argue with prospective jurors. "I'm going to suggest to you that you do more harm than good."

But Francis was adamant that he wasn't doing anything wrong and didn't want the judge to interrupt his questioning.

"Let me have a fair trial, please."

But Smoak was bringing his questioning to a close. Francis was gesturing so strenuously that the bailiffs began closing in on him from three sides. They took steps closer to him while keeping a hand on their belts.

"You have five more minutes," Smoak said. "Choose your questions carefully."

Francis was pretty worked up as he left the sidebar and walked back to the podium.

"It's me versus these eight lawyers over here ..." he said as he passed the jury box.

"Mr. Francis, there will be no more side comments."

"OK."

Francis began on the issue of liability.

"What you might see is there's no way I did anything wrong."

"Mr. Francis."

"I'm just doing what he did," Francis said, waving toward McCloy.

"Ask questions. Put a question mark on it."

Francis asked how many in the panel could put bias aside and award a "damage of a dollar" if they found he'd done nothing wrong. Almost everyone raised a hand, but a few crossed their arms over their chests or gripped their knees.

"How many people go to church on Sunday? Yeah, me too."

How many have seen what goes on in Panama City Beach during Spring Break?

"Are you offended by that?"

One man said he was offended. He was a strict Lutheran and believed that public nudity and public intoxication were wrong. Several others had done a little spring breaking when they were in school.

"It's different now," one woman said.

Francis began a question then stopped. "Am I allowed to ask ages?" he said to Smoak.

"You do it at your peril," the judge joked.

"I think I'll listen to the judge on that one," Francis said then laughed.

One man had worked security at beach hotels and it seemed to him that all he saw out there were naked women. A woman had tended bar at a beach pub and had seen a lot of what goes on during Spring Break. She said she was disgusted by a lack of "morale" among the girls on the beach. She repeated it several times until a few people in the panel corrected her.

"Morals," she said, "the lack of morals."

Francis began to wind down his questioning.

"Sorry to keep you so long, but I've never done this before."

He looked down at his notes.

"Did Joe Francis do anything wrong here, because they're going to try to confuse the hell out of you."

"Mr. Francis, ask a question."

"It's my first time, your honor. I thought I was doing good."

That was it, though, his questions had come to an end. The only thing that was left, was for the parties to question five women in private about whether they knew the plaintiffs.

The rest of the panel was allowed to leave the courtroom and the women were brought into a conference room individually.

During the break a few of the jurors were overheard by a reporter talking about Francis' constant motion, shrugging and twitching, and theorizing that he might be high on cocaine.

When the individual questioning was over, Francis, Smoak and the lawyers stayed in the conference room and went through the process of eliminating those they didn't want on the jury. When they were through, eight women remained, including the woman with the 14-year-old daughter who had a strong opinion about both sides and the Wassau woman who knew nothing about the case.

Someone standing in front of the jury box, facing the jurors, would see a young black woman who worked with numbers for a living, an older woman who had recently become a widow, the woman from Wassau and the woman with the 14-year-old daughter. On the back row, a rather severe looking blonde school teacher, the book keeper for a local pavement company, another older widow and an older black woman with a thick Central American accent.

The common opinion among trial attorneys is that women were usually more critical of female plaintiffs and female victims. An all-female jury was thought to be beneficial to Francis.

"What the plaintiffs want," a lawyer who had come to watch the proceedings said outside the courtroom, "is a jury full of daddies."

Chapter 32

"Ladies of the Jury"

Larry Selander gripped both sides of the podium, leaned forward and began his opening statement in a slow clear tone. It was hard to tell if he was being polite or condescending.

"Ladies and gentle ...., sorry, I mean ladies of the jury," he said and smiled through his beard. At least two of the women on the jury later said they disliked Selander from his opening words. They said they thought he was talking down to them.

"This is a case about a convicted child pornographer taking advantage of children."

That drew a snort from Francis, who was fidgeting in his chair.

"He did this in large part for money."

Francis, he said, made "many millions of dollars" by ignoring the laws in place that regulate the pornography industry and assure that minors are not included in these films.

Selander told the jurors that he would be introducing several long, tedious plea agreements that showed Francis' crimes.

"They show you what happened here. This was not just four mistakes that happened here with these four girls. This is a business practice."

Cameramen will testify that their orders were to "shoot first and ask questions later." Getting scenes was first priority and cameramen were told to save the age questions for later so as to not disrupt the mood.

"Joe Francis is Girls Gone Wild."

And Girls Gone Wild had changed, he said, from a series of videos that primarily featured girls flashing in public places to videos that now promote more hard-core, graphic sexual content.

"Primarily girl-on-girl, hard-core pornography."

There were laws in place, Selander continued, that regulate the type of paperwork that is required to ensure the tapes do not include illegal child pornography.

"If Mr. Francis had followed these laws, it would have denied him his most vulnerable victims: minors."

The plaintiffs in this case were 17, 16, 15 and 13 when they encountered Girls Gone Wild. Selander said the brains of people that young are not as fully developed as those of adults, especially in the area of thinking things through.

"They live in the present. Sometimes they make lousy decisions, that's why we have to protect them."

"So these minors were exploited and they were severely damaged. These stories were both tragic and sad. The evidence will show this is the type of behavior that has to be punished and stopped.

"There's no question how old these girls were."

"Objection. There is."

Overruled.

"Let me tell you about each of these plaintiffs."

Plaintiff B was a straight-A student, accepted to a good college, in student government, outgoing with lots of friends, a stable family and was a regular church goer.

"She was a good kid.

"At the age of 17, she was given alcohol and likely drugs and filmed a scene with Girls Gone Wild with a friend of hers who also was a minor. It's nasty. It's graphic.

"They took that film, produced it into a video and distributed it worldwide."

"Objection, the video was never distributed." Francis might have been thinking about Plaintiff V, not B. At times it was hard to hear the difference.

Overruled.

"She was called a slut. She was called a whore. She was cast out of her school, her community, her family. She was hospitalized three times. She was alone and at one point she was homeless, sleeping on a beach. She became a substance abuser."

He leaned in to the microphone and dropped his voice.

"And then, the deepest tragedy of all," he said. "She had to tell her father. The evidence is going to show that as she was talking to her father, this otherwise healthy father, died. And she blames herself."

The deep, breathless mood Selander had built was interrupted by a snort and sigh from the defense table.

"Objection. Relevance," Francis stood and tossed a legal pad dramatically onto the table in front of him. "How does that apply to Girls Gone Wild? Is he implying that Girls Gone Wild killed her father? Objection."

Overruled.

Plaintiffs S and J were sisters who went to the beach. While stuck in traffic they were approached by a cameraman and bullied into flashing. That footage was put into a video with pornographic material and sold.

"Objection, it was never sold." I'm not sure where that came from.

Overruled.

"Oh, and your honor, it's not pornography under Florida law."

Selander returned to his opening. He said J and S thought the footage was only going to be used for a personal video.

Nine months later, the video was released and suddenly everyone in their community knew. At school, they were called names, groped and asked to perform sex acts on demand.

"They both dropped out of school and they began a downward spiral. The 13-year-old tried to kill herself, twice. Plaintiff J had children out of wedlock at a very early age.

"Both became substance abusers."

Plaintiff V was particularly vulnerable because she'd lost her mother about six weeks before meeting Joe Francis. Her father had physically abused her since the time she was six.

Plaintiff V was 16 when she was driving with four friends on Front Beach Road. They saw the Girls Gone Wild bus and pulled over. Her friends agreed to go to the Chateau Motel where two got into a shower. It was March 31, 2003 and a few days later, Francis would be arrested because of what happened in that motel room.

"Mr. Francis forced that 16-year-old girl to masturbate him, then gave her fifty bucks and then took her driving around in his Ferrari. He then coerced her, and there's no other way to say it, you'll see it, into flashing.

Selander said Plaintiff V only went to the motel room because she was "afraid for her friends."

Later in the day he took her behind the building where a camera crew pressured her into flashing.

She tried to get away, Selander said. He would not let her go.

Francis was arrested and the flashing scene was seized as evidence. It was never distributed. But word circulated that V was involved in the case.

"She was linked to Girls Gone Wild. She began a downward spiral."

She too was called a slut and a whore. She turned to drugs and, feeling isolated, she tried to kill herself.

"She is still struggling to put this behind her."

The sheriff's office went through the films seized in Francis's arrest and identified many girls who were minors when they were filmed by Girls Gone Wild cameramen.

More than 850,000 videos that included the footage of plaintiffs J, S and B were sold around the world.

"They are there forever." Every time some stranger watches these videos, the girls are damaged again.

In addition, there are 174 videos that do not have the proper paperwork attached to them, in violation of federal law. They generated "millions and millions and millions of dollars" in revenue for Francis and Girls Gone Wild.

He said there might be some talk about fake IDs, but there will be no evidence that any of the plaintiffs produced a fake ID. Even if there was, it would be irrelevant. The law does not protect pornographers from minors who lie about their age. It's up to the pornographer to make sure the people in their films are adults.

"This is child pornography we're talking about here."

"Objection, your honor," Francis said, rising again and drawing out each word as if he was weary of saying them.

Overruled.

"While Girls Gone Wild made millions from the sale of these tapes, these four girls' lives were forever altered. Their childhood was ended, they were robbed of it. Their lives had been forever diminished."

At the end of the trial, he said, he would ask them to find there were "significant damages" to these girls.

Selander paused, then turned from the podium and took his seat at the plaintiffs' table.

"Wow, I don't know where to begin," Francis said, walking to the podium and beginning his opening.

"I didn't do anything wrong. I'm just here to defend myself. I object to these eight $500-an-hour lawyers trying to get money out of me. This case is all about money."

That led to the first of more than a dozen objections, sidebar conferences, admonishments and requests to Judge Smoak to have "that stricken from the record."

Smoak had explained to Francis that an opening statement was only to be a guide for the jurors as to what Francis believed the evidence would show during the trial. Smoak reiterated that at sidebar.

Francis trotted back to the podium.

"The evidence will show," he started, believing that phrase would make anything he said after that a proper opening statement, "that my business, Girls Gone Wild, is legal. You may not like it, but it's legal. I would never risk this 13-year empire to film underage girls.

"There's only one victim in this case: me."

He talked about at least one plaintiff in this case who had said into the camera, "'I swear to God, I'm 18.' All of them say that. They swear to God, over and over. Strong statement."

"This case is not about child pornography, it's about money. These guys don't care about the plaintiffs. They're lawyers on contingency, they don't care about anything."

After the objection, Francis returned to the podium.

"The evidence will show, that I am against child pornography."

He talked about how it was legal to film underage girls flashing their breasts in public, which led to another objection. Francis corrected himself and said that Judge Smoak would actually be the one explaining the law to them.

He said Girls Gone Wild films 30,000 girls a year.

"I wouldn't risk everything I have to film two or three underage girls out of 30,000. It doesn't make any sense."

He said the company has safeguards in place to guard against underage girls being included in the videos.

"The evidence will show, the videos will show, that all of these innocent women lied about their ages to be on Girls Gone Wild and at that moment everything he told you" pointing to Selander "will go out the window.

"Are we gonna reward bad behavior? Are we gonna give them a lot of money because they tricked some of my cameramen into getting on Girls Gone Wild? They were not coerced into doing anything. They weren't given alcohol. They weren't given drugs."

He told the all-woman jury that he's discovered that "women have always been smarter than me." He complained about a comment Selander made about teens' brains. Francis interpreted it as Selander saying that women's brains weren't fully formed. That led to another objection.

"I'm just gonna cover some more of what the evidence will show," Francis said when he returned from sidebar.

He told the jurors that just because the companies had been found liable didn't mean the jury had to award significant damages. "Give them a dollar. Stick it to them."

Objection.

When he returned from sidebar: "The evidence will show these women were not harmed or damaged. They don't deserve anything. Look at the evidence. How were they harmed?

"The evidence will show these girls lived the fast life and continue to. None of them ever met me, except for one, so how did I, Joe Francis, damage them?

"And these plea agreements have nothing to do with this case, they're just being used to confuse you guys. I signed those plea agreements because I wanted it to go away, not because we were admitting any wrongdoing.

"The evidence will show that they are trying to fool you."

He started touching back on topics he'd already hit and Smoak told him to stay focused.

"I'm keeping focused, your honor. I just don't want to have a fast one pulled on me by these eight smart people. I believe women should be allowed to make their own decisions, good or bad, without the federal government making it for them.

"The video evidence will show that Mr. Selander is a liar and these girls are liars."

The judge interrupted him.

"Mr. Francis, we don't talk that way in court."

"Oh, we don't say liars?"

He paused, took a breath and started again.

"You have all been ... misled," he smiled at finding the word. "The facts have been misrepresented to you even in Mr. Selander's opening statement. The evidence will show ..."

He looked at the judge, "I can say they lied about their age? I can say that? OK. The evidence will show these girls lied about their age.

"The evidence will show, how do you force a girl to give you a handjob? I'd like to hear that too."

Francis talked about the safeguards that were in place to intercept underage girls.

"They had to work really hard to get through all of the protective barriers. They were smart enough to come through and lie and get through these three protective barriers."

Selander stood up.

"Your honor, may we strike some of this stuff. This has all been objectionable."

Francis spun around on him, looking shocked.

"No it's not. All of your opening has been objectionable."

After the objection was resolved, Francis went back to his closing and his main theme, calling them liars.

"The evidence will show, don't let them trick you. They don't have anything to do with their clients. They're just going to use them to try to trick you."

"Come here Mr. Francis," Smoak interrupted.

When he trotted back to the podium from the sidebar, Francis resumed his opening.

"The evidence will show, the plea agreements have nothing to do with the girls in this case."

"Move to strike," Selander's patience was running out.

Smoak spoke to Francis and Francis returned to the podium. But the constant interruptions were disassembling an already fragmented opening statement. So Francis kept repeating subjects that he felt were important and calling everyone liars, which kept leading to objections and more interruptions.

He came back to another early theme: that he was representing himself because he believed he didn't do anything wrong. "I'm not the person they're saying I am.

"I'm representing myself because I can't afford an attorney."

"Could you instruct Mr. Francis not to say that again," Selander said.

"It's just the truth, your honor."

"It's not the truth," Selander barked. "It just goes on and on."

Francis said again that "the evidence will show" that he wouldn't risk his empire, his life's work, just to include underage girls in his films.

Objection.

The girls were not coerced.

Objection.

Girls Gone Wild does not have a business plan to target minors.

Objection.

"The evidence will show that I give to charities. I'm a generous person."

Admonition from the bench.

"The evidence will show that they've taken this disgusting act and turned it into this lawsuit."

Not proper.

"They (the girls) actually seek out Girls Gone Wild. They plot and scheme to get on these videos. All these girls are liars. We've all been duped by these young women."

Smoak didn't want him using the word "duped." "Mr. Francis, conclude your opening statement."

"The evidence will show that these four young girls are liars."

"Objection. We just went through this."

Smoak sent the jury out of the room about the same time that Francis said he was done. As artless as it was, Francis' opening had scored points with at least one juror, a woman who became something of a leader among the other jurors.

Chapter 33

Juror Number 6

In the jury room, divisions were already forming.

"You know, ladies," Juror 6 said, "they might think I'm a dummy, but I'm not a dummy and I'm not buying into this."

Selander had said something in his opening that caught her attention. She heard him say, 'Someone in this community believes that Mr. Francis should pay.' She believed she heard him say those exact words and they would linger with her throughout the trial.

"I sat there and thought about it as everything else was going on," she said later.

She told her fellow jurors, "I'm gonna tell you something, to y'all right now, I am very straightforward. I will tell you what I think and I'm not easily swayed. I think there's more to this story than we'll probably ever know, but I believe everybody deserves their day in court."

She'd watched Francis closely as he gave his opening. She didn't mind his nervous energy, his sudden shifts in topic. She told the other ladies, "I can't say I would be any different than him."

The woman from Wassau looked over and agreed. They knew they were both on the same wavelength. But Juror 5, the school teacher, instantly disliked Francis and she thought the jury-room discussions should wait until deliberations.

"We're not discussing anything," Juror 6 said. "We're talking freely. I believe I have the right to say what I think."

The division between jurors 5 and 6 remained until the last hour of the last day of trial.

"At that point, I knew that was my number one trouble right there," Juror 6 said later of the school teacher.

Chapter 34

"I object"

Selander approached the podium and told Smoak his first items of evidence were three plea agreements from the 2006 federal records keeping case against Francis, Mantra and MRA Holdings.

Selander made the mistake of saying the documents had been stipulated to, essentially saying both sides allowed them into evidence.

"Stipulated? I wasn't present for any discussions about stipulation. I object," Francis said, standing up and slapping his notepad on the table.

Smoak was confused, too, and Selander, when he was able to say anything around Francis' constant complaints, tried to backtrack.

"Plea agreements," he practically shouted. "Plea agreements! If I said 'stipulated', I misspoke."

Pontikes had gone over these agreements the day before and Smoak had ruled they were admissible. But Francis objected anyway, saying the agreements didn't list any of the plaintiffs in this case. He would argue that over and over.

Pontikes took the podium to explain, again, why she believed the documents were evidence. Yes, there was no mention by name of any of these girls. But, she said, the plea agreements list by name the video titles that plaintiffs B, J and S were featured in. Later in the trial, she said, these plaintiffs would confirm that they were in those videos.

In addition, Plaintiff B's incident was listed by date.

Smoak told Francis that the pleas would be admitted as long as the plaintiffs could tie them in later. If they failed to do that, the judge said, the pleas would come out of evidence.

Francis wasn't satisfied with that. Selander was going to read portions of three pleas, Exhibits 1, 2 and 5. Each time he started a new document, Francis objected on every ground he could think of: relevance, hearsay, time, incompleteness.

Each time, Selander and Francis would be called to sidebar and Pontikes would be summoned to tell Smoak again why the particular document was tied to the case.

Every time Pontikes spoke, as soon as the first words came out of her mouth, Francis would spin around on her and start whispering angrily. His face showed the loathing he felt for her. The muscles in his jaws would bunch like walnuts and the cords in his neck would stand out like twigs.

"Where is Plaintiff B in this document, Miss Pontikes?" Francis spat out during one argument.

"Mr. Francis, you don't talk to her. You talk to me," Smoak said. Pontikes pointedly ignored Francis, who physically bowed to Smoak and apologized.

But the minute she started speaking again he turned on her again: "No, no!"

"Mr. Francis, you will be quiet," Smoak said, his voice rising. "This is fair warning, you're going to get yourself into trouble."

"This is fraud on the court," Francis insisted, bowing and bobbing, his hands clasped in front of him. He was trying to get on eye level, and make eye contact, with Smoak. But there were five people, not including the judge who was on the other side of the bench, packed into this small area and Francis' bobbing and weaving kept bringing him in contact with the people standing beside him. He'd bounce off the judge's judicial assistant, apologize, take a step away from her and collide with Bailiff George Dobos.

Francis would apologize every time, but Dobos was annoyed and at one point he just pointed his finger at Francis.

Francis told Smoak again, "This is about the biggest error in this trial. You're going to get it reversed. If you want to allow them in, fine."

"Mr. Francis, I have made my ruling. There will be no more objections."

That didn't stop Francis from making numerous objections every time a new document was introduced.

Selander spent the morning reading in the pleas.

When it was Francis' turn to address the plea agreements, he wanted to go through every page and show the absence of any direct reference to the plaintiffs in the case. Smoak wouldn't allow it. He kept saying that Francis could only read portions of the documents that Selander had left out and that Francis thought were significant.

He began reading from one document and Selander asked him which plea it was and what page.

"I'm reading from Exhibit C," Francis said, waiving the document at him.

"Exhibit C?" Selander asked.

"These are your exhibits," Francis said, making it sound like Selander should know what Exhibit C was.

"They are exhibits 1, 2 and 5," Selander said slowly.

"Oh, Kristen handed me this," Francis sputtered, indicating the court clerk.

He ended up reading two paragraphs. He emphasized in the first that the girls had dealt with Girls Gone Wild cameramen, not Francis directly. In the second paragraph, he read where he'd paid a fine including restitution for the record-keeping infraction.

They were the two issues he needed to address, but getting there was so convoluted, so painful, that the message might have been lost on the jurors.

Chapter 35

Plaintiff B

After lunch, Plaintiff B took the stand.

Pontikes went to the podium to do the direct examination. "Your honor, the plaintiffs call Plaintiff B to the stand," she said into the microphone. Suddenly, Pontikes' midwestern accent was amplified and she was talking so slowly and so carefully that she sounded every bit like the Church Lady or the women from Saturday Night Live's NPR skit.

"Could you introduce yourself for the record?" Pontikes said to Plaintiff B, who hesitated, clearly thinking about how she should identify herself.

"I'm Plaintiff B," she finally said, sounding like she'd answered a trick question.

"Plaintiff B, we'll take this nice and slow and if you need a break just let us know," Pontikes said, leaning into the microphone.

Francis snorted from his seat, leaned back and covered his grin with a hand. A woman on the jury followed him with her eyes without turning her head. She tried to keep all expression off her face, but she definitely seemed irritated by Francis' antics.

Plaintiff B was now 26 years old. She played with her black wavy hair almost constantly, fluffing it, bunching it at the back, moving it from one side of her neck to the other. When she got upset, she'd bend her head down into a hand that she'd run up and into that mass of hair until she gripped the top.

She was pretty in a sharp, birdlike way. Her arched black eyebrows and downturned lips both pointed to her beak-like nose. Her eyes were her best feature: large, dark and intelligent.

When she talked, her hands were in constant motion, sometimes looking like she was clawing at her chest, sometimes reaching toward the jurors and sometimes plowing through her hair.

Her looks and her movements were noted by Juror 6, who instantly thought of B as both hiding something and being a spoiled rich girl who "got caught."

Pontikes led B through her childhood, which was "pretty normal." B said she was academically driven, hoping for a perfect 4.0 to compliment her athletic endeavors and time on the student council.

Her favorite subject was geometry.

She was accepted to her top college and hoped to major either in communications or veterinary medicine.

But all that changed when, in March 2002, she took a spring break from her senior year in high school and, as she put it, traveled to "Panama City Beach, Florida, USA."

She was a good Catholic girl and hadn't done much drinking in her life. But on the night of March 31, 2002, when a stranger approached her and a girlfriend on the beach and invited them to a party at a nearby hotel room, they accepted.

She said she knew nothing about Girls Gone Wild at that time and had no idea what she was getting into. She lowered her head and ran a hand into her hair, gripping a mass at the top.

"His definition of a party and mine were very different," she said. There were two "older people" sitting on a couch, but B and her friend stayed anyway.

"In hindsight, they were watching us, offering us drinks, watching us get more intoxicated as the night went on," she said. "They were asking us to take off our clothes for the camera. Pouring us more drinks. Our inhibitions were lowering.

"I thought, 'We're not going to do this. We're not going to do this.' I'm also convinced that they had put something in the drink that night."

Francis blew out a big sigh, stood and said, "your honor, objection, hearsay. This is ridiculous."

Smoak called a sidebar and took a minute to explain to Francis what hearsay was. The judge told Francis he had incorrectly used that objection three times already.

"So what is the correct objection?" Francis asked, meaning to B's statement about the drugs. "Opinion? Is the correct objection 'opinion'? She's just stating an opinion, there's no, foundation? Lack of foundation?"

"No."

"Because like, your honor, if she just keeps spouting off, 'I think I was drunk,' these are just ridiculous things. That's never come up in anything, any deposition or anything."

"She testified to that in her deposition," Pontikes said.

Francis was getting himself worked up, gesturing and bobbing. Each word coming out through clenched jaws.

"Mr. Francis," Smoak said, "take a deep breath."

"The jury can hear us, your honor," Pontikes said.

"I think it's fair. People can testify about how they were feeling," Smoak said.

"Your honor," Francis pressed, "but that's like, come on, accusing ... that's accusing somebody of a crime because it's your opinion."

"Mr. Francis, that bell has already been rung without objection."

"No, I objected. I just objected on the wrong ..."

"No. It would be fair game for cross-examination."

"OK. All right. I'll do that. OK. What is the correct objection? So I know. So I don't make the same mistake and say hearsay. Is 'opinion' a correct objection? Is that a basis for an objection, 'opinion?'"

Pontikes objected to Francis asking for a legal lesson. "Mr. Francis is more than able to bring his own counsel."

"I'm representing myself."

"He could have had an attorney on these things. I understand the court is trying to be helpful. But this is not the case of an indigent defendant."

Smoak told Francis to simply say, objection. "Then we'll come up here and you tell me why you're objecting. I'll put a title on it one way or another."

"OK, cool. Cool. Good. All right. So, objection ..."

Smoak explained that opinion testimony can be objected to, but there are times when opinion testimony is allowed.

"There are certain things, just ordinary daily things that lay people are entitled to express an opinion about," Smoak said.

"But, I mean, like 'I was drugged.' Is that ... she's not a doctor. I mean, come on. Like you said ..."

"Somebody can say, 'I've had alcohol before. Alcohol never affected me this way. I was starting to worry that maybe I had been drugged.'"

"She didn't say that."

"That's probably fair game."

"I'll have her on cross."

The sidebar broke up and Pontikes went back to questioning B.

"OK Plaintiff B, you were talking about the fact that you had some alcohol that you believed contained drugs."

"There was no toxicology report to prove that, but I was convinced. It was just completely out of character. It's not something I would have done on a regular basis: have a couple of drinks, take off my clothes and perform sexual acts."

Also, she said she could only remember bits of the night past a certain point. She didn't remember telling anyone she was 18, or even being asked how old she was.

She didn't remember anything from the sexual encounter with her friend. She did have a vague recollection of signing some paperwork and then walking home on the beach.

The next morning she had an extra $100 that she couldn't account for.

She said she's never seen the sex portion of the tape that eventually made it into two "Girls Gone Wild" videos that were sold internationally. Rick Bateman, she said, had shown her the first part of the raw footage during her deposition and she'd "crawled into the fetal position and could not get off the floor."

Shortly into her freshman year in college, she said, the DVD came out and word spread quickly that she was in it. Suddenly, she was receiving phone calls from friends and relatives, who were routinely calling her whore and slut.

Her older brother, she said, called her a disgrace to the family.

Distraught, she'd called her father, hoping that he'd allow her to come home for a time. During that conversation, her 49-year-old father suffered a massive heart attack and died.

"I don't know how much he knew," she said. "I had to go bury my father on top of all this."

"Let's just take this real slow," Pontikes said carefully into the microphone. Francis leaned back in his chair and smirked. "Do you remember what you said to your father?"

"Not at this moment." She said all she was seeking when she called her father was refuge, a break from the constant stress.

Francis objected to the testimony about B's father, but was overruled. Pontikes asked B about the funeral.

B started talking about how isolated she was and Francis objected again.

"This is just ridiculous," he said. He was overruled again.

"I'm not blaming GGW for my father's death," B said, looking at Francis. "I don't know what killed him. A heart attack, yes. I never blamed GGW for my father's death, Mr. Francis."

"Did anyone ever accuse you of killing your father?" Pontikes asked, leaning toward the microphone. Francis objected, but was quickly overruled.

B said her boyfriend at the time had thrown that in her face.

B said "life became too hard." She'd lost her father, her reputation, friends, family, confidence and could no longer concentrate on her studies.

She moved to Southern California with a boyfriend. There, she began drinking every day and using drugs, including cocaine.

It was also there that she did two more porn videos, but, of course, that's not something she mentioned on the stand.

Soon after, though, desperate for some normalcy, she'd packed her belongings in a single bag and driven home to her mother. They had a falling out and B left again, this time taking a bus to Fort Lauderdale, the warmest place she could think of.

She said she knew she would be homeless and at least in South Florida she'd be able to sleep on the beach.

"So," Ponitkes began, bending toward the microphone and dripping each word with sweet midwestern honey, "what happened when you were a homeless, sleeping on the beach?"

She got arrested. But not for sleeping on the beach. She got arrested for underage drinking in a bar. Instead of going to jail, though, B said the cops took her to a mental hospital.

She was medicated and soon after she was allowed to transfer to a mental hospital in her former hometown in Louisiana. She was released from there, but ended up in a third institution before being sent home with a list of medications to take.

She went to live with her mother again, who took her to a pawn shop to buy a new guitar.

"Objection, your honor," Francis said, climbing to his feet and slapping his pad down on the table again. "Relevance. Where is this going? I mean, a guitar shop? Really?"

"Mr. Francis," Smoak snapped, "come up here."

After the sidebar, B resumed her story. She said she weaned herself off the medication that she'd been prescribed in her last hospital stay.

"I got myself back to stabilization, I guess you could say. I was building strength back, to be a part of society again."

Pontikes wanted to use the viewer to introduce a document as evidence. The viewer was supposed to send the image to the attorneys' monitors, and the judge's, so it could be discussed before being shown to the jury.

"My screen is dead," Francis said, looking quickly from one side of his monitor to the other. "Somebody unplugged it."

He went to the other monitor and looked at the small image of the letter on the screen.

"I can't see this. Does someone have some reading glasses," he said, chuckling and turning to the audience. Pontikes looked a little annoyed with the interruptions and asked for help in enlarging the image.

The document was a letter from the Department of Justice informing B that she'd been listed as a victim in the federal records keeping case against Girls Gone Wild. She was asked to submit a victim impact statement and include any monetary damages she thought she deserved compensation for.

She responded to the letter with the victim impact statement that Smoak had insisted Francis read in 2006 when his company had entered the plea.

Francis objected to the letter, saying it was only meant to inflame the jury. Pontikes said the plea agreement that the letter referenced was already in evidence, so it couldn't be prejudicial to him.

"How did you feel when you received this letter?" Pontikes asked B.

"I was just getting my feet under me. I received this letter about the video and it shook me up. Things were working out in my life and I get this letter and, I'm like, 'Wow, child pornography.'"

B said she met with two FBI agents a short time later, who pulled out a stack of forms related to other underage girls who had been included in those films.

"I thought, 'Wow, I'm not alone. There are thousands of other girls out there that GGW had targeted.'"

Objection. They went into a relatively quiet sidebar, which apparently worked out well for Francis who told the judge, "Ok. Cool. Thanks."

Smoak sustained the objection and Pontikes dropped the subject. She moved on to the victim impact statement and B read out loud the same portion that Francis had read aloud nearly five years earlier.

B then told jurors about a few times that she was recognized from the video. She talked about a "big trucker" guy who'd called her a whore in a grocery store.

"What was your reaction to that?"

"It killed me. It just killed me inside."

The name calling and confrontations were taking their toll. She had problems keeping a boyfriend.

"Let me tell you, it's not really easy with a pornographic video in your past to get involved in a relationship. Within two months they were out the door.

"Self image was another thing. When you know that millions have seen you fully exposed, self esteem isn't really high on the agenda."

"Did you develop an issue with your eating?"

"I don't want to talk about it," B said after a pause. She said she didn't sleep much anymore either.

"It keeps me up at night, thinking about what kind of world it's become."

What about depression and anxiety problems?

"This was so close to putting me over the edge."

"Do you regret what happened the night of March 31, 2002?"

"I hate the word regret, but I regret that. It changed the course of the next decade after that day. I was in the wrong place at the wrong time."

Chapter 36

Right triangle

Pontikes said she was done with her questions and returned to her seat. Francis asked the judge for a short break so he could prepare his cross examination. Smoak allowed him a very short break, one minute.

"Can I get two?" Francis asked as he rushed from the room, not waiting for an answer.

A bailiff went into the hallway and retrieved Francis after roughly two minutes had passed. He burst back into the room and asked to approach the bench with a procedural question.

As usual, his sidebar was punctuated with exaggerated gestures, bobbing and the occasional outburst.

"Ah, this is the case," he said loudly at one point. "This is crucial. This is the crux of the case."

Smoak pointed a finger at Francis, but spoke too softly to be heard. After a few minutes, the judge asked the jury to take a break.

With the jury out of the room, the sidebar discussion resumed from the podium.

Smoak told Francis that he had to limit his cross-examination to only things that Pontikes had asked B during her direct examination. Smoak said B "did not testify as to what happened."

"Yes she did, your honor," Francis insisted. If he would be allowed to play the videotape of her encounter with GGW at this time it would contradict everything she said about what had happened.

"She's done, cooked and fried. This jury needs to know, the American people need to know, who this witness is."

He said he had the right to impeach the witness, to ask her about contradictory statements she'd made in the past.

"She has perjured herself for the last hour and a half."

But Smoak was adamant. He would not allow Francis to use the videotape in his cross examination. It was improper, he said.

He then cautioned Francis about his questions and handling of B.

"This would be a challenge for a most experienced trial attorney, to affectively cross examine a victim such as that. What you're going to be doing ..."

Francis began to say something.

"Mr. Francis, shut up until I tell you to talk. You're going to end up with that whole jury hating you and willing to believe anything that's said against you. The best thing you can do is leave her alone."

"Your honor, they are gonna hate her for lying to them for the last hour and a half." He again asked to be allowed to play the video. "I don't understand why I can't show it."

Smoak told him it would be a tactical mistake, that it would backfire on him.

"Let me make the mistake, your honor. Let me make it. I have the right to show that tape." He said he didn't even want to play the sexual portion of it, just the part where Plaintiff B and her friend are walking into the hotel and B says Girls Gone Wild is "her favorite thing in the world."

"That's not true," Pontikes said.

"If it's not true, Miss Pontikes, then let's play it."

"This tape is the crux of the case. This tape is the case. This jury is gonna hate her, hate her. You gotta trust me on this one."

But Smoak continued to argue that Francis was going to do more harm than good. That he needed to go easy on Plaintiff B.

Pontikes objected, saying she understood that the judge was trying to be extra cautious with Francis, because he was representing himself, but she would have to draw the line at step-by-step instructions from the bench.

Smoak ignored her and went back to arguing with Francis over the videotape.

"You don't listen," Smoak told Francis. "You get yourself in a lot of trouble by being a bad listener."

"This is my whole case," Francis beseeched him. "She lied about everything. Every, little, thing. You honor, please, please, this is my case. The video is my case."

Smoak insisted it was improper to use the tape in his cross and he expected Pontikes to put the video in with her evidence.

"What if she doesn't?" Francis asked.

"She's already said she's going to."

"Are you going to play it?" Francis asked Pontikes.

"Your honor, I would like to move on. I'm not going to answer questions from ..."

"You see, your honor. What if she doesn't play it? My whole case is this tape and these tapes of all these girls and she sat here and perjured herself. This is impeachment. This is impeachable evidence that my case is based off. Of course, your honor, she's never going to play that tape."

Smoak insisted that Francis could not use the video in his cross examination, but said he would consider allowing Francis to use it when he presented his defense. He again told Francis to limit his questions to what Pontikes had brought up in her direct examination.

But Francis couldn't let it go.

"I play that video and it's over," he said, then pointed to Pontikes. "She's never, never, never gonna play that video."

Smoak said he'd made his ruling. He told Francis he would be smart to keep his cross-examination to just four questions.

"You may be as smart as any entrepreneur in the world, but you're not a trial lawyer." He said Francis would end up making B look better with a brutal cross examination.

"I don't think they feel bad about her," Francis said. "I don't think they're buying it. I'm gonna look great. I'm gonna be great."

B was brought back into the room. Then the jury returned and Francis approached the podium.

"Hello," he said to B. "So, Plaintiff B. So, right off, have we ever met before? Have you ever seen me in person before?"

"I don't think so."

"Was I there that night, that this happened to you, that you have nothing to do with?"

She didn't think so.

He then asked for her birthdate. June 1, 1984. That made him stop. He thought her birthday was in early April and she had been a few days shy of turning 18 when she did the video. Now he had to do the math.

"How old were you?"

"I would have been 17."

"And when would you have turned 18?"

"I turned 18 on June 1, 2002."

"So, you were a couple of months away from turning 18. Do you know what the age of consent is to be involved in pornography?"

She said she thought it was 17, but Pontikes was already objecting to the question.

"So you were of the legal age?"

Objection.

"So how old were you when you posed for GGW?"

"I was 17."

"Seventeen. And you turned 18 a few months later?"

"I was 17."

"Do you feel like you were the victim at 17 and 10 months? Do you feel like you were the victim of child pornography?"

"Yes."

But isn't age just a number?

Pontikes objected again. The questions were improper and Francis was arguing with the witness.

"Do you have any tattoos?"

Objection, relevance.

"What's your relevance of the tattoo?" Smoak asked Francis at sidebar.

"She lied. She lied about her age."

"Why?"

"She lied about her age to get the tattoo. She forged it."

"So, she got a tattoo."

"She was underage."

Plaintiff B listened to the sidebar discussion, which was taking place a few feet away from her. She scrunched up her face, then recoiled, putting a hand over her heart like she'd been offended.

Smoak sustained the objection and Francis dropped the subject.

After the sidebar, Francis asked her about where she was living when she did the video. He asked her if she'd ever lived in Southern California.

"Did you do any acting?"

"Yes."

"Modeling?"

"Yes."

"Were you ever paid to be on camera?"

"Yes."

"For what?"

Objection. Outside the scope of Pontikes' direct examination.

At sidebar, Pontikes accused him of trying to get the other porn films in. But Francis insisted he was not.

"I'm not going there. She also did modeling and all this other crap."

Smoak said it was beyond scope of Pontikes' direct examination.

Francis dropped it and went back to how old B was in March 2002.

"Did you lie about your age to a GGW camera operator?"

"I don't remember."

Did you sign a release after the taping?

"I remember signing something. I don't remember what it was or what it was for."

"You don't remember."

"Mr. Francis, you will ask questions. You will not make comments as you go along," Smoak said.

"Did you lie about your age?"

"I don't remember."

What did you know about Girls Gone Wild before the taping?

"I don't remember even knowing about Girls Gone Wild. You heard my story."

"Ha," Francis laughed. "And now I'm asking you questions about your story."

Had she heard about Girls Gone Wild?

"Mr. Francis," Smoak said from the bench.

"What?" Francis asked, looking up at the judge. "Do you want me to approach? All I'm asking is whether she'd heard or not heard about GGW. It goes to the credibility, the credibility of this witness."

"Stop and move on to another question."

Did you lie to the cameraman about your age?

"Mr. Francis, this is your last warning. Move on to your next question."

"How did I harm you?" he asked Plaintiff B. "You're suing me. How did I harm you?"

"You know what," she said. "You had your ticket to the top of the world, but you know where you went wrong? When you took video of underage women."

"How much money are you seeking here? Give me a number."

"How much would I like? I'd like to be compensated for lost time. I'd like to go back to college."

"How much money do you think you deserve?"

Pontikes objected.

"She's the plaintiff. She's suing me."

Smoak allowed the question.

"How much do you want?"

"It's up to the jury to decide what would be fair."

"How much do you want?"

"Mr. Francis," Smoak interrupted, but B went on answering it.

"It's not up to me."

Smoak was running out of patience. "Your time is about up," he told Francis.

"What would be a fair amount?" Francis persisted. "You're suing me."

Objection. Asked and answered. Francis hunched his shoulders over the podium and flipped through his notes.

"What is a right triangle?"

"Pardon?"

"What is the definition of a right triangle?"

Objection, beyond the scope.

"No it's not. She said her favorite subject was geometry. Who doesn't know the definition of a right triangle if your favorite subject is geometry? It goes to credibility, your honor."

It was close to 5 p.m. and Smoak called a break for the night and sent the jury home.

"Mr. Francis, you are just about to be held in contempt and taken into custody. No more warnings."

"She said she was an A student in geometry, but she doesn't know what the definition of a right triangle is. Now who the heck is an A student in geometry that doesn't understand what a right triangle is?"

"It's meaningless," Smoak said, his voice rising.

With the jury gone, they took a few minutes to go over Francis' witness list. The judge had allowed him to submit a list of people he wanted to call, even though the deadline for that had long passed. But if Francis wanted to call witnesses who the plaintiffs' lawyers had already spoken to, and knew what they were going to testify about, then the judge would be more likely to allow it.

Steph Watts had handwritten the names on a sheet of paper. Pontikes said she recognized a few, but objected to several others including private investigator Jack Palladino.

Francis had hired Palladino shortly after the original 2003 lawsuit was filed. Years later, he called it the greatest private infiltration ever undertaken.

Francis said Palladino planted three young women in the Panama City Beach community where the original plaintiffs, and Plaintiff B, lived. They got jobs with the plaintiffs, made friends with them, and in many cases they attended the wild parties that were going on before and after the settlement.

But they were spies and they were all ready to testify as to the things they'd seen.

Pontikes said Palladino's investigation was what Francis had threatened them with during his deposition. Smoak had already ruled that anything not already entered into evidence was not coming in as an ambush on the plaintiffs.

All that dirt would never see the light of day.

Francis also wanted to enter into evidence the releases the plaintiffs had signed after their episodes with GGW. Pontikes argued that the releases were irrelevant. The releases weren't valid because the girls weren't old enough to legally sign them. In addition, it didn't matter if they signed them or not. Legally, the only issue was whether underage girls had been filmed for pornographic uses; it meant nothing if they'd lied about their ages.

It was the first of numerous arguments on this subject throughout the trial. It was a clash between the common sense argument of personal accountability of minors versus the law.

Francis' argument was that lying about their ages to get on "Girls Gone Wild" went to their credibility as witnesses.

"Had they not lied they never would have been on GGW. This is the most important issue, your honor, because it goes to the core of the case. They created this situation, then they sued me for an intentional tort. When you see these videos, you'll be on my side. It will be over."

Smoak said the releases were immaterial, but if they had evidence that the girls had produced fake IDs, then that might be something he'd consider allowing into evidence.

But the issue of whether they lied about their age, without producing a fake ID, was immaterial.

"Whether they were truthful does not absolve the defendant of liability. There will be no further inquiry into it."

"That kills my entire case," Francis interrupted.

"Stop talking!" Smoak snapped.

Francis apologized and said he was very tired. He asked that Smoak not make any rulings until the next day, so everyone could "sleep on it."

"We're not going to sleep on it," Smoak said.

He would allow Francis to make his argument the next morning, with case law to support it, as to why evidence of fake IDs should be allowed in.

Francis continued to repeat his argument, his voice rising the whole time until Smoak told him to stop yelling.

"If I'm yelling, it's only because I'm tired. Can we do this tomorrow?"

Francis then went way back to an earlier argument and began asking Smoak to change his ruling about keeping out Plaintiff B's video.

"She lied in this courtroom, your honor, and that should piss you off. I wouldn't be standing here today if she didn't lie about her age. That's the most material thing ever."

Smoak stood by all his rulings. Lying about age would not be an issue and Francis would not be allowed to use Plaintiff B's video tape to impeach her.

"You might as well default me, your honor. You might as well default me. You might as well default me."

"Unless I have clear proof that false identifications were produced, no one says another word about age. Just because children fibbed is not a significant issue."

"It's not a significant issue to lie in a federal courtroom? And that happened today. Not when they were minors."

Pontikes said there was no evidence that fake IDs were produced.

Francis said that wasn't true and could prove it. Smoak said, again, that he would have until the next morning to produce his evidence and the caselaw supporting his argument.

He then cautioned Francis, again, to calm down.

"We're not going to have a repeat of the day. You're on the verge of being out of control."

"How have I been on the verge of being out of control?"

Smoak paused. Francis had certainly been manic at times, but it was hard to identify specific instances.

"I told you not to get into certain areas. You've interrupted opposing counsel. You've badgered witnesses."

"If you want to default me, if that's your endgame, then default me,"

"You need to calm down and quit flying off the walls. You're doing more harm to your own case in the eyes of the jury."

"I think I was effective."

"You did yourself so much harm."

"I respectfully disagree."

Steph Watts, standing behind Francis, tried to distract him from his argument with the judge. He kept repeating, "Joe. Joe." But it had no effect.

"I think I did an OK job."

"I'm going to take a real serious look at entering the default against you. That motion was just held, I didn't deny it. One of the things I have to look at is whether you have a meritorious defense."

He said he'd already ruled that there was no merit to the defense that the girls lied about their age.

"I'm growing increasingly convinced that you do not have a meritorious defense."

"Basically, you've already defaulted me by taking away all my witnesses, my ability to produce the videos, the releases and my ability to talk about age. It's not fair. It's not fair." Francis slumped forward onto his arms, which where crossed on the table in front of him, and put his head down as if he was going to nap.

"You talk real good," Smoak said, "but you don't listen too well and that's going to get you ..."

"I do," Francis interrupted. "I do listen."

Chapter 37

"Joe Calm Down"

The storm that had been threatening finally blew in Wednesday morning, both inside and outside the courtroom.

A steady drumming could be heard as the rain pummeled the courthouse roof. Francis was supposed to be at his table by 8:15, ready with caselaw to prove why he should be allowed to use at least one of the girls' fake ID in his case, but he was late. He didn't arrive until 8:35, which would have been late even for the start of the trial.

"Did you get my message?" he asked the court clerk as he unpacked his satchel onto his table. "No? OK."

He waved around a handful of documents, his precedent, that he would like the judge to review. He handed them to Elizabeth, but said he didn't make copies for the plaintiffs' attorneys.

He strolled over to the plaintiffs' table, smiling, and said he'd found what he needed to get in Plaintiff B's fake ID.

"How many times has he said you're wrong?" Selander asked, referring to Smoak's rulings on this issue.

"I don't care what he says, I read the law," Francis said, smiling and hitching up his pants. "I mean, I care what he says."

"No you don't," Selander said.

"The law is the law and I know this is Good Ol' Town, but it's still the United States of America and the *law* is the *law*," he said, adopting an exaggerated Southern accent for the last few words.

"Here, I'll just read you the case numbers and you can look them up yourself."

"No," Selander said, smiling. "Why don't you just let us look at them for a few minutes."

"Well," Francis hesitated, "I could just read you the case numbers."

"Why don't you just let us look at what you've got."

Francis hesitantly handed the bundle to Pontikes and walked slowly to his table, not comfortable with leaving his documents in the attorneys' possession. His anxiety propelled him out of his chair before Selander and Pontikes had made a dent in the stack.

"I'd like my papers back," Francis said, holding out his hand.

"No," Selander said, staying in his seat but looking steadily at Francis. Pontikes continued to study the paperwork and ignored Francis.

"I want my papers back. Give me my papers." Francis tried to snatch the documents away from Selander, who jerked them out of Francis' reach.

"Do not grab my papers," Francis said, his voice rising into a strained, childlike plea. "Can I get a marshal. Sir, hand me my papers back. They won't give me my papers back. Marshal."

Two bailiffs walked over from different ends of the room.

"Enough Mr. Francis," George Dobos said.

"He won't give me my papers back. I want my papers back."

"Just hold on. We'll take care of this," Dobos said.

Dobos led Francis to his seat then talked to the bailiff who had been sitting at the front of the room closest to the altercation. After being briefed, Dobos turned to Francis and said, "We'll just wait for a few minutes. Let them have a look and then we'll get your papers back."

"Oh. My. God," Francis said, standing. "I'll be back."

"That's probably a good idea," Dobos said, letting him pass by and through the knee-high swinging gates. Francis shoved open the door and stepped through into the hallway

Before the door closed, Francis could be heard saying, in a loud voice, "Oh my fucking God."

"That did it," Dobos said, moving quickly to the door.

George Dobos was a retired Panama City police officer who took his position with the federal courthouse very seriously. He believed that people in court, including lawyers, should not wear anything on their heads, including their glasses and sunglasses, when inside the courtroom. He did not allow people to open candy, or cough suppressant wrappers, while they were in court and would always tell reporters to take pens out from behind their ears because it was disrespectful to the court.

Francis, who wouldn't wear a tie, could never get to court on time, routinely argued with the judge, raised his voice and was just a general ass in court, had gotten on Dobos' last nerve.

The reporters sat for a second until they heard what sounded like Francis squealing from the hallway. We all filed out to find Francis pressed up against the wall near the open elevator doors.

Dobos was gripping Francis' left arm and had his face inches from Francis's, who refused to look at him.

"This is a place of business," Dobos said. "You will not go around yelling like that."

"I'm going downstairs. I'm going downstairs," was all Francis could say, and he repeated it over and over.

"Joe, calm down," Steph Watts said. "Calm down."

The hallway was now filled with press, two marshals, another bailiff and Francis' people. Dobos stared at Francis for another second, but then let go of his arm.

Francis darted into the elevator. When he got to the first floor he fled outside and sought some shelter from the rain and the bailiffs.

Within fifteen minutes, he came back into the courtroom, looking composed.

"Mr. Francis, where have you been?" Smoak asked as he took his seat at the bench.

"I was just a few minutes late. I called the clerk and left a message on her machine. We had some weather delays."

Francis then went right into his argument on the fake ID issue, apparently assuming that his explanation was going to satisfy the judge. It did not. Smoak told him that this was his last chance. He was not to be late again. If he was, the judge would impose sanctions.

"Do you understand?"

"Yes sir."

"Sit down."

Smoak said he'd read the cases that Francis had provided and they were not specific to the issue. Francis wanted to argue, but Smoak wasn't in the mood. The trial was already delayed and he wasn't going to allow Francis, or Pontikes for that matter, to go on and on after they lost an argument.

"I have ruled," he told Francis. The cases did not support his argument and therefor nothing about age or the girls lying about their age would be allowed into the trial.

Francis said the videotape of Plaintiff B, which he so desperately wanted in, had nothing to do with the age question. He said it was evidence that B was not plied with drugs and alcohol and had lied about that to the jury.

"If I could just play this video we could all go home."

"Tell me what that video shows."

Francis apparently didn't understand the question because he started talking about something else.

"What is on that DVD?" Smoak repeated, keeping his voice even.

"It's the lead up to the sex scene. We don't even have to put the sex scene in ..."

"Tell me what is on that video." Smoak said again. What he wanted to know were specifics.

"It's going to show that she lied yesterday, on the stand, and this proves that."

"What is on it?" Smoak said again, still not getting frustrated.

Francis still didn't give him an answer, saying only that it shows B was sober and knew about Girls Gone Wild prior to the filming.

"You let me play this and we can all go home."

"Because she said she'd never heard of GGW?" Smoak asked.

Francis said it was more than that. B said she'd been coerced, but the video disproved that. She said she was drunk, but she appears sober. She said she was too drugged to know what she was doing but the video showed someone who was fully involved in the activities around her.

Smoak said it didn't necessarily matter if she'd told the truth about everything. If, for instance, she said she was wearing a blue dress when she'd actually been wearing a white dress, that was immaterial and would not be proper for impeachment.

He said the video had to impeach B on relevant issues. Since age was no longer material, as was her prior knowledge of GGW, then what other evidentiary value did the video have?

"This is not about one small inconsistency," Francis said. He was talking loudly now, not listening to what anyone else was saying, and gesturing angrily at the notes he'd taken. The bailiffs were standing on three sides of him and Smoak was trying to get his attention. "I counted forty-seven inconsistencies. This witness is a liar. Forty-seven is an overwhelming number of inconsistencies for an eight-minute video."

"Mr. Francis. Mr. Francis. Mr. Francis, be quiet!" Smoak finally raised his voice.

The only thing that mattered, Smoak said, was that B was a minor at the time she was filmed and the footage was then published to the world. That was liability in a nutshell.

"Then it goes to the damages question," Francis insisted, still unable to calm down. "I don't want to give her anything."

"Not everything is fair game."

Francis could not accept where the judge was going and couldn't stop himself from continuing the argument.

"Mr. Francis, you're out of control," Smoak barked at him. "This kind of thing makes me concerned about your mental state. Did you take your medicine this morning?"

"No. I just drank a lot of coffee," Francis giggled. He then told the judge that he didn't appreciate the bailiffs standing every time he did and crowding in around him every time he spoke. "The jurors are watching that, your honor."

He said he should be allowed to show the jurors the release B had signed after the sex scene.

Smoak said the release he was looking at was barely legible.

"She authenticated this document in her deposition. It's on the internet. It has been for seven years."

That drew a gasp from the plaintiffs' lawyers and launched Pontikes to her feet, but she didn't say anything.

Smoak asked Francis again what the release was supposed to prove. It didn't matter that she listed her date of birth as 1983 instead of 1984, lying about age was immaterial. This document, he said, only had the potential to mislead the jury about the issue of age.

"It goes to credibility," Francis insisted. "She wasn't coerced or manipulated. She was a willing participant!"

Consent didn't matter, Smoak said. A minor cannot legally consent to a sex act or being filmed for pornography. It was immaterial.

"It's not immaterial to lie to a jury," Francis said. "She lied yesterday, in this courtroom, before your honor. It goes to her credibility. I counted fort-seven lies and the credibility of a witness is always on trial."

Smoak didn't budge from his ruling.

He talked with Pontikes for a while about the releases. Then he asked Francis to address the issue of how the signed releases or any aspect of consent went toward the issue of liability.

Francis said he was being sued because the plaintiffs claim he did an intentional bad act that destroyed their lives. He said the issue of consent, or any evidence that the girls sought out Girls Gone Wild or lied to get onto a video went to the issue of his intentional acts.

"They have to prove malice," he said, especially if they hoped to get punitive damages. How can there be malice if the girls sought out his company, lied to a cameraman and then falsified a release to claim they were adults? "How can you ask a jury to go and determine punitive damages without seeing this video? This clearly disproves malice, especially on my personal part."

"Just because she signed the release should not bar the award of damages," Pontikes said.

"Your honor, the jury needs to decide that. They need to see that she was a willing participant. She created this for herself."

It still came back to strict liability, Smoak said. By law, it didn't matter that a minor consented to a sex act.

"She was the one that initiated this process," Francis said. "She sought out GGW. This is what she dug for herself. This is the grave she dug for herself."

Smoak ruled that the signed release was out, it couldn't be used as evidence in the trial.

"Whether she lied about her age is immaterial, Mr. Francis," Smoak said.

"But it shows there was no malice. GGW didn't run up to her, rip off her clothes, tie her down and film her," Francis insisted. He then turned to the issue of the videotape, which he still wanted to use in his cross examination of Plaintiff B.

What he didn't realize was his cross examination of Plaintiff B was over. Smoak had ended it the day before.

"I wasn't done. I still have plenty more to ask her," Francis said when that was made clear to him.

Smoak said Francis can write down what questions he wanted to ask B. The judge would review them and decide whether they were appropriate.

"Frankly, I'm not going to turn you loose after yesterday and how badly things got out of control," Smoak said.

Francis said he couldn't get the questions written out until after lunch and he objected to the requirement. Smoak said he would also review the portion of the Plaintiff B videotape that Francis wanted to use.

Then they moved on with the trial.

After the jury came in, Pontikes called Plaintff B's mother to the stand. She described her daughter as her "most passionate child, filled with love."

Francis moved some papers around on his desk, then propped his elbow on the table and sank his cheek onto his palm.

Pontikes asked her a lot of the same questions she asked B, about her daughter's background and plans for the future.

Then they got to Spring Break 2002. Why did you allow her to go to Panama City Beach for Spring Break that year?

"Before this happened I didn't realize there were perverts out there," B's mother said.

Why didn't you warn her about Girls Gone Wild?

"You trust your daughter. You try to raise them up right. Why would you warn them about something I didn't even know existed? I never dreamed my daughter could ever have been a part of something like this."

They moved on to her husband's death.

Francis was getting restless. He tore out some pages from his legal pad, crumpled them up and threw them in a box. Then he let out a big sigh.

B's mother was talking about her daughter's phone calls the day her father died. She said B was very upset and wanted to come home. B's mother said she didn't know anything about the video until someone at her "Bible study fellowship" told her.

"They said they'd heard about it, or seen it, and it was really bad."

She said she didn't think her husband knew about the video. She said his death was a shock to everyone.

"It was just one of those things that happen so quickly."

And how did B react at the funeral?

"She kept hanging on to the coffin and screaming, 'I'm sorry daddy. I'm sorry.'"

But, like her daughter the day before, she did not blame GGW for her husband's death.

"This incident did not kill my husband. My husband died of a heart attack. Bottom line."

B's mother said one interesting thing about her daughter's drinking: "She'll tell you, after two drinks she's drunk. Three drinks and I don't even recognize her. It's a total personality change."

Since 2002, B's life had changed significantly, her mother said.

"She's disgusted in herself. She just couldn't cope. She was so depressed and lost a lot of friends through this."

B's mother went on to say her daughter became paranoid and sometimes thinks people are watching her. She told about a time when some children were playing with laser pointers outside their home. The laser dots flashing through the window and on the walls made B think someone was outside with a rifle trying to kill her.

Francis laughed.

"How do you think that being sexually exploited as a minor by Girls Gone Wild has affected her?" Pontikes continued.

"It has changed her life. It will always be a part of her life. She will always be embarrassed about it."

Then B's mother turned to the jury.

"If you've got a daughter or granddaughter, warn them. I hope you never have to go through what I've gone through."

Pontikes sat down and Francis began his cross-examination.

Do you feel like B has taken any responsibility for her actions?

"She's taken full responsibility for her actions."

"Then you don't blame Girls Gone Wild?"

"I think she was coerced and manipulated."

"Were you aware that your daughter has been on other videos?"

"Mr. Francis," Smoak interrupted. "Come up here."

"Your honor, this question is important."

At sidebar, Smoak told Francis he wanted to know what the rest of his questions were going to be.

They went back and forth for a minute before Smoak could be heard saying, "that's immaterial."

"Oh, no, no, no," Francis said, backing away from the bench with his hands up. But Smoak was adamant.

After the sidebar, Francis returned to the podium.

You don't think B was responsible for her actions?

"She was manipulated. I don't feel she's totally responsible."

"You don't think that at 17 years and 10 months ..."

Objection.

"How old was your daughter?"

"17."

"And you don't hold her responsible for her actions?"

And her husband's death?

His death certainly contributed to her mental problems, as did the "guilt and stress" she felt over the GGW incident, the mother said.

Francis began on another topic, but Pontikes objected, and Francis' cross-examination began to wind down.

"I have nothing further."

The next witness was B's former boyfriend. A portion of his videotaped deposition was played for the jurors. He too talked about her change in personality and the guilt she felt. They had been together before the GGW filming and after. They moved to Southern California and both tried to get into the music industry.

"Yes, she was a girl I would have married."

"Did you contemplate that?" Dent asked him from off-camera.

"Not seriously."

Chapter 38

"Mr. Francis, you are out of control"

Before the next witness took the stand, Ross McCloy asked Smoak if they could approach and discuss something quietly.

"Mr. Francis," Smoak said, inviting him to join them. Francis was rifling through the notes and files on his desk.

"Mr. Francis?" when he didn't come up to sidebar.

"I'm on my way, your honor," Francis said, finally breaking away. He jogged past the jury box and glanced over at the jurors with a wry smile on his face.

When Francis joined McCloy and Smoak at sidebar, they started a hushed conversation. It didn't take long for Francis to get agitated. He began dancing around, bobbing and emphatically pointing into the courtroom.

Smoak said something in a low growl and the bailiffs closed in on Francis again from three sides.

"Mr. Francis, you are out of control," Smoak said, this time clearly understood by even those in the audience.

With two bailiffs standing at either shoulder, Francis put his hands up and stopped gesturing and moving.

When they'd resolved the issue, McCloy and Francis went to their respective tables.

Plaintiff S came in the courtroom, hesitated, her eyes scanned the room but looked above the spectators. She didn't want to look anyone in the eye.

Ross McCloy approached the podium as S took her seat in the witness box. Francis was standing at his table, shuffling papers, slapping note pads on the table. McCloy gave him a long look, but didn't say anything.

Plaintiff S had already been sworn in and McCloy wanted to start asking her questions, but Francis was still standing at his table. He didn't look like he wanted to say anything, he just looked like he forgot to sit down.

McCloy started, hesitated, looked at Francis expecting an objection, started again and finally got to his first question. Francis finally sat down.

Plaintiff S was the most emotional of the girls who took the stand. She choked up almost immediately, as McCloy asked her how old she was when she flashed for Girls Gone Wild.

"15."

And what does the video show?

"I exposed my breasts, and I was just smoking a cigarette, laughing."

She appeared in "Girls Gone Wild College Girls Exposed/ Sexy Sorority Sweethearts."

"What grade were you in?"

"Ninth grade."

"Were you in college? Had you been a member of any sororities?"

No.

Plaintiff S was blond with streaks in her hair, a small upturned nose and, without makeup, her eyes seemed small and featureless. She had thin lips and a small mouth, which gave her a hard look. Her voice, however, was high and clear and even when she got upset, her tone never lost a bell-like quality.

She'd grown up in Northwest Florida, the second youngest of seven kids. Until the filming, in 2000, she'd had a normal scholastic career and a boyfriend.

The day of the filming, her older sister had asked their mother if she could take S and Plaintiff J, who was 13 at the time, and J's 12-year-old best friend to the beach. Her mother was initially opposed to her children going anywhere near Spring Break, but eventually she was talked into it.

The four girls spent the day swimming and sunning, before getting back in the car to get some food. They were in bumper-to-bumper traffic on Front Beach Road when a cameraman approached the car.

He first asked the driver, the 18-year-old older sister, to flash. She said no and he came around to the other side of the car where S and J were sitting, S in the front seat and J behind her.

S said the cameraman badgered them, pestered them and would not leave.

"Finally, I just did it."

She said she didn't think the cameraman would leave unless she flashed. She said she covered her face and leaned forward afterwards.

She said she had no idea that the video was going to be used and sold by Girls Gone Wild.

"I felt that if I didn't do it, they weren't going to go away. They just kept saying, 'Do it, do it, do it.' And traffic was stopped, we weren't going anywhere. I just didn't think they were going to stop so I just did it so they would just leave us alone."

How did it make you feel?

"Ashamed. I was embarrassed more than anything."

J and the 12-year-old also flashed. The cameraman tossed some beads to them and left. The girls continued their day and when they went home they didn't tell their parents.

S said nothing came of it until sometime in January or February of the next year. The video had recently been released and suddenly, she said, it seemed like everyone knew about it.

"Someone ran up to me and said, 'You're on the 'Girls Gone Wild'. You're on a porn tape. Ha ha ha. Everyone's gonna know now.'"

And that was the beginning. Her high school career, she said, was a nightmare of insults and gropings in the hallways.

Someone even spit in her face. Her boyfriend broke up with her, saying he was ashamed of her.

"There was plenty of times that going to the bathroom, you're just sitting on the toilet and crying and not knowing what to do, who to talk to. It was hard," she said, wiping tears away.

The women on the jury were watching her very carefully. At the time of the filming, she'd been close to the same age as one of the juror's daughters. She watched S with a sad look. Another juror wiped tears from her eyes, but the others were unmoved.

"Did you lose most of your, what you thought were your close friends at that time?"

"I lost everything. There's no one wanted to talk to me anymore. I lost my best friend from ... I've known since like five years old. We went to grammar school, everything, we did everything together. I even lost her."

"Did this change affect your grades?"

"Yes, because I didn't care anymore. I mean, I kind of gave up. Like my grades just went downhill."

She started using drugs: marijuana, Xanax.

S told them about having to tell her mother, which she did after her mother found out about the video from someone else and confronted her.

McCloy asked her how that conversation went.

"Humiliating," she wailed. "That's your mom. That's not something you ever imagine having to talk to your mom about, being on a pornography tape, when you're 15. It's embarrassing."

S dropped out of high school, left home and got involved in a series of abusive relationships.

"What did this guy turn out to be?" McCloy asked of her first boyfriend after the Girls Gone Wild incident.

"I don't even know how to answer that. A nightmare."

He was controlling to the point where "I couldn't even wash my body," she said.

Francis laughed, "Objection. Relevance. This is a joke. What does this have to do with her showing her breasts on Girls Gone Wild? This has gone on long enough."

Smoak called Francis and McCloy to sidebar.

"Mr. Francis, this is your last chance," Smoak said. "Next outburst and you're going into custody."

"Please work with me. I'm trying really hard."

"No you're not. You're totally out of control."

Smoak turned to McCloy and asked him about the testimony. "Are you going to link this up? Because right now it doesn't appear to be particularly relevant."

"We will, with the expert witness."

"Are you saying that because of this experience she was more prone to an abusive relationship?"

"Yes, your honor."

"That's such a stretch," Francis said. "He's having fun making her cry in front of the jury. This absolutely irrelevant and ridiculous. And by the way, it's not even a violation. In Florida law minors can show their breasts. This is not even a violation of Florida law. I want to make a motion for directed verdict right now, because this isn't a violation of Florida law."

He said the last part so loudly that it could be plainly heard throughout the courtroom.

"Be quiet," Smoak said. "The claim that they have made is for intentional infliction of emotional distress. The fact that it isn't a crime is irrelevant."

"I think the jury needs to be instructed, your honor, that they're to disregard the fact that she was underage and showed her breasts because that's not a violation of Florida law."

"Their claim is not for a violation of a criminal law. It is for the common law tort of intentional infliction of emotional distress."

Smoak turned back to McCloy. "Are you representing to me that you have an expert who will tomorrow testify about why this plaintiff got into or stayed in an abusive relationship and will connect it to the experience?"

"Yes, your honor."

"On that representation, I am going to permit it to go on. If it does not come to pass as represented, I will instruct the jury accordingly and in very strong terms."

Smoak thought it was a good time for lunch and released the jury until 1:30.

After lunch, Francis was late getting back. Smoak had warned him that morning, but didn't say anything to him when he took the bench.

Before bringing the jury back in, Francis, Pontikes and Smoak had another heated discussion on whether evidence of fake IDs, signed releases and the introduction of the videotape would be allowed as evidence.

Francis' argument, didn't make sense considering the defendant on the stand – saying the video would show they weren't drugged or drunk – but there had been no testimony from S about drugs or alcohol, just an annoying cameraman. There hadn't been anything mentioned, either about anyone asking S for ID or to sign a release. It sounded like Francis was just going back to the same argument he'd had for the last two days, about getting Plaintiff B's video in.

Francis was facing a lot of restrictions on what he could do, but part of that was due to the fact that he hadn't submitted the proper witness list and evidence exhibits before the pretrial deadline.

"If I'm not even allowed to question these witnesses about what they said, it's pointless to be here. We might as well take it up with the 11th Circuit" Court of Appeal, he said.

The argument ended and an assistant brought Plaintiff S back into the room.

"Mr. McCloy are you ready to proceed?" Smoak asked.

McCloy simply pointed to the empty jury box. Smoak laughed.

"I can't even blame that on a senior moment."

A minute later, Hughes announced the jurors' entrance and McCloy resumed his questioning of S.

"Why did you marry him?" he asked her, referring to her "nightmare" boyfriend.

"I thought maybe things would get better."

"Did it?"

"No sir."

She ended up divorcing him, but then her drug problems got serious. She talked about the types of narcotics she tried.

"I even ended up smoking crack cocaine," she said, dabbing a tissue at her eyes. "It's so embarrassing."

McCloy paused as S sobbed into her tissue. She regained her composure and McCloy asked her if any of her boyfriends had abused her during high school.

"No sir."

"How has your life changed since the release of the videos?"

Francis sighed and ripped a page out of his legal pad.

"I don't like to take my bra and stuff off," Plaintiff S said. She added that she couldn't even shower with her ex-husband while they were married because she always felt like she had to cover her breasts. "I just get that paranoid feeling, like someone is watching you."

Did her ex-husband have an opinion about her incident with Girls Gone Wild.

"He said Mr. Francis was a pedophile and the biggest scumbag on Earth."

"Objection, your honor, this is just absurd."

"Sustained."

Francis began to sit down, then bounced up again.

"I'd like you to instruct the jury to disregard that last comment."

Smoak did so.

Plaintiff S's relationship with her mother was strained.

"I have my good days and I have my bad days. It's always gonna be there, the shame from what I've done."

McCloy asked her when she was last recognized from the video and she said November. Her district manager asked her about it.

It was maddening that the video was available for rent at her local Blockbuster and she would see it advertised on TV.

"Do you think you could benefit from some form of therapy?"

Yes.

"Can you afford it now?"

"No. Not really."

Do you regret what happened that day?

"I don't feel like I had a choice in the matter. If I'd know it was Girls Gone Wild, I would have never have done it. I didn't have a choice in the matter. They didn't tell me. It's not fair. I was 15."

She wailed the last few words, then cried into her tissue again.

McCloy asked her if she and her sister had a "scheme to target GGW?"

"I didn't know who they were."

McCloy said he was done and turned back to his table. S continued to cry into her tissue as Francis walked to the podium.

He asked her how long the video was that her footage was a part of. She had no idea. Guess.

"I have no idea. An hour and a half?"

"OK. Good. An hour and a half. And how many girls do you think appear in this video?"

"I'm not sure Mr. Francis."

"Can you guess? Would you say there were 50-100? 200-250? Would you be surprised if I told you there were 250 girls on that video?"

McCloy objected and they had a brief sidebar.

"And you exposed your breasts on this video willingly right?" Francis asked when he returned to the podium.

"Yes."

Francis seemed a little surprised by the answer.

"Did someone force you to expose your breasts?"

"No one physically touched me."

"So you did it on your own free will?"

Yes.

"Do you know the total amount of time your breasts were exposed?"

"It felt like forever to me."

"Was it one second? Two seconds?"

She didn't know.

"Two seconds." Francis announced for her. "It was two seconds."

He'd gotten pretty worked up and was talking loudly while leaning in toward the microphone. Smoak told him to tone it down.

"The total time was two seconds. Would that seem like a long time to you?"

"I'm not for certain that it wasn't longer than two seconds."

"How long was it then?"

McCloy objected. "She has answered the question."

"What am I supposed to do? I can't make her tell me."

"Now Mr. Francis is badgering the witness."

"I don't mean to badger."

He dropped the subject and moved on.

You were smoking a cigarette? And how old were you? And you were smoking a cigarette because you thought it was cool?

McCloy objected. "This is not about children smoking."

Francis whipped his head around and said to McCloy, "I think I'm entitled to an answer."

"You are not to talk to Mr. McCloy," Smoak snapped at him.

"I'm on trial here." Francis said. He turned back to S.

"Have you met me before?"

"I don't believe so."

"Have you ever seen me before in person?"

She said he kind of looked like the cameraman.

"Now she's claiming I was the cameraman?" Francis burst out.

"Maybe," she said. "I was 15. Maybe it was you."

"This is ridiculous. It's established who the cameraman was."

Smoak called another sidebar. He told Francis to calm down and stop making statements. He was to ask questions only. If he couldn't control himself he would be removed from the courtroom and held in a cell.

"I'm the one on trial here. I'm only representing myself because I can't afford a lawyer."

"You are not represented by counsel because of your own actions," Smoak said.

"I'm on trial. They're not on trial. They're suing me."

After the sidebar, Francis's jaw was set in a tight line and he was obviously fighting back tears. He went to his table and sat down, pretending to write some notes in his pad while he composed himself. Dobos handed him a tissue and he blew his nose.

After a few minutes, Francis returned to the podium and took several deep breaths.

"I'm emotional. I'm on trial here, not you. You're suing me."

McCloy objected to the comments.

"You're suing me," Francis said somewhat absentmindedly, but the statement got him back on track. "What have I done to you? Why are you suing me?"

"Your company, you film underage girls. You have no idea what we girls go through."

"What have I done to you? Tell me, please."

"It's just so hard to answer that, Mr Francis. For allowing your company to manufacture and produce videos of underage girls. It's your company."

"How have you been damaged? How much should this jury pay you? How much do you want? How much money do you want?"

She didn't have a ready answer.

"Do you want money?"

McCloy objected.

"Were you in a public place when your exposed your breasts willingly?"

Yes.

"Did you take your top off yourself?"

"Well, yes sir. I did it. Yes sir. But those guys were pressuring me to do it."

"Didn't you just say you willing flashed your breasts?"

"Yes sir."

"Is flashing a common practice for you?"

She looked at him without understanding.

Have you flashed before or after this?

"No sir."

Francis asked her again what she did on the video.

"I already told you, I pulled my top up."

"For less than two seconds?"

"Mr. Francis," Smoak cautioned.

"We've got the video. We can show it if you'd like."

"Yes," she said, the word dripping with frustration. Yes as to the question about how long the flash was. "My gosh."

When was the last time you smoked marijuana?

"Probably two years ago."

"Remember, you're under oath. You're under the threat of perjury."

"What are you talking about?"

Objection. Move on to another subject.

"You were teased in high school? Boys wanted to get with you. None of that ever happened before you willing exposed your breasts for Girls Gone Wild?"

No.

"And Girls Gone Wild destroyed your life? It made you smoke crack cocaine?"

"Yes sir. It led up to that."

"Exposing your breasts willingly in public was the cause of all your problems?"

"It was the start of it. Yes sir."

How?

"Because I was 15 years old and I was violated." She was wailing now, wiping tears from under her eyes constantly. "I was pressured into it. I didn't think it was going to go nationwide."

"Mr. Francis, it is time for you to stop and sit down," Smoak said.

Francis pressed on. He asked her about a statement she made to law enforcement. He wanted to read a portion of it, but McCloy objected.

"Mr. Francis, I've already ruled on that."

"I apologize. I'm almost done here."

"Had you ever heard of Girls Gone Wild?"

"No sir."

You said a guy spit in your face.

"He called me a whore and spit in my face."

"What was his name?"

McCloy popped out of his seat and objected.

"Mr. Francis, this is not material."

"It's material if I want to call him in here and ask him if this really happened. I don't believe the witness. I don't believe she's credible."

"You're so rude," S exclaimed, sniffling into her tissue.

Have you accrued any medical bills "because of this two-second exposure of your breasts, willingly, on Girls Gone Wild?"

"I'm not sure of that."

"Have you spent anything on medical bills as a result of willingly showing your breasts for two seconds on Girls Gone Wild?"

She had to buy some medication for depression.

OK. What kind of medication?

She wasn't sure.

How much did you spend?

She wasn't sure.

"How much are you claiming in lost wages? In total dollars, how much have you lost in wages?"

"I haven't lost any wages."

McCloy objected, saying Francis was just repeating himself.

"I have nothing further," Francis said, collected his notes and sat down.

McCloy asked S a few more questions.

It really wasn't about the two seconds she was on video, was it?

No.

Didn't the trauma stem from the 11 years that the video has been out in the public?

"It's been out there most of your life."

"Yes sir."

McCloy was done. Francis wanted to ask her a few more questions.

"No sir," Smoak said. "Sit down."

S got up, dabbed at her eyes, and walked quickly out of a door that was beside the jury box. Before the door closed, S said in a loud wail, "He's so mean." The door eased shut on the sound of her sobbing.

Plaintiff J entered through the same door. She was harder looking than her sister, a little huskier and wearing dark eye liner. Her blonde-streaked hair was cut in a short bob.

They went through her background as well: straight-A student, daddy's girl, normal family and not much of a trouble-maker. She also repeated much of what S had said about the actual flashing: they thought it was for personal use; the cameraman pestered them for 15-20 minutes. But J said the cameraman also asked her to pull her pants down. Then the cameraman tossed some beads into the car and left.

"I thought it was just some random guy with a camera and we'd never hear about it again."

A few months later, when the video was released, they heard about it from a friend. She was labeled a "whore" and a "slut."

"I got the nickname 'GGW' for the longest time."

Boys started asking her to do sexual favors and grabbing her in the school hallways. She began to skip school and failing her classes.

Her friends abandoned her.

"I felt very ashamed. I was disgusted at myself for the choice I had made. I was the one that had liquor in the locker because it could get me through the day."

She tried to kill herself twice, in 2003 and 2004. She was hospitalized both times and received psychological treatment.

She'd also gotten involved with abusive men and had three children out of wedlock with two different guys.

"Objection, your honor, relevance." Francis said. He scoffed when the judge overruled him. He was not trying to hide his contempt for Plaintiff J.

She was now working security for a private company.

Would she benefit from therapy?

Sure.

Does it bother her that her video is still out there?

"I'd give anything to have them, every single one of them, back."

Does she blame Girls Gone Wild for all her problems?

"I made a bad choice. I have to live with that every day. I'm trying to move on."

Did you know who Joe Francis and Girls Gone Wild were at that time? Did you and your sister conspire with one another to target GGW?

No.

Joe Francis began his cross-examination with a cordial greeting.

"How ya doin?" he said to J.

He asked her about her family and her parents' marriage. Then he asked her about the video. It was the same question he hammered her sister with a short while before: how long did the incident last?

But J had the answer ready.

"Two seconds."

Have you ever met me before?

"You do look familiar."

"I was not there."

"You do look similar to him (the cameraman), yes."

"Had you ever heard of me before this litigation?"

"I cannot be sure."

"Do you have a problem telling the truth?"

No. He asked her to describe the flashing incident again. She was in the backseat, behind S who was in the front passenger seat. She saw S flash and thought, "Why not?" She's not sure why she did it.

Had she talked to anyone about her testimony before taking the stand, or during any breaks?

Smoak wasn't happy with that question and instructed Francis to move on. But Francis thought she'd been coached and asked her again if she'd discussed her testimony with anyone.

"All they told me was to be strong and tell the truth."

Smoak told him again to move on to another subject.

Was she working now? No, she'd taken time off.

Her 18-year-old sister had been driving the car that day, right?

Yes.

Did she show her breasts?

No.

Why isn't the 12-year-old a plaintiff in this case as well?

Her mother is in the military and it would have damaged her career.

Had she had any alcohol during the day prior to flashing?

Objection.

You admit that the total length of time you were on film was two seconds?

"It doesn't matter about the length of time. I still did it. I was still made fun of. I was still groped."

And all of your problems stem from this incident? He made a snide comment about her three kids and having never been married.

Smoak told him to stop with the comments.

"Just ask questions and get it over with," the judge said.

You're still recognized?

No, not really.

"So, this is over for you?"

"I didn't get to go to college. I didn't get to go to prom."

And all of that is GGW's fault?

"I did make that choice. I take full responsibility. But I was 13 years old. I should not have been allowed to make that choice. You are the one that sold it to hundreds of thousands of people. Not me."

So you take full responsibility?

"I would say there was some pressuring."

"You're suing me in this lawsuit. How have I, Joe Francis, damaged you?"

"You sold thousands of tapes with me on it, when I was 13 years old."

"I did?"

"Your company."

"How have you been harmed? How much have you spent in medical bills because of the two seconds you were on tape?"

She had some bills from her suicide attempts, but didn't know how much.

After every answer, Francis would repeat back what she said.

Smoak wanted this over with and kept telling him to move on with his questioning.

"I feel like I could have done better for myself," Plaintiff J said.

You tried to kill yourself twice? Why?

"I was tired of life. I made a bad choice being on GGW. That one choice led to a lot of other bad choices in my life. I don't directly blame GGW. I made the decision. But what 13-year-old makes a decision like that?"

Francis went back to the cost of her medical bills and damages.

McCloy objected and Francis conceded.

"I will move on."

Was she a willing participant in Girls Gone Wild? Yes or no?

Objection, she's already answered that question.

"Are you asking for a percentage of the profits from the DVD in which you showed your breasts, willingly, for two seconds?"

"That is not a proper question," Smoak said.

Francis paused and asked to approach sidebar, to ask Smoak if his next question was a proper one.

"Have you done illegal drugs?" he said when he returned to the podium.

Objection, outside the scope.

"We covered it with the other witnesses?"

Objection sustained.

"Do you take personal responsibility for your decision?"

Objection, asked and answered.

"How did I, Joe Francis, intentionally harm you?"

"I don't know how to answer that." She'd dropped out of school and lost job opportunities.

"Was I there?"

"Mr. Francis," Smoak interrupted.

"What's wrong?"

Move on.

Did you know that the footage of you flashing was licensed from a third party?

Objection. Smoak instructed the jury to disregard that statement. He told Francis if he continued going over material that he knew was off-limits he'd be held in contempt of court and sanctioned.

Francis resumed his questioning.

"How have I harmed you?"

"I don't know how to answer that."

Francis made another comment and Smoak again warned him to just ask questions.

But Francis was done. He ended his questioning and went back to his table.

McCloy went over a few more things with J.

You were depressed enough to try to kill yourself twice, he asked. And this whole episode in your life has lasted more than two seconds, with the video still out there. Do you expect it to stop anytime in the near future?

No.

Plaintiff J was done and Smoak called McCloy and Francis to the bench.

He could be heard scolding Francis for his behavior.

"You were abusive."

More of that, Smoak said, and they would be talking about sanctions for contempt of court.

Chapter 39

"I was vulnerable"

McCloy and Francis returned to their tables and Plaintiff V was shown into the room.

She had short black hair, a small upturned nose and large, but tired looking eyes.

Pontikes went through her history: high school sports, decent student, "just a normal high school life."

But V's home life was a mess. Her father had beaten her since she was 6 years old. Her mother had died about six weeks before she'd had her encounter with Girls Gone Wild.

How did her mother's death affect her?

"It made me feel lost. I was vulnerable. I didn't know, really, who I was."

She said she and four friends went driving on Front Beach Road after school when they saw the Girls Gone Wild van in front of them. The van's driver, she said, asked them to pull into the parking lot of a gas station. Within a few minutes, he'd convinced two of her friends to go to the Chateau Motel and allow him to film them showering together. All five of them followed the cameraman to the motel room and while they were filming, she sat in another room.

Then Joe Francis came into the room and introduced himself.

"I don't know how long it was before he walked into the bedroom and asked us to come in. He pulled us into the room. He had us sit down on the bed next to him and asked us to masturbate him."

How did he get you into the room?

"He grabbed our hands and pulled us into the room. He sat on the bed and started to take his pants off. He was taking our hands and rubbing it on his penis." She mumbled the last word and Pontikes asked her to repeat it.

"Penis," V said into the microphone.

"And then what happened?"

V just looked at Pontikes with a blank stare and didn't answer.

"Did it come to a conclusion?" Pontikes asked, attempting to help her out.

"Yes."

"He ejaculated?"

"Yes."

"Then what happened?"

"I got him a towel and threw it at him so he could clean himself up."

He then took out a "wad of money" and tossed it on the bed. She never said she picked any of it up, but apparently $50 found its way into her pocket.

"He asked us if we wanted to go for a ride in his Ferrari and we said yes. We just drove around."

They then returned to the motel and went around back where a camera crew was waiting. They wanted her to flash.

"I said 'no.'"

They kept at her and she kept saying no.

"How many times?"

"A lot."

She had a boyfriend at the time and she didn't want to be on a video flashing.

Did you tell Joe Francis you were underage before he took you into the bedroom?

Yes, he knew. And she really didn't want to flash but they kept pestering her and wouldn't let her leave.

"I felt like it was the only thing I could do to leave, to get out of that situation."

It didn't matter that the tape was seized and would never be released. Francis was arrested a few days later and it became common knowledge at school that she'd been involved in the case.

Francis objected and they went to sidebar. Plaintiff V put her cheek in her hand and listened to the conversation without looking in their direction. She rolled her eyes and shook her head as Francis gestured and argued in a strident whisper. But the argument didn't go his way and Francis backed away from the bench until his back was against the wall. He then slid down until he was squatting on his haunches as Pontikes made her point.

He stood and threw up his hands as the sidebar broke up.

Pontikes asked V what happened with her boyfriend.

He broke up with her and called her disgusting.

"I got really depressed. I took a bunch of painkillers and tried to kill myself."

She ended up at Bay Behavioral, a treatment center.

"I just didn't want to live anymore. I didn't have anybody. I felt disgusting."

She started drinking and using drugs. The situation with her boyfriend continued to bother her for years. In 2007, four years after the GGW incident, she asked him to meet her so they could talk. She told him the whole story, about how she'd been forced into her actions.

"How did he react?"

"He was really upset."

And since then, you've gained a lot of weight?

"I'm disgusted with myself. I feel dirty and disgusting and just being here right now makes me sick. I'm so depressed, I just let myself go. I don't care about myself any more."

She said she also has problems sexually.

"I don't do anything with the penis. I have flashbacks."

Her boyfriend broke up with her again, just a week ago, because she was going to trial.

"He said it had been 11 years and it was still in our lives. He called me trash. He said I was disgusting and I shouldn't be doing this."

This was the first time, she said, that she'd actually confronted her feelings about her encounter with Joe Francis.

"I've denied it for a long time. Now, I have to talk about it. I've never really talked about how I feel until today."

Could you benefit from therapy?

"Yes, a lot."

Are you doing therapy right now?

"No. I don't have the money."

When you and your friends were driving around that day, did you have a "scheme to find GGW and get on GGW?"

No.

Do you have any regrets?

"I wish I had never drove down that road and saw that van."

Chapter 40

"Does that make you a prostitute?"

Joe Francis was "early" by 90 seconds and he only accomplished that because his consultant, Lisa Dufort, can drive an orange Dodge Grand Caravan like a NASCAR stock car.

He swept into the courtroom and slung his satchel onto the table top. Black pinstripe suit, white shirt open at the collar.

Plaintiff V resumed her seat on the witness stand. She fidgeted slightly, trying to get comfortable around the nervousness.

"Good morning," Francis said, walking to the podium. He repeated that greeting to the judge and jury before beginning his questioning of V.

"Plaintiff V," he began slowly, leaning toward the microphone with his hands on the podium and his elbows splayed, "Do you know who I am?"

"Yes."

"What's my name?"

"Joe Francis."

"Do you know a woman named Felicia Carr?"

"Yes."

"Is Felicia Carr in this courtroom?"

"Yes."

"What's your relationship with Ms. Carr?"

Objection, outside the scope. Sustained.

"Your honor, how is this not relevant?"

"That was not part of direct examination."

"I'm allowed to impeach the witness on cross, your honor, if she lied ..."

"Your honor," Pontikes shot up from her chair, "I move to strike those comments."

"Mr. Francis, that is outside direct. You will not go into it. Members of the jury, you will disregard the statement Mr. Francis just made about a witness lying. It was improper. Mr. Francis, you are instructed that you are not to do that again."

"All right, but can you tell me specifically what I did so I don't do it again?"

"Referring to a witness lying."

"Oh, saying they lied. But if I show that they lied ... I got it. I understand. So you're saying I can't use the word lie, but I can prove it."

"I move to strike those comments, your honor," Pontikes said, rising from her seat again.

"They are stricken and the jury is instructed to disregard this exchange with Mr. Francis."

"Let me adjust my notes real quick," Francis said, shuffling papers on the podium. Then he asked V, "Had you heard of Girls Gone Wild prior to 2003?"

"Yes, from friends."

"Did you have any firsthand personal knowledge of Girls Gone Wild?"

She stared blankly at him. "Firsthand, how do you mean?"

"How do I mean firsthand? Is that your question?"

"Could you repeat the question?"

"You don't know what the word 'firsthand' means or the phrase 'firsthand?' Did you have any personal ... did you know what it is? Had you seen a Girls Gone Wild television commercial?"

She had.

"What was your personal understanding of what Girls Gone Wild was about?"

She said it was a company that featured girls on videotape.

"Girls doing what?"

She stared blankly at him. "Being on videotape."

"Doing what?"

Pontikes objected, saying V had answered the question.

"Girls being on videotape is not a sufficient answer, your honor," Francis protested.

Smoak overruled the objection and told V to try to answer the question.

"What are they doing on these tapes? Being on videotape is why we're here today."

Blank stare.

"You're suing me."

Objection.

"Mr Francis, come up here."

Smoak admonished him, again, to ask questions and to make no comments. "Everything you say needs to have a question mark after it."

"Don't worry, I have plenty of questions for this witness today," Francis said back at the podium.

Pontikes objected to that comment and asked that it be stricken.

V was asked again what the videotapes portrayed.

"Basically, women flashing and getting naked," she finally said.

And you knew this prior to 2003?

"I had seen commercials and have heard about it from friends."

After a brief sidebar, during which Francis accused Rachael Pontikes of using hand and eye signals to communicate with V, he asked her how many other girls were with her the day she encountered Girls Gone Wild. Four.

"What were their names?"

Objection.

"Why, they're not under the protective order."

Sidebar.

Francis went back to the podium and told V that her friends will be known as "Friend 1, Friend 2, Friend 3 and Friend 4."

"Where you ever, at any time, alone with me?"

Yes.

"When was that?"

"When I was in the bedroom with you."

Wasn't there another girl in there too?

She was in the doorway.

"So you were not alone with me ever, is that correct?"

"Not in an enclosed door, no."

"I'm going to jump back to Girls Gone Wild and that day. When did you hear Girls Gone Wild was in town?"

"I don't know."

Francis asked Smoak if he'd be allowed to read something from a police report. Smoak called Francis and Pontikes to a sidebar.

"You want to quote something from a police statement?" Smoak asked Francis.

"No, what I want to say is she just said that – in her Bay County statement she said that her friends and her met at the beach, they heard Girls Gone Wild was in town and they targeted Girls Gone Wild, and this is a huge part of this."

"She never said she targeted Girls Gone Wild," Pontikes said.

"You can't use a police report," Smoak told Francis.

"What about her own deposition? She said – and her friend said in her deposition ..."

"That they targeted – you need to get on to something else. You are not making that an issue in this case," Smoak said.

"It goes to intentional infliction of emotional distress, because if I intended to do something versus they came to us, they met and they came to us ..."

"Doesn't make any difference."

"For malice it does, because if you commit malice you're going after them. They came after us."

"We're not going to spend a whole lot of time on that. You can ..."

"Fine. I'll get through that part quick. I'll get through that part real quick."

Francis loped back to the podium.

"Does that make you a prostitute?"

"Is it correct that you and your friends sought out Girls Gone Wild that day at the beach? Weren't you driving around saying, 'It would be so cool and fun to be on Girls Gone Wild'?"

At this point, V started to get upset. She said they were driving along Middle Beach Road when her friends, who were dancing and screaming in the back seat, told her to go down to Front Beach Road. When they saw the Girls Gone Wild van, she said, "Yes, I pulled over."

Didn't they get together earlier to talk about finding Girls Gone Wild?

"I don't remember doing that."

Francis asked her if she met with her friends and discussed looking for Girls Gone Wild that day. Pontikes objected.

"It's in her deposition your honor," Francis said.

Smoak sustained the objection, but Francis asked it again. "I want to know the answer to that question."

"I don't remember."

Pontikes objected again, but this time Smoak overruled her.

"You don't remember? You don't remember. It's an answer. You don't remember?"

"I don't remember doing that. No, I don't."

"Mr. Francis," Smoak interrupted. "Time out. You are to make no comments about that. You are simply to ask questions. Members of the jury, you will disregard the gratuitous comments made by Mr. Francis."

"How old was I for this handjob in 2003?" Francis asked V.

Twenty-something.

"I was in my twenties, that's correct," Francis said, nodding his head and showing that he was proud that she'd gotten that question right. "And how old were you?"

"Sixteen."

"And how old did you tell me you were?"

"Sixteen, about to turn 17."

"Did you at any point tell me you were 18 years old and you were going to college?"

Objection. Sustained.

"Your honor, it's reasonable ..."

"It's immaterial," Smoak said sternly, ending the discussion, but not the questions.

"Did you tell me you were in college?"

"No."

Did you and your friend tell me you had just enrolled in junior college?

"I don't remember."

"Take a second, because this is really, really important."

"Mr. Francis," Smoak said.

"I just wanted her to think about it."

"Mr. Francis."

"All right."

Turning back to V, Francis asked, "What did you say to me when you first met me?"

"I don't remember. That was almost 10 years ago."

"You seemed to have a pretty good memory yesterday when ..."

Objection. Sidebar. Plaintiff V sat in the witness box, slumped forward, rolling her eyes and shaking her head at what she overheard.

Francis returned to the podium and asked her again what she said at their first meeting.

"I said I don't know. I don't remember."

"Do you remember saying, 'You're cute.'? Do you remember saying, 'I saw you on the Maury Povich show last week and you were so cute.'?"

Blank stare.

"Had you seen me on television?"

"I don't know. I don't remember."

"Do you have memory problems?"

Objection. Overruled.

"I don't know."

"You don't know if you have memory problems?"

"I don't know if I ever have. I don't know."

"Have you ever had anyone tell you something, maybe the next day, that you did the night before that you didn't remember?"

"Yes."

"How often does that happen?"

"I can't count up the times that I've forgotten something. I tend to put things away when things happen. That's why I don't remember them."

How often?

"I don't know," she said, appearing frustrated. "How can I count up the times when I haven't remembered something?"

"I'm gonna jump around a bit," Francis said, changing tracks.

He asked about how she got into the bedroom with him, was she pulled or coerced?

"Both."

"I physically pulled you into a room? Show me how I did that."

Before they got into that, he asked her how big the motel room was. The best she could say was that it was a standard size. But Francis pressed for more detail. He asked her to describe it in relation to the courtroom, but she couldn't do it.

"I don't know. It was just an average hotel room. I don't know."

"Like an average motel room, right? Just a motel room? We've all been in a motel room. I think that I can stipulate to 'it's an average motel room.' So there's eight people ..."

"Move to strike that comment, your honor," Pontikes said.

"That wasn't a comment. I'm just trying to help her along."

"Mr. Francis," Smoak said, sounding tired, "you are to ask questions only. In other words, everything you say needs to have a question mark after it. Do you understand that?"

"I'll make it like Jeopardy, your honor."

Francis then got back to how he brought her into the bedroom.

"How did I pull you? Did I grab you by the hair?"

"You grabbed our hands."

"How were you pulled? Show the jury how you were physically pulled."

She said he pulled both girls into the room.

"How were F1 and PV pulled onto a bed?"

"You grabbed our wrists and eased us into the room."

"Eased? Now it's eased? I thought it was pulled."

Objection.

"I don't understand the word eased. Can you explain what you mean?"

"You were touching my hand and you eased me into the room."

Francis continued to ask her what eased meant.

"What's the difference between eased and pulled?" V yelled, at the end of her patience. "You were still touching my hand. What is the difference? I still said 'no!' God!"

"It's a straight question."

Objection, arguing with the witness. Smoak called the attorneys to sidebar. Francis bobbed and gestured, trying to lock eyes with the judge to plead his case.

Smoak said to him, "It's a matter that is very small. You are this close for me stopping the cross-examination. Now, get on to straight questions."

"Got it," Francis said. "The jury deserves to understand what happened in this room. She said 'forced masturbation' 40 times yesterday, and I deserve to defend the fact it wasn't forced."

"She's given you an answer."

"The ambiguity, what the hell does that mean?"

"This is not rocket science. She's made it very clear that you got her by the hand or by the wrist ..."

"No, no," Francis said, bobbing and clasping his hands in front of him, "she later, she retracted that just now, your honor."

"Doesn't matter."

"It really does, because ..."

"Not that material, Mr. Francis, just move on."

"OK. Fine. But I want to object because I think it's proper. Ms. Pontikes said no less than 45 times yesterday 'forced masturbation' to antagonize and ..."

"Move on to the masturbation. It doesn't matter whether you were grabbing her hand or wrist," Smoak said.

"The jury needs a picture."

"You're not doing a very good job."

"OK, you're right."

"I would like to just make a statement for the record as well," Pontikes said. "First, I renew my motion for default.

Second, I would like the record to reflect, as we discussed yesterday, and Mr. Francis knows, that he has been convicted for procuring this minor girl into prostitution, which included the masturbation."

"But not forced," Francis insisted.

"That is a conviction," Pontikes countered.

Francis insisted that it was a plea of no contest, meaning he didn't admit guilt.

"Mr. Francis," Smoak said, "we're about to end your cross-examination. You better be as careful as you can be and get onto something important."

Francis walked back to the podium and began again.

"What happened next?"

"We were eased into the room and then we sat on the bed. I don't know if you started taking off your pants and pulling out your penis and rubbing our hands over it."

"How does someone force someone to masturbate them?"

"By taking their hands and stroking your penis," She's crying now and yelling at him across the room. The microphone only makes the yelling more penetrating.

"Would it be correct to say, and truthful to say, that you were not forced to masturbate me? Is that the truth, Ms. Plaintiff V? Is that the truth?

"Yes, I felt like I was forced."

"Thank you, what? You felt like you were forced, but is it the truth ..."

"You were touching my hands, yes."

"Holding your hand or touching, or forcing someone to masturbate me?"

"You were grabbing both of our hands at the same time and rubbing it on your penis. Doing the motions of jacking you off."

"So you're saying that I was forcing two women, with eight people in the room, to masturbate me? Is that your testimony today? After the allegedly forced masturbation, you got up to get a towel. If you felt like you were a victim, or had been violated in any way, why did you do that?"

"I was stuck in that situation," V said, starting to calm down. "I remember getting you a towel, yes. I don't remember why I did it. I didn't know why I was doing anything that day.

"How much money are you claiming you received for this handjob?"

"One-hundred dollars for both of us."

"Are you a prostitute?"

Objection.

"That's a fair question your honor. If somebody says they were given money for sex ..."

Sidebar.

Pontikes told Smoak that he'd specifically barred Francis from asking these kinds of questions.

"Your cross-examination is now finished," Smoak said.

"Your honor, please ..."

"You abused it."

"Your honor, please let me just ... I won't ..."

Pontikes interrupted, "Your honor, I need to say this for the record. The ruling in this court is that someone who violates Rule 412 is taken into handcuffs."

"No, your honor," Francis was pleading now. "No, your honor, I have not violated 412. Your honor, she said ..."

Pontikes tried to continue, "I'm sorry, I'm talking ..."

But Francis wouldn't let her talk, "I'll ... you have to let me finish this."

"Go sit down," Smoak said to him, and as Francis and Pontikes were walking back to their seats, the judge turned to the jury. "Mr. Francis's cross-examination of this witness has been concluded."

"I'd just like to object for the record," Francis said weakly.

Pontikes, however, had her own issue to bring up. The jurors were sent from the room.

Chapter 41

Contempt

She told Smoak that Francis had violated the 412 rule, preventing litigators in a sex case involving child pornography to go into the plaintiff's sexual history.

She reminded the judge that Francis had brought up this exact point, the issue of prostitution in regards to Plaintiff V, earlier in the week and had been told he could not go into it.

The courtroom had to be cleared of everyone who wasn't involved with the case so they could openly discuss details of the issue, which included examples of Plaintiff V's history. A few minutes later, Francis came out in the hallway to talk to his crew. He had lost all of his usual swagger and looked slightly unsteady on his feet.

Smoak had agreed with Pontikes and found Francis in contempt of court. Those words alone coming out of Smoak's mouth were unnerving for Francis. But Smoak had not ordered him to jail. Instead, the judge had fined him $2,500 to be paid by 8:30 the following morning.

But Francis was obviously shaken. He ordered Steph Watts to immediately begin looking for a lawyer.

The reporters drifted back into the courtroom. When Francis came back in, he looked over and gestured for me to follow him into the hallway.

"You know all the local lawyers, can you get somebody here to take this case?"

"I can make some phone calls."

Lisa Dufort had followed us out.

"Go with David while he makes his calls. Get me somebody here now. As soon as I get a lawyer I'm getting out of here. I am not going back to jail."

After the 412 hearing, he'd told the judge he wouldn't say another word during the trial. He cleared the table of all his files and slumped down into his chair. Alone and defeated.

I went to my truck and got my cellphone. I knew who I wanted to call. I'd known Rachel Seaton-Virga for six years. I was also dating her mother. We'd talked several times about Francis's case over the last few months and I knew that she had an understanding of the issues.

She was also quick on her feet and had the type of situational command that would work well in handling Francis.

"Want a job?" I asked her when she answered her phone.

"What job?"

I couldn't play this out. I had to get to the point.

"Joe Francis needs someone to come out today and take over the case for him. I'm not kidding. You need to give me a flat fee amount that you would do it for."

"I don't know how effective I would be; I don't know enough about the case."

"You don't have to be very effective. I think all they want is for someone to sit through the rest of the trial, try to make the appropriate objections to the plaintiffs' introduction of evidence and do what you can to protect the corporations. They don't expect you to be able to argue the case."

"I don't know what to ask for, how high I should go?"

"Go as high as you want. We'll see what happens."

She threw out a number.

I passed it along to Dufort.

“What about Gerard?” Rachel asked, talking about her husband and law partner.

“The fee would have to cover you both, but sure.”

I told Dufort that the flat fee would buy them two lawyers who could rotate in and cover each other’s cases. That way the office didn’t suffer during the trial.

Dufort walked off quickly to get the message to Francis. She came back with his offer. Half.

It was laughable. And incredible considering the tight spot he was in, but also entirely in character. Terrified of going to jail, he still wanted to lowball the lawyers who would be saving him.

I nearly did laugh, but said, “I’ll pass it along.”

Mantra’s business manager, Eric Deutsch had recently flown in from California and was standing next to me during the phone conversation. He suggested that the number Francis offered could be for just that day and the next, which would be Friday. If the trial went into the next week, they could renegotiate for more money.

“No can do,” Rachel said instantly. She knew Francis’ history with lawyers and she wasn’t going to put herself in a situation where she might be stuck on his case working for free.

The negotiations began. Deutsch strolled away with my phone pressed to his ear, trying to hammer out a price with her.

A few minutes later, they struck a deal. In less than a half hour, the time it took Rachel to change into a suitable outfit for federal court and drive to the courthouse, she became Joe Francis’ latest lawyer.

I stayed downstairs to wait for her so I could make introductions. She pulled into the parking lot with her cellphone pressed to her ear.

Only 30, Rachel had been a lawyer for six years and had never done a civil trial, let alone a federal civil trial. She’d worked a few years at the State Attorney’s Office where she developed a reputation as a hard-nosed trial attorney and a person who had no problem speaking her mind. But whatever she lacked in tact she made up for in loyalty to her clients.

Francis had just left the courtroom for the midmorning break. He trotted down the steps to meet his crew who were talking to Rachel at the door of her Toyota.

He took her elbow and led her away from the SUV, and kept her walking away from the television cameras. They continued to walk until they'd gone around the corner of the old public library across the parking lot. Dufort got in her Grand Caravan to go pick them up.

When they returned, Rachel was fully and easily in charge.

"You're freaking me out a little," she told Francis, who kept trying to lead her around by the elbow and tell her every thought that crossed his mind. "You're going to have to settle down."

When they entered the courtroom, Rachel took the seat that Francis had been sitting in all week. He bounced up from his chair to say something to her, but she did a pushing motion with her right hand and he sat. Good boy.

Smoak entered the courtroom and Francis stood, pointed a finger in the air and said, "Your honor ..."

"No," Rachel said. "You don't speak."

Francis sat.

Rachel introduced herself and said that her husband was e-filing their notice of appearance. She was now the attorney of record on the case.

"We don't want to slow things down. We're ready to proceed."

And the trial went on. The nervous ticks and twitches that plagued Francis earlier in the trial, faded away. He stayed active, leaning over to whisper in Rachel's ear or talk to Steph Watts and Palladino. When Gerard Virga arrived, slipping quietly into the room and sitting to Francis' right, Francis drew him into a long one-sided conversation.

When the lunch break was called, Gerard Virga announced that Francis had decided that he wouldn't be returning to the trial until closing arguments. Francis would remain in the area for consultations.

"We don't have any objection, your honor," McCloy said.

"I have to listen to my counsel," Francis said, making it sound like he was reluctant to leave. "This table isn't big enough for three lawyers."

"By no means do we mean to suggest that we prefer that Mr. Francis was not present," Seaton-Virga said. "Mr. Francis would prefer that he not be present."

"They've told me if they need me they'll let me know. I don't want any more trouble," Francis said.

"Mr. Francis, you understand that you are welcome to return at any time," Smoak said. He was sincere. Despite everything, Smoak was not angry. But the tension that had been on his face all week was gone now as well.

And the trial would change radically from that point on. The Virgas were polite to opposing counsel, made appropriate objections and argued without getting upset.

"What's wrong with these lawyers. Don't they know how to do a proper sidebar?" I joked with News Herald reporter Chris Olwell.

He looked at the quiet debate going on at sidebar. No one was gesturing, no one raising their voices.

"Really," he said, smiling. "I can't hear a damn thing."

The energy level and tension declined throughout the day, lulling Judge Smoak and a juror into a light, often-interrupted sleep by late afternoon.

• • •

After the prostitution question, the jurors had been ushered from the room. They had no idea what was wrong and wouldn't find out until they received all the evidence in the case why Francis had suddenly left. One of the documents they received was the order finding Francis in contempt of court.

But the exchange between Francis and Plaintiff V had shown Juror 6 all she needed to see. When Francis had asked V how much money she wanted in damages, V had looked at Pontikes.

"It was very obvious those girls had been coached," Juror 6 said later.

When Francis had asked V about taking money for the handjob and being a prostitute, then the uproar that followed, all that rang a bell inside Juror 6's mind. She felt like things were being kept from her and it would have been much worse if Francis had not been representing himself.

"That's where he brought things out that probably ... well, I think probably it never would have come out. In that sense in the manner, I think he did himself a justice, not an injustice. He showed someone fighting for themself. I think he's always pretty much gotten what he's wanted, that's my take on it. I sat and I watched him. He was arrogant, but I could read that he was intently nervous. He was up against all these powerful lawyers."

During the many, many sidebar arguments that took place in the four days that Francis represented himself, the jurors would watch closely. Juror 6 said she immediately disliked the way Pontikes acted toward Francis. She felt like Pontikes was looking at Francis as someone who was beneath her, someone she didn't mind being rude to.

"Whether he's a lawyer or he's not a lawyer, you have to be fair," Juror 6 said.

Chapter 42

"Money grubbing whores"

Joe Francis left the courtroom peacefully, but he didn't leave the case quietly.

Outside the courthouse doors, he was intercepted by the reporters.

"I've been representing myself, and I think I was doing a very good job," he said. But, he said, Judge Smoak was out to get him. He said every time he objected, every time he sought to enter evidence, any time he looked to defend himself, "about 20 times a day," Smoak would threaten to lock him up. "He held me in contempt this morning. I can't risk going to jail. I've got too much to lose. This is a good old boy legal system."

He leaned back and ran this next phrase around his mouth before he spat it out.

"These girls are money grubbing whores, and that's what this case is about. Do we reward bad behavior? Should this jury make these girls rich for bad behavior?"

When he had questioned them on the stand, not one of them could tell him how they'd been damaged, he said.

"I'd ask them, 'Why are you suing me?' 'I don't know.' 'You're the plaintiff. You're suing me and you can't explain to the jury?' Two seconds they showed their breasts on GGW and that changed the course of their lives?"

He said he was very happy with his new lawyers.

"They came in and really believe we're gonna win. They came to me through someone in the courtroom and they're into it. Its great."

He said when he went to lunch that day he'd gotten a standing ovation from the crowd in the restaurant "and a bunch of shout-outs."

"The community is behind me, they're not gonna reward these girls for their lies."

The only reason he was leaving was he didn't think he'd get a fair trial.

"I was gonna win this case by myself. I was perfectly capable of winning this case by myself, even with the corrupt nature of the legal system in Bay County."

He said Smoak's finding that he was in contempt of court was unfair. He said he'd asked one plaintiff if she was a prostitute after she admitted taking money for a sex act.

"That was a perfectly legal question."

But the court had found that he violated federal rule 412, which essentially prohibits any evidence of sexual conduct other than what is directly alleged in the complaint.

"I decided to leave instead of going to jail. Joe Francis is not gonna win here."

• • •

Much of the testimony in the afternoon was from former Girls Gone Wild cameramen. They didn't take the stand. The plaintiffs played portions of their videotaped depositions that benefitted their case.

All of them said their orders were to shoot video first and then ask for proof of age.

"What Joe really liked was the spontaneity of the situation. He was the scene master. He was always good at getting a lot of scenes. A lot of girls were a little star struck by him." Bill McCoy said. "He wanted spontaneity. He didn't want to kill the moment with trivial things like age."

Francis had a typical type of girl that he wanted in his videos: blonde, natural breasts, no tattoos. "The girl next door that you'd never expect to do GGW." McCoy said.

"He wasn't interested in the stripper look with breast implants and tattoos and looks like she does that for a living. I think that's what the allure of Girls Gone Wild was."

McCoy said he thought he saw Francis with cocaine on two occasions. Once, he said, he had to pay for it out of the operating budget.

• • •

Former cameraman Mark Schmitz's deposition was being read into the record.

Dent was reading the questions he'd posed to Schmitz and Robert Fleming, a young lawyer in McCloy's firm, was reading Schmitz's part.

Schmitz had said many of the same things McCoy did, but he went a giant step further.

Francis wanted scenes and he preferred young girls.

"The younger the better." If they were minors, Fleming read, Francis would cut the footage and keep it for his private collection.

Did Francis ever tell you what his personal preference was?

"He said he liked 16-year-old blondes," Fleming read, then looked at the jurors.

Chapter 43

"Big. Fat. Mistake"

I left the courtroom at 5 p.m. Angela was taking care of Rachel's two kids, 6-month-old Tre and 23-month-old Vivi while Rachel was in court. I was eager to go see them. I was there when they were both born and they were a big part of my life.

When 5 o'clock came around things were wrapping up and the videotape depositions were pretty boring.

Angela lived two minutes from the courthouse and as I got out of my truck I heard Vivi squeal my name. She was standing at the screen door, her nose flattened and cross-hatched by the screen.

I smiled and felt the day ease out of my muscles. I opened the door and Tre looked up from his play mat. He gave me a grin, which was a big greeting for him.

When Rachel arrived an hour later, she tossed her purse on the counter and walked around the couch to where I was playing with Tre. Each step she took was deliberately slow, but not from fatigue, heal click then toe tap on the floor. She was in trial mode, which meant every conversation was a debate and every encounter would be a confrontation until the trial ended.

"This was a big, fat mistake," she said. "I should never have taken this job. I am so unprepared. We're gonna get our asses handed to us."

"No one expects you to win, Rach. You just have to do your best to make the right objections."

As usual, she acted like I'd never spoken. She didn't go into any situation just to do her best. The only thing that would satisfy her was a win.

"What do you think a win would be in this case?" It wouldn't be the last time she asked that question. "There's no way they're going to give them nothing. Less than a million? Less than a million each?"

Angela didn't want her to talk about the case in front of the kids. Vivi was a word sponge and Rachel had a tendency to use strong language when describing her opponents in a trial.

Vivi picked up descriptive words in a very short time and was excellent at using them at the worst moments. I had to give her credit, though, she put them in sentences where they were supposed to go.

"Big. Fat. Mistake," Rachel said, pointing a finger at me to emphasize each word, and to make it clear that if this went bad it was my fault.

That evening, Rachel and Gerard ordered pizza at the office and met with Eric Deutsch and Steph Watts. Joe Francis had gone to bed early. He was pretty close to a physical collapse by the time he left the courtroom.

Gerard got to work on the first draft of a closing argument. It helped him organize his thoughts and come up with a game plan for the next two days. Gerard's strength was in research. He normally didn't sleep much and would use the quiet hours of the night and early morning to read.

Rachel was far more frenetic. She went into the conference room with Deutsch and bantered with him through what she thought could be his testimony as their only witness. Deutsch learned quickly that if he wanted to make a point with Rachel he had to talk fast and keep it short. She had no interest in listening to lengthy explanations and usually cut people off after five words. It wasn't unusual for her to ask someone a question, listen to 10 seconds of the answer, then interrupt them with another question on another subject.

But she absorbed nearly everything and had perfect recall of information and, more importantly, where the information had come from.

Rachel worked until 1 a.m., then went home to rest. Gerard stayed at the office until 3:30 a.m. They both had bleary, bagged eyes when they came into court the next day.

Chapter 44

"Millions"

Rachel Seaton-Virga stepped off the elevator ahead of Jim Batton, their law clerk, who was towing what documents they had in a bankers box on a dolly.

"So, what do I do?" she said to Batton.

"What do you mean?"

"Do I shake it up? Do I have to pour it over ice?"

"You just drink it. You can shake it up if you want to."

He handed her a tiny black, yellow and red 5-hour Energy bottle.

Rachel took the small bottle and looked at it warily. She began shaking it and looked over at the reporters.

"It's my first. I'm a 5-hour Energy virgin. Ha, I'm glad I'm still a virgin of something."

She twisted the small cap off the tiny plastic bottle and took a tentative sip. She scrunched up her face and handed the bottle to Batton.

"Oh. That's disgusting." She looked like she could barely get the words out.

Batton was laughing. "It's an acquired taste."

"I'm not sure I want to acquire that taste," Rachel said, moving toward the courtroom.

• • •

Michael Burke's face filled the monitors Friday morning. His deposition testimony had been the last evidence Thursday and they picked it up where they'd left off. It was time to talk money.

He was asked if he'd helped prepare the interrogatories that answered the question of how much money GGW had made off the sale of the two videotapes at the center of the trial. They'd netted $7 million between the two of them.

More than 230,000 copies of "Ultimate Spring Break Vol. 3" had been sold worldwide, for a gross of just over $4 million. "Ultimate Spring Break Vol. 4" hadn't done as well, with only 159,000 in distribution for a gross of a little more than $3 million.

Burke said he hadn't participated in preparing the figures, only instructed those who did to compile the numbers as precisely and accurately as possible.

He was not the person to ask if they were, in fact, correct.

Chapter 45

Dr. Leslie Lebowitz

She wasn't tall. She wasn't short. She was pretty, not beautiful, but her makeup was applied to even out, not to enhance her best features. She had thick, wavy brown hair shot with gray and everything about Dr. Leslie Lebowitz spoke softly. Lebowitz was the unobtrusive observer.

Her testimony was the longest of the trial, but essential to understanding how the plaintiffs viewed their encounter with Girls Gone Wild and how they blamed Joe Francis for even the smallest shortcomings of their lives.

Lebowitz, a clinical psychologist who examined all four plaintiffs, took the stand. After going through her qualifications, Pontikes asked her to explain to the ladies of the jury, "How Girls Gone Wild harmed these plaintiffs."

"In my opinion, Girls Gone Wild was like a stone that fell into the center of these women's lives. And like a stone, a big, heavy stone, falling into a pool of water, it initiated a sort of radiating levels of harm that spread from, you know, their sense that they were bad and extended to the destruction of their social world and their relationship with their social community and they just kind of radiated from there."

At first, she said, she didn't think the allegations in this case were too terribly serious. She usually dealt with victims of rape, incest and combat.

"I sort of thought, well, how could this event be so harmful? What could be so harmful about a brief, you know, unpleasant experience? But that was predicated on not really understanding the nature of this particular event.

"When you look at a traumatic event, the question you need to ask is: What was the meaning of this event to this person? So I, you know, came to understand that this was a very different kind of trauma.

Shame was the central theme of Lebowitz's testimony. She distinguished shame from guilt by saying that guilt was a constructive feeling of remorse for one's actions that could be used to promote positive behavior changes.

"Shame is the sense that the self is bad in a way that makes you want to cringe and crawl away and hide yourself. Shame is like a kind of tar that is stuck to you," she patted her chest, over her heart, as if to indicate that the tar was smothering that organ, "that you can't – can't get rid of. And shame is understood in the psychological literature as a really, a really harmful emotion."

Shame, she said, is what all these women were feeling. Shame caused by Girls Gone Wild. Shame was also something their friends, families and communities felt.

In Plaintiff B's case, she said, it had also led to an eating disorder. "She feels like if she doesn't eat, all the loathsome parts of her will just evaporate."

Pontikes asked her what effect being sexually exploited by Girls Gone Wild at the age of 17 had on B.

"It filled her with regret and made her feel that she was loathsome and disgusting. It made her feel a literally toxic level of shame and exposure. It led to her being rejected by her community and lose her social supports and meaningful social contacts. And that led her to feeling a kind of emotional pain which, in the absence of friends and family to turn to, I believe that led her to use drugs and alcohol as a way to soothe that pain. And the whole thing took on an extraordinarily destructive downward spiral, resulting in a nervous breakdown, hospitalizations and a whole host of psychiatric symptoms, many of which are continuing."

"Do you believe to a reasonable degree of medical certainty that being sexually exploited by Girls Gone Wild caused this breakdown of Plaintiff B?" Pontikes asked.

"I guess the other thing that I would say about her nervous breakdown is that, you know, the structure of our lives, school, work, all those routines that not only structure our lives in the world they structure us internally, what happened to Plaintiff B because of the way in which Girls Gone Wild impacted her life is that she lost all the customary structures of her life. At one point she was homeless. She was very nomadic."

She lost jobs and every time she lost a job it made her feelings worse.

"The self hatred, the loss of community the excessive use of drugs and alcohol and the kind of destructuring of her life I think unmoored her to such an extent that a nervous breakdown was the result."

What about the death of B's father? Pontikes asked.

"She was already psychologically devastated by Girls Gone Wild and then she experiences this profound loss. Because she was on the phone with her father, asking to come home because of Girls Gone Wild, and because she already felt like she'd done something terrible and was a bad person, when he died, at an emotional level she came to feel that she had been responsible for his death. While I don't have any question in my mind that this would have always been an incredibly painful loss for her, there's nothing about it that would have led to her, you know, completely falling apart."

Usually, when a child loses a parent the family and community rally around them for support. But B had been ostracized because of her association with Girls Gone Wild and didn't get that support.

"The whole fabric of her life was destroyed."

The sexual incident, Lebowitz said, was not something Plaintiff B would normally do.

"It was a behavior that was completely outside of anything she ever imagined herself doing, anything she would have ever endorsed doing, anything she ever could have, you know, planned to do."

What B needed, what all the girls needed, was a skilled professional to help them through this. A good one, she said, would run about $225 an hour and there shouldn't be a cap on when it should end.

"You know, if somebody else can say to you, 'I see it. I hear it. I know it. This does not have to define you for the rest of your life. You know, it was a momentary – it was a brief mistake that you made when you were 17 years old. You know, you can be a much bigger person than this.'"

• • •

Pontikes moved into the subject of Plaintiff J's suicide attempts.

"Yes, she had two," Lebowitz said. "You want me to talk about them?"

"I was going to ask a question. Just wait for a second," Pontikes said quickly. She then dropped her voice into its slow, midwestern-laced, question-asking tone. "Did the GGW incident, to a reasonable degree of medical certainty, cause these two suicide attempts?"

"I think," Lebowitz said, "but for (the incident with) Girls Gone Wild there was no reason to expect that she would have tried to kill herself twice."

Lebowitz said J was under pressure because her parents were threatening to divorce, but "the kind of shame and guilt and self-condemnation that she's feeling from Girls Gone Wild makes it sort of the straw that breaks the camel's back."

Pontikes moved on to Plaintiff S.

"How is Girls Gone Wild and this Girls Gone Wild event responsible for the very abusive relationship that Plaintiff S found herself in?"

"It's the same link. I mean, Girls Gone Wild caused her to drop out of school, which means she didn't have the same choice of partners. It made her needy and alone and desperate and a target. And it made her a good target for somebody looking to prey on a woman who could be controlled and dominated."

"What Girls Gone Wild stole from them was the most valuable resources that a young woman has going forward: friends, family and education."

Chapter 46

The Key

The reporters and lawyers filed out into the hallway for the lunch break and most left to grab some food. I stayed behind to talk to Rachel Seaton-Virga. She'd gone into the room that was set aside as their base of operations, but came out after a few minutes.

"Did they think we wouldn't find it?" she asked as she walked up to me. I had been standing at my favorite spot, the second-floor window that overlooked the bay.

"Find what?"

She didn't answer that. It had something to do with the medical records.

"Did they really think we wouldn't find it?"

"Yes, Rachel, whatever it is, I'm certain they didn't think you would find it."

I'd seen her like this before. She was committed, not because of Joe Francis, but because she felt personally insulted. Whatever was in those records was good and Rachel was going to have fun.

I walked over to my favorite lunch spot, around the corner from the courthouse. On the way I noticed I'd missed a call from Angela, Rachel's mother.

"I assume you're calling to find out when a good time is to come to the trial?"

"Actually, I was just calling to find out how it was going."

Angela did want to come out, though.

"After lunch would be an excellent time; Rachel is going to eviscerate a psychologist."

"Really?"

"She found something. I don't know what it is, but she's all fired up."

• • •

Rachel Seaton-Virga was huddled with Gerard at the table when Angela and I walked into the courtroom after lunch. They were both flipping through the thick volumes of records pertaining to a different plaintiff.

Usually, Rachel doesn't like it when Angela comes to court to watch her, but this time she was too distracted to do anything more than give her mom a smile.

Pontikes resumed her questioning after the jurors were brought in. She asked Lebowitz if she'd watched Joe Francis' cross examination of V.

"What did I observe during the cross-examination?" Lebowitz asked. "She came into that with every intention of maintaining a perfect composure. She did not actually want to give him the satisfaction of becoming distraught. His aggression, his insinuation that the fact that she may or may not have thought he was handsome was somehow responsible for what subsequently happened, her feeling of inadequacy because she couldn't remember certain trivial details, which were actually pretty unimportant and pretty validating of the fact that she has been traumatized because people who have been traumatized can never remember unimportant details, it's part of the nature of traumatic memory."

I don't know when this woman breathes, I thought to myself while I struggled to take notes.

"Watching her be so activated by her exposure to him that she absolutely could not maintain composure spoke to the way in which that prior exposure lives inside of her in a form that, when it is triggered or activated, it begins to feel just the way it did the first time it happened," Lebowitz continued. "You know, afterwards, I left when she left to try to check in with her and she was so hysterical. It was probably 45 minutes before I think she could hear anything I was saying, but what she kept repeating over and over again was, 'I feel like I'm such a bad person. I want to die now.'"

Lebowitz said in V's mind she'd taken responsibility for what happened that day because Joe Francis refused to.

"This is one of the tragedies that you see anytime somebody has been victimized, you know, wherein they take undue responsibility."

Children, she said, must have a sense of moral completeness in their world. If something bad happens, someone must be held accountable. If an adult will not accept the blame then the child accepts it to compensate.

"He's the grownup," Lebowitz said of Francis.

I nearly laughed out loud. I was sure that was the first time Francis had been accused of that.

Plaintiff V had been particularly vulnerable to Francis' charms and had suffered in a unique way. She wasn't traumatized by a video image that was out in the public, because her footage had been intercepted by authorities and never released. V, however, was traumatized by the *fear* that someone would find out about the footage and about what she'd done.

Because V's father had been physically abusive to her, and her mother had died about a month before the Girls Gone Wild encounter, she was an "easy target" for Francis and his crew.

Lebowitz said V had struggled with many of Francis' questions because she believed that he really wanted an answer to them.

"But that isn't actually what was happening. He was not earnestly seeking the truth in that encounter. He was trying to make his case. I mean, he was engaged in an adversarial process. And even though she knew that intellectually, emotionally when she couldn't make herself heard, when minor details got picked upon as if the implication being that somehow she was being unclear, it all went right inside and she came away saying, 'I'm a bad person. I knew I was a bad person, now I'm really a bad person and I need to die.'

"So, I'm not sure if I answered your whole question, but that's some of what I observed."

Pontikes asked her to explain the "power differential that Plaintiff V felt in what you observed in this courtroom. How do you think Mr. Francis' celebrity status and his power play into that power that Plaintiff V feels that he has over her?"

"Just enormously."

What V was especially upset about were Francis' questions about why she'd brought him a towel after he forced her to masturbate him.

Lebowitz said V's concern for Francis after the incident was a sign that Francis had captured her mentally. "His size, his looks, his celebrity status, money, all of those things enhanced his stature to the point where (Plaintiff V) was psychologically captured by him."

Rachel Seaton-Virga leaned toward Gerard and, in a whisper, said, "I bet she says something about Stockholm Syndrome next."

"You know, we see it when people are literally taken hostage, as in the Stockholm Syndrome," Lebowitz said.

Seaton-Virga smiled behind her hand and leaned back toward Gerard, "Told you."

Pontikes asked how V was harmed.

Lebowitz said V was traumatized by the fear that people would find out what had happened, would then reject her and she would live her life alone.

"It led her to cling to the man that she was involved with at that time for fear that she couldn't imagine that anybody else would ever accept her."

That's why the breakup and attempted suicide were Girls Gone Wild's fault.

According to Lebowitz, all of the girls could benefit from consistent, long term counseling. But it would be bad to put a timeframe on that counseling. It should be for as long as the girls needed it to be.

Lebowitz then began to talk about how the girls would benefit from a verdict that included significant amount of money for punitive damages.

"They all wish that they could prevent other people from being harmed. They all, like all victims of all kinds of interpersonal traumas, they long for some kind of measure of justice.

"The problem with being exploited or taken advantage of or diminished is it makes you feel small. It makes you feel less than. What justice does is it, you know, it's a moment in which, you know, in which the community basically says to the victim, 'To the best of our ability, we're going to give you back some of what was taken from you because we agree that a wrong was committed. And we're going to try to restore something to you symbolically.'

"But, you know, he can't be shut down and he's not going to apologize. So, in the absence of that, you know, the closest they get to justice is the hope that money could draw some kind of boundary on his bullying behavior. You know, bullies will bully until somebody stops them. Being forced to pay for what you've done is, you know, a potential border. It signifies to them that somebody in the community agrees that a wrong has been done and that amends should be made. So, psychologically, I think it would mean a lot to them.

"You know, one of the things that they all experienced is the sense of being cast out and thrown away."

Seaton-Virga stood, "Judge, I would like to object to narrative."

Overruled.

Lebowitz, who had stopped speaking but stayed in the same position, as if someone had a hit a pause button, resumed as if Seaton-Virga had never spoken. "And one of the things that I believe all victims who have been interpersonally injured need is some kind of path back into the human, into society, back into the human fold, some sense that they are welcome back.

"So when, you know, the community in whatever way is possible says, 'You know what, we agree that was wrong, that shouldn't have happened and we're going to put something behind it to really, to really represent our belief that, you know, teenagers and girls should not be exploited in these ways.' It's kind of like saying to the victims, 'You can come back now, you know. We see that injustice was done and we're going to extend a hand that leaves you more included and less cast out.' Yeah."

Pontikes asked her why this wasn't a case about rewarding the girls for "bad behavior."

Lebowitz crossed her arms as if the question was personally insulting.

"If you want to call what they did bad behavior, which I will argue with in a moment, but if you want to call what they did bad behavior I think they've been adequately punished for it and then some.

"You know, in terms of rewarding bad behavior, my understanding, you know, and I don't have independent knowledge of this, but my understanding is that, you know, Mr. Francis made, through his company, made $17 million on the release of these videos."

Seaton-Virga stood, causing Lebowitz to pause again, and said, "Judge, again, I object to foundation and hearsay."

Overruled.

"Now that's a reward for bad behavior," Lebowitz continued. "Also, in terms of it being bad behavior, I mean I think the way I think about it is that, you know, you know, they made the, you know, they were young and they were manipulated. And within that vortex of vulnerability they made a mistake. They did something they regretted, that's all.

"In the litany of things that human beings do to each other that constitutes bad behavior that's pretty low down on my list. And if I compare that to having a professional commitment to mainstreaming pornography into popular culture, to trying to make the degradation of young women so normal that it becomes increasingly difficult even to figure out what you're supposed to do. I mean, when I think about a life enterprise that consists of waking up in the morning and seeing how many girls you can get to do something they really don't want to do and how much you can lower the bar, I actually think that's bad behavior."

Chapter 47

Medical Records

Rachel and Gerard Virga stayed seated at the defense table after Pontikes ended her questioning of Lebowitz. They huddled over one of four white jacketed binders, each about three inches thick. Rachel took an extra second, then took the binder and approached the podium.

Gerard had prepared two sets of questions for her. Rachel's cross-examination would hinge on whether Lebowitz admitted reading the medical records and using them in forming her opinion. She said under direct examination that her methodology was simply to talk to her subjects.

Seaton-Virga approached the podium and told Lebowitz good afternoon.

"You don't like Joe Francis or Girls Gone Wild, do you?"

"I don't."

"You find it personally offensive, don't you, to women such as yourself?"

"I don't feel personally at risk."

"I didn't ask if you felt at risk, I asked ..."

"Do I find it offensive?"

"...if you find it personally offensive."

"I do."

"You come into it with certain perceptions that may affect your ability to render an unbiased medical opinion in this case?"

"I actually came into this case with no opinion."

"OK. Let's talk about the basis of your opinion. You've reviewed all of the evidence in this case?"

"I've reviewed the evidence available to me."

"What evidence was available to you?"

"Medical records."

"So you're familiar with the medical records of these victims," Rachel said, waving at the thick binders on the table in front of Gerard. "You've reviewed the records on some of these involuntary commitments?"

"Yes I have."

"Have you also reviewed their previous testimony in the form of deposition testimony?"

"I have."

"You've reviewed hundreds of pages of documentation?" Rachel gave a small laugh, like they were sharing a joke.

"Yeah."

"Right here I have four binders with what I believe is, at best, the majority of their testimony and medical history. You've reviewed at least that much?"

"Yes."

"Then let's talk about what you didn't mention to the jury when you reviewed their medical documents. Let's start with ... why don't you tell the jury what bipolar disorder is."

Lebowitz went into a description of a disorder that is characterized by drastic emotional highs and lows.

When Plaintiff B was institutionalized in March of 2004 she was having a nervous breakdown, Lebowitz said, and was ultimately diagnosed as bipolar.

"When she was admitted, she was having grandiose delusions?"

"Yes."

"Hallucinations? She said she was seeing ghosts and dead people?"

"Yes."

She said she was a designer for Guess Jeans?

"She told a variety of bizarre and delusional things. The evidence is pretty clear that she was psychotic."

What is psychotic?

"When you've really broken with reality."

Lebowitz said Plaintiff B was acting, in common terms, "crazy, and what we used to call a 'nervous breakdown.'"

"Actually, you called it a nervous breakdown today. So what is the clinical term for it? You said you used to call it a nervous breakdown. So what do we call it these days? Is it a psychotic episode?"

"A brief psychotic episode is a formal diagnosis. I didn't, you know, diagnose her at that time. Nervous breakdown is just sort of a colloquial phrase that captures a gamut of a sort of psychiatric collapse. That's just being the broadest possible term."

Lebowitz said that while others had diagnosed B as bipolar, which is characterized by periods of mania punctuated with poor-decision making, she did not believe that B was bipolar.

"When people don't know somebody's been traumatized, which happens all the time because people are ashamed or they don't think to say or people don't think to ask, then this sort of florid disorder is often thought to be something else and bipolar is one of the things that people have historically been misdiagnosed with," Lebowitz said. "That said, I do think she was psychotic at the time."

"Are you suggesting," Seaton-Virga began, "that the other doctors, the numerous other doctors who have previously diagnosed her as bipolar are incorrect and that it was in fact this traumatic incident that is masquerading as bipolar disorder?"

"I didn't interview her at the time so I can't, you know, retrospectively diagnose her."

But two things made her think that B was not bipolar. The first was the "historical fact that people are diagnosed with all sorts of things when trauma is kind of the unrecognized core."

B also hadn't showed any signs of bipolar in years.

Seaton-Virga turned to a tabbed page in her binder. B was hospitalized for a month and during that time, she spoke with numerous mental health professionals.

"Licensed professionals, I'm sure, doctors and, perhaps not of your caliber but certainly capable of making these determinations, and is there anywhere in those doctors' notes where she indicated anything about Girls Gone Wild or any sort of trauma related to Girls Gone Wild or Joe Francis?"

"I agree with you," Lebowitz said. "People don't talk about what they're ashamed of."

"Right. Not until they're suing someone."

The comment came out a little sharper than Seaton-Virga intended and actually drew a gasp from one of the jurors.

Jury, meet Rachel Seaton-Virga, I thought with a smile.

Pontikes objected, but Lebowitz answered anyway.

"No, that's not actually true. People don't talk about what they're ashamed of until all sorts of things happen: they think that they might get a sympathetic hearing; they feel like the shame has devastated their life for so long that they're like, you know, they can make a different step."

Lebowitz said she'd treated military veterans who didn't disclose their deepest shame until 10, 20, 30 years after the fact.

Seaton-Virga leafed through the binder on the podium. "When she met with a counselor she seemed to focus on the death of her father."

Lebowitz said mental health services at hospitals were primarily concerned with prescribing the right drugs to suppress the problem and send the patient out the door. There was little effort, she said, to get to the root of the problem.

"Saying that her father died is a non-shaming non-humiliating way to account for some of the stress."

But, Seaton-Virga persisted, when B's mother met with these counselors during one of B's commitments, she didn't say anything about GGW either. The mother, who by this time knew about the filming, told the counselors that her husband's death was probably the primary cause of B's breakdown.

B's mother was experiencing the same shame her daughter was, Lebowitz said. It was more salient for her to say her husband's death was the cause of her daughter's breakdown, instead of the girl's participation in a pornographic film.

How long did you examine B?

"I met with her twice and spoke with her on the phone."

"Can you estimate a total amount of time?"

Fourteen to 20 hours.

And in 14 to 20 hours, you were able to get her to open up to you where the other professionals had failed?

She was an expert on trauma. The other psychologists were not. And B was unwilling to face her real problems early on.

"Did you confer with any of these other doctors that diagnosed her?"

"No, I did not."

"Is that something that could have assisted you in your diagnosis?"

"I think those doctors were dealing with what was right in front of them and without knowing precisely what kind of drugs she was taking and without knowing the big picture, they made a completely plausible diagnosis."

"At what point did, this is going to sound facetious but, for lack of a better word, this epiphany that the root of her problems or her issues was the incident in 2002? At what point did she have that, I guess, breakthrough?"

"I think she always knew, absolutely, that that was there. I think it was a just a long time before she did anything about it."

"What was the trigger in her particular case?"

"I don't think I know the answer to that."

When B was hospitalized, it was recommended at that time that she engage in counseling, but she chose not to. Lebowitz blamed that on poor health insurance in America.

"Do you have any reason to believe at this point that she was not insured when they offered her those services?"

"I don't think she was."

"You know that she wasn't or you don't think she was?"

"I don't think. I don't know for sure."

Seaton-Virga walked B's file to the table and took V's file out of Gerard's outstretched hand. Before she got into specifics, though, she asked Lebowitz about the tests the plaintiffs had taken. The test that had shown that they weren't lying and weren't exaggerating their problems.

"These are standardized tests? They don't have any questions on them about this particular case?"

In other words, the test showed the girls weren't lying about the answers they'd given on the test, not necessarily about the allegations they were making.

"No, no, no. It's a standardized test," Lebowitz said.

Seaton-Virga had V's file open and referenced her involuntary commitment to a mental facility in May 2003 after a suicide attempt. At that time, she said her mother's death and the fact that her father had already moved his new girlfriend into their home were the cause of her breakdown.

Lebowitz asked if that was the first or the second suicide attempt. Seaton-Virga flipped through some pages and said it appeared to be the second one. She'd apparently been hospitalized in February 2003 after her first suicide attempt.

Neither Seaton-Virga nor Lebowitz seemed to realize that the February suicide attempt happened before she met Joe Francis.

Seaton-Virga pointed out in the file that V had said the February suicide attempt was because her boyfriend was "hanging out with his ex-girlfriend."

"It was motivated out of anger, not depression, anger with her father and of course the death of her mother," Seaton-Virga told Lebowitz, reading from the doctor's notes.

"I think she was undoubtedly very angry with her father," Lebowitz said. "I think she was in grief about her mother. I think she was in shame. I think there were a lot of things on her plate."

Lebowitz didn't elaborate on what V was ashamed of prior to her Girls Gone Wild incident.

Plaintiff V went to counseling and at no time did she bring up Joe Francis or Girls Gone Wild as being a problem.

"I do not find that to be inconsistent in any way with what we know about sexual trauma," Lebowitz said calmly.

They moved on again, this time to Plaintiff J.

Plaintiff J was involuntarily committed in March 2003 and June 2004, both times after suicide attempts. In both instances, she'd told the doctors that problems with her boyfriend led to the suicide attempts.

Seaton-Virga asked Lebowitz if she'd read in the file where J had supposedly tried to kill herself on one of these occasions by overdosing on Benedryl?

Pontikes stood and objected. At sidebar she told Smoak that she'd been willing to give Seaton-Virga some leeway in her cross-examination, but she didn't think it was appropriate to have these unauthenticated medical records read line-by-line into the record.

"Were these records part of what she reviewed?" Smoak asked.

"That is correct and she somehow glossed over some of these details when she was testifying on direct about these suicide attempts and their origins," Seaton-Virga said.

"That's clearly not a, that's clearly a mischaracterization of her testimony," Pontikes said.

"None of this came out on direct," Seaton-Virga stressed. "I'm simply trying to get to the basis of her opinion and how she formed her opinion and whether or not these things played in the formation of that particular opinion that everything leads back to Girls Gone Wild."

"These are records that she did review?" Smoak asked again.

"That is correct."

"I'm going to overrule the objection."

The sidebar broke up and Seaton-Virga returned to the podium.

In both hospitalizations, Plaintiff J had said nothing about flashing for Girls Gone Wild?

"You don't talk about what you're ashamed of."

J had blamed her suicide attempt on a fight with a boyfriend.

"You would agree with me," Seaton-Virga said to Lebowitz, "that young love can be very tumultuous."

"I would, but I would also argue that young love, in the absence of other serious stressors or vulnerabilities doesn't result in suicide attempts."

"She didn't indicate any other stressors in her life at that time did she?"

"There's nothing in the medical records."

In June 2004, J was hospitalized again after overdosing on drugs. She again blamed a breakup with a boyfriend.

"And, again, she also indicated that she had not been suffering from any depressed mood," Seaton-Virga pointed out.

"Right. Given that she took a near lethal dose of drugs you would at least want to question that."

"Do you recall in reviewing her medical history, particularly in the June 2004 commitment in Bay Behavioral, that she indicated that she didn't feel like she could talk to her mother? And that she would like to? And that her mother probably would not do that?"

"She felt like she had really let her mother down. She felt like, you know, that day that they went to Panama City Beach, it was really over the mother's pretty strenuous hesitation. She was very concerned about her two teenage girls going over there and the mom had been kind of pressured and she had let them go. Plaintiff J felt very guilty and very badly about, essentially, you know, in exchange for her mother's trust doing something that had been so bad. It drove a wedge between her and her mother."

Pontikes stood and objected.

"On what basis?" Smoak asked.

"On the basis we discussed at the sidebar."

"Relevancy? What?"

"Let's come up," Pontikes said, indicating she'd like a sidebar.

"I think she's objecting to the form of the question," Seaton-Virga volunteered. "So let me rephrase. Am I right Ms. Pontikes?"

Pontikes did not answer her and only asked again for a sidebar.

At sidebar, Smoak told her he'd like a little head's up next time.

"All I ask is that you give me a code word like 'form', 'relevance' or something like that so I can be shaking the cobwebs out while you're coming up here."

"I'm sorry, your honor," Pontikes said, "I wasn't sure what the code word should be here."

"I was thinking you thought form," Seaton-Virga volunteered again, "because of the ..."

"Just let me state the objection," Pontikes cut her off. "Because of the discussion we had, basically instead of having the opportunity to publish these records, which would require authentication and the defendants identifying them in the pretrial order, we're going line by line with the medical records to get them into evidence through our expert."

"If I may, judge," Seaton-Virga said, "she's indicated this was part of the basis of her opinion. I'm just inquiring as to whether or not these things were taken into consideration when she made the determination that GGW was responsible for these girls' damages."

"As I understand correctly," Smoak said, "these were part of her review."

"She did review them, your honor," Pontikes said. "She hasn't testified they were the basis of her opinion. She did review them."

"Then I think it's proper to question her about them," Smoak said.

"In a line-by-line basis?"

"I think a little bit of that has gone a long way, quite frankly," Smoak said. "It might be a little better to get a little more focused and get to where you're going. Keep in mind that we're getting into late Friday afternoon."

The sidebar ended and Seaton-Virga returned to the podium. She returned to the subject of Plaintiff J's stated reasons for trying to commit suicide: her boyfriends.

"I think it was one of the hospitalizations," Lebowitz said in response, "where her counselor was a male. In the groups they were in, they were encouraged to focus on – they were not encouraged to talk about their feelings. They were not encouraged to talk about the etiology of their problems. And, more to the point, saying I'm having relationship problems is socially acceptable. Saying that, you know, I've been in pornography is something that they were – you don't talk about what you're ashamed about."

"Did you confer with any of these doctors about their treatment programs and their groups?"

"I did not."

"So you didn't have any professional conversations with these treating physicians?"

"No, I did not."

On to Plaintiff S.

Plaintiff S failed the ninth grade before she flashed.

"Was that Joe Francis' fault too? Was Plaintiff S skipping school in the ninth grade his fault? I'm assuming that you don't find it unusual that none of these women indicated to the medical personnel and the psychiatrists and the doctors that evaluated them prior to this lawsuit that they never disclosed anything about Girls Gone Wild or the issues they faced because of it."

"I don't find that remarkable, no."

"Some of these issues that some of these young ladies faced as children, be it alcoholism, fighting parents, child abuse, those don't play a role in any of their issues either?"

"I'm not saying that."

"Should the father who abused his child, should he be punished financially and fined?"

"It would be a nice thing if he took some responsibility for what he had done."

"Do you know whether he has?"

"I think they have reached a more peaceful place. In an ideal world, everybody who does something that harms somebody would, you know, fix it or make amends or say they were sorry. It's not every day that somebody profits so remarkably from the harm they have caused."

"I guess it depends on what you classify as profit. Certainly, the father that is beating his child is reaping some sort of reward for that."

"I don't know that I could speak to that one way or the other."

Pontikes stood and objected to the line of questioning. Smoak sustained the objection and Seaton-Virga moved on.

"Would you disagree with me that there are thousands, perhaps tens of thousands of women that have performed in some way or exposed themselves in some way to these cameras?"

"I wouldn't disagree."

"Do you believe that all of these women have been traumatized?"

"No."

You said you thought all these girls would benefit from therapy?

Yes.

"All these young ladies were given the opportunity for counseling and only one opted to pursue treatment."

Pontikes objected, saying Seaton-Virga was assuming facts not in evidence.

"You've read the medical documents?" Seaton-Virga asked Lebowitz.

"Uh-huh."

"In that document, those doctors recommend continued treatment?"

"Uh-huh, some of them did that."

"And only one of these young ladies opted to pursue treatment."

Pontikes objected again. Smoak called a sidebar.

"What's the basis for that objection?" the judge asked.

"I know that counsel's new in the case, but the medical records, although they say 'treatment' it was drug treatment, not counseling."

"Actually," Seaton-Virga said, "it refers to counseling and I'll be happy to show that to counsel."

"This is again using the medical records as if they were admitted as exhibits and they're before the court. I have given counsel a lot of leeway on the medical records," Pontikes said.

"I'm letting her use it on cross-examination only," Smoak said. "They were part of what (Lebowitz) did review." He brought up Seaton-Virga's specific question that Pontikes had objected to and asked Seaton-Virga for some clarification.

"She's conferred with each of these young women. She's reviewed the reports. It's clear in these medical records that they suggest ongoing counseling. I mean it actually refers to counseling."

"I would like to see that," Pontikes said.

"I'll be happy to show it to you."

"I'm going to allow that question, if this is the only one that sought treatment."

Seaton-Virga went back to the podium and asked the question again. This time, Lebowitz disagreed with her about who sought counseling. She said she thought both S and J met with counselors.

"So, Plaintiff J and Plaintiff S have already sought counseling?" Seaton-Virga asked.

"Uh-huh."

"And they did not disclose that to their therapist?"

"Plaintiff J definitely didn't. I don't recall if Plaintiff S mentioned it or not. I don't think so."

"Did you talk to their counselor?"

"No."

"Is there a reason you didn't talk with any of these treating physicians or these counselors?"

"There wasn't a burning question that it would have answered for me."

"Is that because you had already made up your mind that this was all Joe Francis' fault?"

"No. Because it's not clear to me what question it might have answered. I didn't disbelieve that these women had gotten into psychiatric trouble and had been in the presence of medical professionals and had not disclosed the kind of information that, you know, would have been helpful."

"But, miraculously, at the time it was time for you to meet with them, someone they never met, they all disclosed the trauma they had faced with Girls Gone Wild?"

Pontikes objected, but Smoak overruled.

"They disclosed it to you," Seaton-Virga persisted. "They were able to somehow find the wherewithal to disclose it to you but to none of these medical professionals?"

"Yes. It's not at all unusual in my field, particularly when you have a specialty in trauma. I'm not suggesting there's anything miraculous about me as a therapist. What is true is that if people are deeply ashamed about something, they tell it to the person

– if they're going to tell it to anybody, they tell it to somebody who they believe will receive it in a compassionate way. It happens all the time that people have not disclosed things in spite of not just a brief encounter with mental health professionals. And it isn't until they meet somebody who they believe really will get it that somehow the story is made available."

"And apparently with you they believed it right away, that you would get it."

"Well, they knew what I was there to do. I mean, they already had – they knew that I was a trauma person. They knew that I had experience with sexually victimized women, so they had a reason to expect a compassionate hearing."

"They knew that this case was about Girls Gone Wild," Seaton-Virga said, driving home the point. "You talked with them after suit had already been filed?"

"Yes."

"So they knew what this was about and what your purpose was?"

"Yes, yes, absolutely."

"That's why it didn't make it relevant that, you know, those other doctors had evaluated them within a couple years after this happening: those opinions didn't matter," Seaton-Virga said. "What mattered was Girls Gone Wild?"

Pontikes objected and Smoak sustained it. "Let's get on to something of substance."

Seaton-Virga asked Lebowitz if she'd looked at the qualifications of any of the other doctors that had treated the girls, "or whether or not they would be compassionate?"

"No. I don't mean to suggest they weren't compassionate professionals."

"Is that maybe why one of the plaintiff's mothers who was aware of the trauma history didn't bring it up to the doctors then? Did she feel that person wasn't going to be compassionate?"

Smoak interrupted, without an objection from Pontikes, and called the lawyers to sidebar.

"I do not see how this is going to help the jury," he said about Seaton-Virga's line of questions. "We are running late on a Friday afternoon and I think the jury is going to get numb with much more of this fairly obtuse bit of questioning about communication with the people – I mean, you know, if we push this. I'm going to probably get pushed to instruct her that it would be – it is not common practice by a retained expert to communicate with treating physicians."

"I would like that instruction now, your honor. I was about to get up and object. I think this line of questioning has gotten argumentative," Pontikes said. "It isn't common practice for experts to communicate with treating physicians."

"My old hero, Irving Younger, said about cross-examination you pick your one best topic, two at the most, and this is sort of turning into a discovery exercise. So please, let's get on to something productive," Smoak told Seaton-Virga.

Pontikes asked for the instruction that Smoak had mentioned earlier, but the judge ignored her.

Back at the podium, Seaton-Virga asked Lebowitz her last question.

"Doctor, is it fair to say that, based on your informed medical opinion, that the source of a lot of the issues that these young women have faced is due to Girls Gone Wild?"

"That would be accurate."

Seaton-Virga gathered up her notes and sat down.

Pontikes tried to repair the damage, but ended up asking a lot of the same questions and getting the same answers. Lebowitz said the word "shame" more than a dozen times as she answered Pontikes' last few questions.

Why didn't B, J and V talk about Girls Gone Wild in their prior encounters with mental health professionals?

"Because they were ashamed. People don't easily talk about things they are ashamed about."

And Plaintiff J failing the ninth grade, what could account for that?

"She said she had a really sexually creepy male gym teacher. So she failed gym and decided that, rather than going to summer school, she would just repeat ninth grade."

Chapter 48

"Tactical disaster"

Rachel Seaton-Virga worked until 6:30 Friday night, but picked up the kids after that. She wasn't going to pull another all-nighter.

"Lebowitz killed us," she said, sounding well past the point of exhaustion.

"Are you kidding me? She was awful. She was a tactical disaster. I guarantee you she did more for you than she did for the plaintiffs," I said.

"You think so? I don't know. She had an answer for everything."

"That's exactly it. If the video was released, they were traumatized by the release of the video. If the video was seized, they were traumatized by fear that the video would be released. Plaintiff B was diagnosed with bi-polar, but they're wrong and I'm right.

"And what was all this crap about a 'nervous breakdown'? No one uses that phrase anymore."

"Right. It's a psychotic episode or a psychotic break."

"The only reason she was using it was because it sounded better. It fit her theory better than saying B had a psychotic break. She had a 'nervous breakdown'. She obviously had an agenda.

"And the jurors smelled it. They don't want someone to come in there and manipulate them. They want someone to tell them, this plaintiff has this symptom or had this happen to her and you can reasonably say that a part of her problem was GGW."

"And what was that catch line she kept saying, 'To a reasonable degree of medical certainty'? What the fuck does that even mean?" Rachel was getting into it now, smiling and warming to the topic.

She didn't believe that Lebowitz's testimony would help her, but she was enjoying the witness bashing just the same. She wasn't going to feel good about anything until the trial was over.

"You gonna work all weekend?"

"On what? We don't have anything."

This was a first. Rachel and Gerard had never gone into trial and not worked 18-hour days before and during. They couldn't help it. They couldn't separate themselves from the argument, from the competition. And while Rachel was beginning to feel a creeping indignation, that low, persistent protectiveness toward Francis that she felt with most of her clients, she just didn't have the reports, depositions and documents that would have absorbed her during a normal trial. They were waiting for the plaintiffs' testimony to be transcribed so they could start working on their closing.

Francis was on his way to a benefit dinner in Miami and she'd heard very little from him all day. She was beginning to think that he wasn't such a bad client.

Chapter 49

It was Monday, the beginning of the second week of trial. Rachel Seaton-Virga, Gerard Virga and Jim Batton walked in to the courtroom together. Rachel stopped just through the gate, before she'd even put her files down.

"Did you bring it?"

"It's out in the car," Batton said.

"Out in the car? How does that help me?"

"I'll go get it."

She looked over at the reporters. "It's my second day of 5-hour Energy and I'm hooked. I can't get enough."

She laughed.

"I still can only drink a half a bottle."

• • •

Larry Selander approached the podium and told Judge Smoak that they had two more video depositions to play and then their paralegal, Victoria Ter Bush, was going to testify about a summary she'd compiled explaining GGW's financial gain in selling the videos.

Gerard Virga stood and said he believed the plaintiffs would have to submit all the documentation used to compile the summation.

Selander disagreed and Smoak overruled Virga's objection. The financial data would come in basically unchallenged.

But before that happened, the plaintiffs would like to show the jury the interview that Francis gave Thursday morning as he was leaving the courthouse. They'd subpoenaed the footage from Channel 13 News.

Francis's "money-grubbing whores" comment was the only thing they were really interested in.

Smoak had seen it and denied their request. What he'd said outside the courtroom wasn't much different from what he'd said inside the courtroom. But he did issue an order preventing any of the parties from making derogatory comments about the plaintiffs, or opposing counsel, for the rest of the trial.

Joe Francis was going to have to stay quiet or face serious sanctions from Smoak. There had been little threat of Francis going to jail during this trial, other than watching the proceedings from a holding cell at the federal courthouse. But this order could change that.

Otherwise, the trial was on track to wrap up soon.

Selander believed they would finish that day and Seaton-Virga said they would have one witness and then they would have to address the issue of whether the Girls Gone Wild footage of the plaintiffs would be allowed in as evidence.

That argument was to take place later. Smoak was eager to bring in the jury and get things moving. When the jury was finally brought in, the plaintiffs played a portion of a video deposition of Donald Guttman, Francis' former corporate attorney.

It was a somewhat awkward deposition. Guttman didn't want to answer their questions because he felt that his answers would violate the attorney-client privilege.

What they got out of him, essentially, was that he'd never told Francis it was all right to videotape underage girls and that there were many videotapes from GGW's early years that didn't have the paperwork required by federal law to prove that the girls depicted were adults.

Dent, who had questioned Guttman during the deposition, asked him why he'd left the company, which Virga objected to. The implication was that Guttman had resigned for ethical reasons.

Selander's paralegal, Victoria Ter Bush was the last witness on the stand. She explained her summary that showed GGW had made $17 million off the sale of the three videos at issue in this trial.

That was based off the number of videos that GGW's records showed had been shipped. She estimated the dollar amount off the usual price per video of about $19.99. The attorneys had complained last year that they couldn't get the exact amount because they didn't know if any of the videos had been discounted or sold as a package with other tapes.

But there was little that the Virgas could do to challenge the number.

Ter Bush then said that GGW had made more than $160 million in profit off the sale of all the videos that had been found to be in violation of the federal compliance law. The gross was closer to $330 million. And that was just off the 150 or so titles that were on the list and not the hundreds of "Girls Gone Wild" videos that were in compliance with federal law.

She was done and the Virgas had no questions for her.

Selander announced that the plaintiffs rested their case.

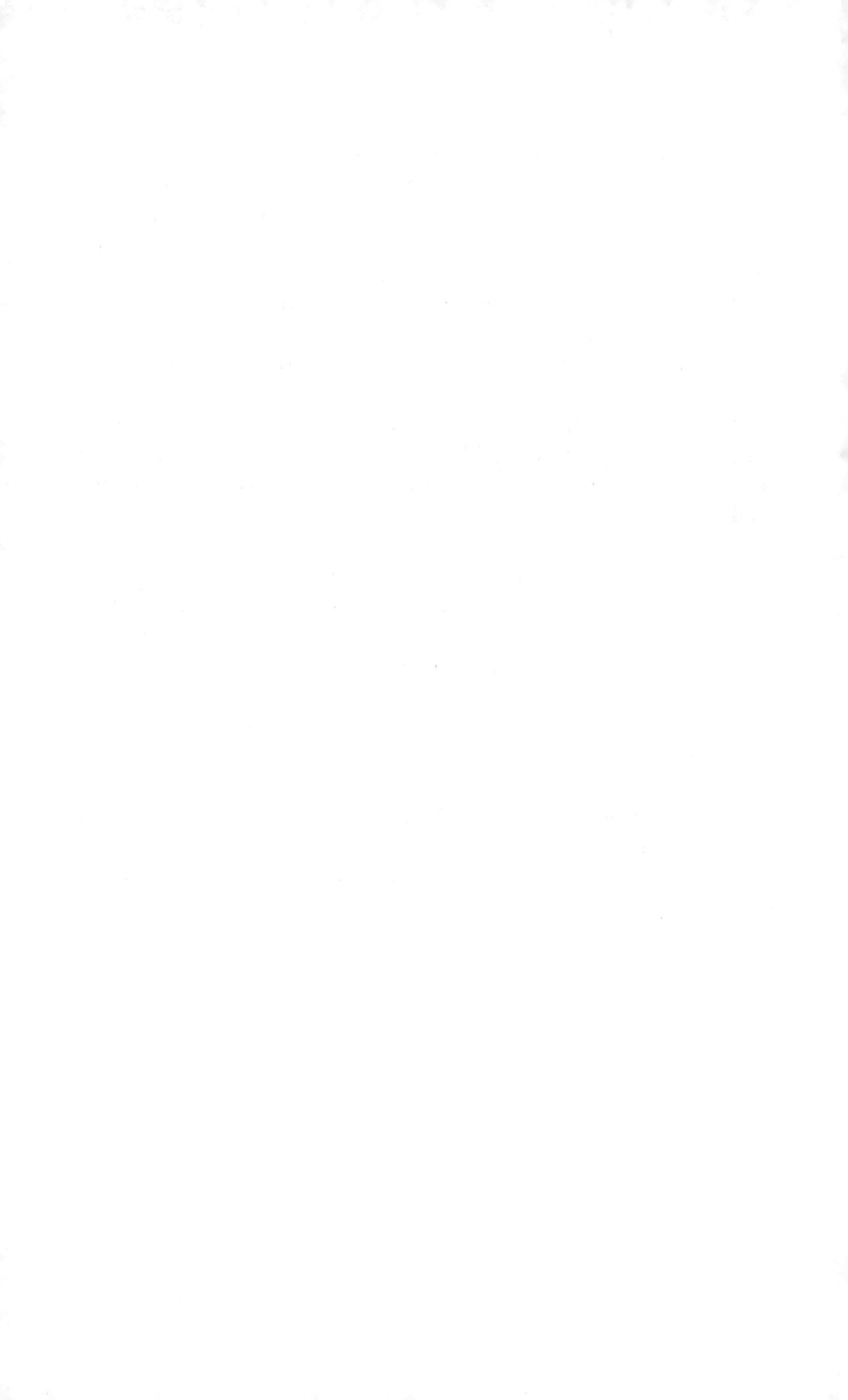

Chapter 50

Mr. Deutsch

"Mr. Deutsch, would you introduce yourself to the jury?"

"Hi jury, I am Eric Deutsch and I am the executive vice president of Girls Gone Wild."

Deutsch was easily 6-foot-4, slim and with hair cut so close he appeared bald. He had an open, honest face and a sincerity that was going to be essential for the defense if they hoped to make him the face of the company.

He was a 1986 graduate of UCLA and had been vice president of worldwide distribution for Playboy before coming to work for Girls Gone Wild.

"I met Joe in 2002 and we became friends."

A part of his duties was to meet with the cameramen and instruct them on the policies and procedures they would follow in the field.

He talked about the safeguards they have in place now to catch footage of underage girls. It was a three-step process: the cameramen would card them, employees in Los Angeles would go through all the raw footage and sort the scene according to available identification and then a private investigator would check each girl to ensure she was an adult. In Los Angeles, the company used a program called Pilot Ware to sort the material for the next step in the process.

They hadn't had an incident, he said knocking on the wooden arm rest of his seat, since 2003.

There is also a phone number, a "remorse line," that the girls can call, before the video they're in goes into distribution, to have their footage removed.

"How hands-on is Joe, I mean Mr. Francis?" Seaton-Virga asked.

He's busy with other projects so he's not that involved, Deutsch said.

Has he ever instructed you to disregard the law or cut corners on getting sex scenes? Seaton-Virga asked.

"We don't joke about underage girls," Deutsch began, but Pontikes stood and looked like she was going to object, so he paused. But when she didn't say anything, he went on. "We don't talk about underage girls. Joe will fire anyone who does."

Pontikes objected to hearsay.

What about compliance efforts?

GGW has a federal monitor who was ordered into her position by Judge Smoak in 2006.

"Have you had any issues?"

Pontikes stood again, but this time instead of pausing, Deutsch answered more quickly.

"We have not."

Pontikes again objected to hearsay.

Have the safeguards changed since 2002?

Pontikes stood again.

"It has," Deutsch said then rushed through some of the changes.

Pontikes objected to relevance.

Is it important for the cameramen to understand the rules when it came to shooting scenes and getting the proper identification? Seaton-Virga asked.

"Failure to follow these policies can lead to termination or worse."

"I tender the witness," Seaton-Virga said, gathering up her notes and sitting down.

Pontikes asked Deutsch some background questions and then asked if he had any first-hand knowledge of what the policies were at GGW from 2000 through 2004?

He did not.

Was he aware that Francis had pled to producing 134 videos without the proper age identifying records?

"I am not."

She brought up a printout from GGW's Pilot Ware program, the second safeguard in the three-step process. She pointed out a name on the printout and asked him if, on the printout, there was a green light next to the name. A green light, she asked, would indicate that this footage had been cleared to go into production?

He agreed that there was a green light next to the name and a green light meant it had been cleared.

Pontikes asked him if the printout was dated April 1, 2009?

He looked at the date and agreed, that was what it showed.

"And a green light means go?"

Deutsch tried to get out that the software was just the second step in the process, but Pontikes only wanted to know if green meant go. He had to agree that it did.

Pontikes didn't identify the name on the printout.

She then asked him if he'd read Ryan Simkin's newly released book on GGW? He hadn't, but he'd heard about it.

"Did you know that he talks about the remorse policy and calls it a joke?"

Seaton-Virga had objected several times to this line of questioning and Smoak finally sustained her objection. But it was out there.

Pontikes was done and Seaton-Virga approached the podium.

"Do you know Mr. Simkin?"

Yes.

While he was working for GGW, did he ever express any concerns over the remorse policy?

Not to me.

"Is GGW in litigation with Mr. Simkin over that particular book?"

Yes.

Deutsch was done on the stand. He could now go home to Los Angeles, his beloved Lakers and the family he missed so badly during his time in Panama City.

Smoak allowed the jurors to take a break so he could handle some issues with the lawyers.

• • •

Seaton-Virga's next items of evidence were going to be portions of the plaintiffs' depositions that she was going to read into the record. After that, they were going to have to resolve the issue of the videotapes.

Selander said they were still reading over the portions of the depositions that Seaton-Virga wanted to read. They would have to make their objections, and they were also entitled to have other portions read if they felt it presented a better balance to the testimony.

He suggested that they let the jury go home for the night, but they'd stay and argue the last big issue of the trial: the tapes. Smoak agreed and the jurors were sent home.

When the door closed, Pontikes rose from her seat.

"The defendants would like to admit the videos, over our objections," she said.

"Plaintiff J and S's footage," Seaton-Virga said, walking toward the podium to stand beside Pontikes. "Also the footage of Plaintiff B, but not the actual sex act; the raw footage leading up to the point where Plaintiff B disrobes and, afterwards, where she states what she would be doing the rest of the night."

B, she said, had testified that she was plied with alcohol and possibly drugged by GGW in order to get her to perform. Her statement after the sex, Seaton-Virga said, was indicative of her state of sobriety.

"She said," Seaton-Virga began, then hesitated. "Well, I'll just say it, she said, 'I'm gonna go get fucked up tonight.'"

"We do object to that," Pontikes told the judge. "We don't see what purpose that serves."

She said B and the other girl could be seen drinking out of red cups, which supported her contention that she was drunk. And, Pontikes pointed out that right before she made the "fucked up" comment B had said, "Did that really happen?"

"That shows that she hasn't processed what had occurred," Pontikes said. "Whether she was drunk or drugged, any small material things in these videos is outweighed by the prejudicial factors. Despite what the defendants will tell you, their real purpose in wanting to introduce these videos is to try to show that Plaintiff B was consenting."

Strict liability, she said, makes the issue of consent irrelevant. Pontikes argued that consent was far more wide ranging than simply saying yes. She said showing that Plaintiff B was sober was implying consent. Showing that Plaintiff B willing went with the cameramen, willing disrobed, willing did anything in relation to being videotaped having sex was immaterial because it all implied consent and consent was irrelevant.

Nothing on the video will show anything that is relevant and would only go to confusing the jury as to the issue of consent, Pontikes argued.

"No matter what she's doing on this tape, it's inappropriate to show it."

"But the tapes are the crux of this case," Smoak said, echoing what Francis had said days before.

"Why wouldn't it be material that the plaintiffs were lucid and steady and not offended and not weeping in shame?" Smoak asked. It had now become a debate between him and Pontikes. "The claim before this court is a damage claim, wouldn't that have a bearing?"

No. The claim for damages was from the dissemination of the footage, and in V's case the fear of dissemination, not the actual act that was filmed, Pontikes said.

Seaton-Virga reminded the court that the damage claim includes the filming, not just the aftermath.

Smoak said the plaintiffs had "painted a very dire picture" of their experience being filmed.

"The devastation they all testified about came about after the fact. Wouldn't it be material to show that on the heels of exposure everybody was feeling pretty cool?" Smoak asked.

"I don't see how that is relevant, your honor," Pontikes answered.

"Why wouldn't it be unfair to the defendants not to give the jury the best evidence of what really happened?"

Because the defendants are not allowed, by law, to argue consent, Pontikes persisted. The law plainly says that pornographers are responsible for making sure that the performers in their videos are adults. It doesn't matter if a minor lies about her age or seeks out Girls Gone Wild, the onus is on the cameramen, producers and disseminators to make sure they don't get on tape.

Smoak said he understood that, and if there was any misrepresentation of age included in the videos they would have to be taken out.

But Pontikes insisted that didn't go far enough.

"Kids make mistakes," she said, her voice catching a little. This was her most impassioned argument of the trial and while she wasn't one to show her emotions, she certainly felt strongly about this. "Teenagers do stupid things. Things they regret. Allowing the defendants to use the videos in an effort to show consent is far more prejudicial than probative."

She said the law doesn't allow pornographers to defend themselves in child porn cases by saying there was a mistake of age.

Pontikes said the defendants want to challenge B's claim that she was drunk. But showing that she didn't appear to be drunk would only imply that she consented.

"Not being drunk means she wanted to do this, means consent," she said.

Seaton-Virga said there is a claim by the plaintiffs that Joe Francis acted with intent or acted in an outrageous manner beyond the bounds of normal behavior. Those were things the plaintiffs would have to prove and one way of doing that was for Plaintiff B to tell the jurors that Girls Gone Wild had drugged her and then taken advantage of her.

She insisted that the jurors be shown the tapes to put the entire incident in perspective.

"The plaintiffs put this at issue, your honor," Seaton-Virga said. "Plaintiff B said she was plied with drugs and alcohol. It goes to the outrageousness of GGW's conduct. If it wasn't relevant, they shouldn't have put that at issue. Miss Pontikes asked the questions, and now she's coming into court and asking you not to show the jury the tapes, which put this incident in context.

"The jury should be given the opportunity to judge for themselves whether she appears to be drugged."

"I remember that testimony," Smoak said. "I woke up at the time that was said and I was wondering why no one objected."

Francis had objected and been overruled.

Smoak said the testimony about being drugged could certainly bear on damages. "It would seem to be so much more serious to say she was drugged and plied with alcohol. It's more shocking."

Seaton-Virga said the film showed Plaintiff B appearing lucid and sober, both before and after the sex scene.

"No one seems to be upset. It didn't appear to phase her in the slightest. It was almost like she was proud of herself."

Pontikes resumed her argument.

"Consent is not at issue. The child is not on trial here, the pornographer is. Miss Virga wants to put the child on trial." It didn't matter if she looks lucid or proud, Pontikes said, "she's been exploited by a pornography empire."

Smoak asked her to address the argument that the videos would be relevant as to damages.

"Would the footage lead the jury to believe there is less injury than they claimed, in that there in the immediate aftermath everybody seemed all right?" he asked.

Pontikes insisted that the footage only went to the issue of consent and consent was irrelevant.

Smoak said he understood her argument on consent and she no longer had to keep arguing it. Wouldn't the footage of B leaving the sex scene go to the argument that she wasn't immediately damaged and this "claim of injury is a more recent fabrication?" How do the defendants prove that the plaintiffs weren't as damaged as they claim?

Pontikes started back in on consent.

"We're not talking about consent," Smoak said.

"I respectfully disagree, we are only talking about consent."

Smoak told the lawyers on both sides to get together and watch the pertinent portions of the videos to come to some agreement on what was relevant.

"It may be that the videos are fraught with danger for either or both sides."

• • •

I got to Angela's that afternoon to find her dealing with a decidedly agitated baby girl. It wasn't that Vivi was fussy, she just seemed frustrated. She was focused on organizing her toys and any disruption of that, especially if she couldn't find something, caused her to wail.

Rachel was going to be a few hours late and Vivi kept asking for a bath. I gave Angela the much more subdued Tre to bathe while I ran the water for Vivi. She stood alongside the tub, fully dressed, and tried to hitch a leg over to climb in.

"Silly girl. When do we ever have a bath with our clothes on?"

She started jerking her dress over her head and when I tried to help, she got her arms and head lodged. That produced another wail until I got her free.

Normally bath time is relaxing for Vivi, but she was too tense. She didn't want to play, only organize her bath toys. Rachel came into the bathroom as I was shampooing Vivi's hair.

"So what do you think?" she asked.

I was impressed with Pontikes' argument. Bringing everything back to consent was a smart move and she never wavered. She was a believer too, she really felt these girls were victimized.

"What do you think the judge is going to do?" Rachel asked.

"I think the judge sees the basic unfairness of keeping the videos away from the jury, but it's hard to say what he's going to do."

"I think the judge doesn't like these plaintiffs, he doesn't like this case," Rachel said.

While we talked, Vivi refused to look at her mother, concentrating instead on her toys.

"Out," she said standing up in the water and trying to climb back over the side of the tub.

"OK baby, hold on." I wrapped a big towel around her and tried to dry her hair, which resulted in more wailing and struggling. I held her still long enough to dry her and then wrapped her securely in the towel, tucking the end in at her neck to hold it in place.

"Hold you," she said, meaning she wanted to be picked up.

"You want mama to hold you?" Rachel asked.

"No."

"No? Can mama have a smooch?"

"Home. Vivi. Take me home."

Rachel's eyes immediately watered.

"Take you home? Oh baby girl, don't say that, you'll make mama cry. Everything will be back to normal tomorrow. I promise."

Chapter 51

"We're gonna be porn stars"

"You all were instructed to have portions of the videos identified and keyed up, and to have reached some kind of agreement about that," Smoak said. It was Tuesday morning and he was all business.

Rachel Seaton-Virga got to her feet and said she'd talked to Dent until 10 the night before.

"It's not that we're not working together, I just don't think we're going to be able to come to an agreement. They want none of the video in. Miss Pontikes is not gonna budge on that."

They cued up the portion that they wanted to play, but it wouldn't go through Gerard Virga's computer. Eventually, they got it to play on Ter Bush's laptop.

Pontikes went around to each video monitor on the plaintiff's and defense's tables and turned them away from the audience. She shot the reporters a look that accused them all of being voyeurs. She also wanted the audio sent only to the judge's computer, but that didn't work and eventually they had to play it loudly enough for everyone to hear.

The early clip started off with a startlingly high-pitched, vigorous and drawn out "wooooo" from either Plaintiff B or her friend, an unidentified female.

"We're gonna be stars, man" B said.

"Porn stars," the other one said.

"That's where it all starts." They slap hands, a low five.

Smoak stared steadily at his monitor, his hand rubbing his lower lip.

Pontikes objected because the other girl, another minor, is exposed. Nothing has been done to try to cover her face.

"There's nothing illegal about having a minor in a video." She's clothed, no sexual conduct, Seaton-Virga said.

Pontikes, however, objected again.

"We don't have this," she said of the footage being shown. "We got an edited version."

This has more content, it has a time meter, and appears to be shot from a different angle, Pontikes said. She said they made numerous requests to Francis during the three years of discovery in this case for all footage related to the plaintiffs and they never received this film.

She wanted the entire video excluded as punishment for the discovery violation.

Smoak said nothing from the defendant's video would be used, but he would still review the clips from the plaintiff's copy.

It took a few minutes to get the plaintiffs' version of the video to the right spot. They began playing it and Seaton-Virga told the judge that it didn't appear to be different from the copy they have. She disagreed with Pontikes' claim that it looked like it was shot from a different angle.

"This is a discovery violation and very serious discovery violation," Pontikes said, ignoring Seaton-Virga's assertions. "I'd like to have them sanctioned by having it excluded."

"Present counsel have my sympathy," Smoak said to the Virgas. "Mr. Francis is a scoundrel of the first order, but we can't deal with that right now."

When the "before" clip finished, and the chatter of excited girls was suddenly cut off from the speakers, Smoak looked out toward the lawyers.

"Our main objection is that this occurs before anything has happened," Pontikes said. "Their only possible reason for wanting it admitted is, again, to show consent. Those two minors look like they want to do this. There's nothing to do with damages. Nothing has happened yet."

"Tell me why this is material," he said to Seaton-Virga.

"She was the same person walking in as walking out. The jurors should be able to see whether her demeanor was any different than when she left."

Pontikes started in again on consent.

"Miss Pontikes, we're not gonna finish by Friday unless we get on with this," Smoak said, holding up a hand to stop her. "I think I know where you are going."

They played the "after" clip.

"I'm getting fucked up after this," B said in a high giggle.

She said she'll need a taxi to take her home after this night and then asks the cameraman if she can have another drink.

"That's about unintelligible," Smoak said after the audio suddenly stopped. "What is probative about that scene?"

"I don't want to be repetitive," Seaton-Virga said. "The plaintiffs have sensationalized what happened here. They have vilified Mr. Francis. The jury should be allowed to see the tape to see for themselves the context of the event, not just what she testified to. Despite the plaintiffs' attorneys' clever spin, this has nothing to do with consent. Credibility is always an issue. This goes to the damages. She's substantially the same person after as she was before. She's ready to go on and continue her night. I understand why the plaintiffs don't want this in, it doesn't paint Plaintiff B in a very favorable light."

Smoak was still looking at the monitor, rubbing his bottom lip and chin.

"We only see a small bit of face," he said. "We don't see expressions. They're speaking in an excited tone, you can't tell what they're saying. They're very excited about what just happened. I wasn't sure I could pick out what they were talking about. I don't know if what I saw was excitement or hysteria."

"That is a question for the jury. The video is what the video is," Seaton-Virga said.

Smoak said he didn't see the value in the footage. He ordered that the after-scene would be excluded.

There were two segments to the before clip: one where the girls are walking into the hotel and a later part where they're leaving the party and going into the bedroom.

Seaton-Virga said the part where they're going into the bedroom is essential to disputing the drug allegation.

"This is to refute the contention that she'd been drugged. She said this was so out of character for her, she felt numb the next day. This was testimony that was elicited by Miss Pontikes in the direct. She put her character at issue. And it goes to the intentional infliction of emotional damage. It is outrageous if she is drugged by Girls Gone Wild. That is an outrageous claim for the jury to hear and would certainly go to boosting her damages if the jury found that she had been drugged."

Smoak said the jurors might be expecting to see someone who was "zombie like. It may go to the contention that she had been drugged. That was a pretty serious accusation. These two clips will be permitted."

Pontikes had no intention of letting it go. She again objected, but Smoak was ready to move on.

While Ter Bush cued up the footage of plaintiffs J and S, Pontikes went over to have a whispered conversation with Selander.

"While we're getting things ready I'd like to return to Plaintiff B for just a minute," Pontikes said to the judge.

"Miss Pontikes, I'm done with B for now. Let's get this out of the way."

They watched the tape of J and S flashing.

"Plaintiff S claims she hid her face in embarrassment after flashing, but the video doesn't show that," Seaton-Virga said.

But Pontikes said S disappeared from the frame when the cameraman shot J. Pontikes saw S leaning forward which would be consistent with her testimony.

Pontikes said Francis had already pounded the plaintiffs in his cross about the length of time they were actually shown flashing. Two seconds. "We're looking to put the least amount of nudity into this case. Everyone knows what happened in this video."

"Their demeanor is certainly something the jury can consider," Smoak said. "This segment will be allowed."

Pontikes held some files to her chest as she stepped carefully back to the podium. She was going to bring B up again and was leery of an angry response. She asked the judge to clarify his ruling on the Plaintiff B video. She said she assumed that Smoak was allowing the footage in without audio.

Smoak said he didn't hear the audio so they cued it up for him again. The sound wouldn't play through his monitor so he came around and stood behind Ter Bush and watched the video over her shoulder.

Seaton-Virga said the dialogue is important so the jury can hear her speech pattern. "As we know from DUI investigations, that is pertinent."

"That dialogue is very prejudicial," Pontikes said.

"That was unintelligible," Smoak said. The girls had been excited, talking fast and loud. "Did anyone understand what was said."

Seaton-Virga tried to carefully go through the dialogue.

"Plaintiff B makes the comment, 'We're gonna be stars.' The other girl says, 'We're gonna be porn stars.' Plaintiff B says, 'That's where it all starts.' And that's when they're high-fiving each other, I guess low-fiving is more accurate."

She returned to the sobriety issue. They put her sobriety at issue. They put consent at issue. If drugs and alcohol didn't matter for consent, then why did they ask her about it.

"They opened the door. Your honor has said that I can't use this to argue consent and I won't. Maybe any confusion could be cured with an instruction that the jurors are not to consider this as evidence of consent."

Smoak was starting to reconsider his prior ruling. He asked whether the clips would do more to confuse the jurors because it's so hard to hear what they're saying. After some consideration, he decided that the best way to handle the drug question was to simply tell the jurors to disregard B's testimony about drugs.

"That's not enough," Seaton-Virga said. "They should be able to see the tape, the context, the circumstances so they can also address the issue of B's credibility. Once that jury heard that testimony, there's no un-ringing that bell. There's no guarantee that a jury instruction will undo the prejudice done to Mr. Francis."

But Smoak had decided. B's clips, all of them, stay out. He'll tell the jurors before they begin deliberating to disregard testimony about drugs.

Chapter 52

Flash

It was time for Gerard Virga to do his thing. He stood and approached the podium, slightly hunched over his notes. He had a tendency to mumble and every time he stood to make an objection, the court reporter and Smoak would lean forward and cock an ear in his direction.

Smoak insisted that he make all his arguments while speaking into a microphone.

Sometimes even that didn't help.

Virga had worked well into the night, nearly every night since they'd taken the case, trying to catch up to the plaintiffs' attorneys as far as where they stood with the law.

His first argument was to address the age of the allegations. He said the plaintiffs were barred by the statute of limitations from going forward.

"This has already been argued," Pontikes said to him quietly. "This has already been dealt with."

He nodded without looking away from his notes, and continued on with his argument. He had two reasons for going over this ground. First, he hadn't argued it the first time and second he needed to buy time for Seaton-Virga to write her closing argument.

Pontikes said they were well within the statute of limitations because the sale of the DVDs went on for years after the actual filmings.

Virga then touched on something that Pontikes had brought up the day before. She'd been trying to prove a point about how seriously the legislature thought of these cases. She said it had raised the minimum award of damages for the intentional infliction of emotional damage in 2008 from $50,000 to $150,000. The plaintiffs were proceeding under the new rule, meaning if the jurors found that there was intentional infliction of emotional damage they couldn't award anything less than $150,000 per defendant to each plaintiff. Considering there were four defendants, for a total of $600,000, and four defendants, it would mean a minimum award of $2.4 million.

But Virga noted that when the legislature changed the rule it did not apply it retroactively. He said it was meant for lawsuits that were filed after 2008. These cases, he said, should fall under the old rule.

Smoak agreed.

Seaton-Virga turned to Deutsch, sitting in the audience, and stage whispered to him, "He just saved Joe Francis $1.6 million."

They took up a few more issues before allowing the jury back into the room. When they were seated, Seaton-Virga moved the video of J and S into evidence and played it.

What it showed was a view from outside the passenger-side window, looking in on a laughing, giggling Plaintiff S with a cigarette dangling off her bottom lip. She jerks up her bikini top, jerks it back down and laughs some more.

The cameraman asks if anyone else wants to flash and J immediately says, "I'll do it."

The camera swings to the back and J slides her top up and down a little more slowly.

The cameraman tosses in beads still balled up in a plastic bag and, that's it.

There was nothing to say so no one said anything.

Selander had one housekeeping item to take care of. He told the judge that the computer printout that Pontikes had shown Eric Deutsch in her cross-examination the day before, the one in which she asked him about the green light next to the name, that name was Plaintiff B's.

Both sides rested.

Chapter 53

Closing arguments

"Now it's time to argue," Larry Selander said after taking the podium and facing the jury. It was his way of introducing the next phase of the trial, closing arguments.

"This is a case that is solely about damages. You'll have to decide whether the four plaintiffs suffered damages and who should be held accountable for them, and whether punitive damages should be awarded."

Joe Francis had presented no evidence that the plaintiffs weren't damaged; That was a theme in Selander's closing. Because Francis had missed the evidentiary deadlines and the Virgas had come in to the case so late, they hadn't been able to present much evidence or challenge the plaintiffs' evidence. Selander would refer to much of his evidence as "uncontroverted," unchallenged, as a way of saying that the defendants were powerless to argue against their facts.

"You have to judge who is responsible. The plaintiffs are damaged. Seriously damaged. Valuing it remains your task," he said.

The defendants, Selander said, want to blame the plaintiffs, say they did something wrong, that they conspired to expose themselves on Girls Gone Wild.

"Should the responsibility belong to the victim or should the responsibility belong to the pornographer? We protect minors. We should protect minors. We always have protected minors."

"Mr. Francis said in opening that he was going to show you that these girls had given false ID. Absolutely untrue and irrelevant anyway."

He tried to describe how liability applied to Francis.

"Mr. Francis knows the law that applies to his business. He knows you don't film minors. You don't do it. Nobody thinks child pornography is OK. But Mr. Francis pled guilty to it. He violated the law. Why did he violate the law? Money, fame, prestige, women. And money. Lots and lots of money."

Francis targeted the young because they were naive, easy to manipulate, Selander said. He only stops when he gets caught.

"Supposedly he straightens up his act. Mr. Deutsch seems like a good man, but he was not told a bunch of things that went on here. He didn't know there had been guilty pleas, that there were hundreds of tapes out of compliance."

Selander picked up the Pilot Ware printout.

"We get down to a line over here," Selander said, tracing downward with his finger. "That person is Plaintiff B. On April 1, 2009, when this document was printed, GGW had her as a 'go'."

So Francis pleads out to his charges.

"Mr. Francis admits he's violated the law. He doesn't do any jail time. He has to pay a $2.1 million fine. For someone like him, that's not a substantial amount. He didn't pay a whole lot of attention. It's like the maybe $40 I have in my wallet right now, it doesn't attract a lot of attention."

GGW sold about 850,000 of the videos that include the footage of plaintiffs B, J and S, for a total of $17,098,307.

"Those tapes are still out there. That is the real problem with those crimes."

He said a part of the problem was the availability of these images on the internet. He said there were cases of teens committing suicide after private, embarrassing photos of them were posted without their knowledge.

"Our children are killing themselves over this and it's going to get worse. There are all sorts of problems related to the internet and this is a big one."

He said Girls Gone Wild made $160 million off the sale of videos that were found to be in violation of the law.

"This is a big-dollar business."

He called minors, "targets of opportunity. They are the most vulnerable people for his business."

Selander mentioned his experts. Dr. Costanzo called Joe Francis "the pied piper of fun."

"He plays the pipe and leads children, leads people, leads animals over a cliff," Selander said.

Adolescents' brains aren't fully developed.

"Teenagers, minors, are not capable of making the kind of mature decisions we expect adults to make."

They are opportunities for "predators seeking vulnerable targets."

Dr. Lebowitz was as qualified in the field of trauma as any you will find, he said.

"She didn't come in with an ax to grind. She sees a problem."

And Francis was the heart of the problem. Selander said Francis set the policies at GGW, he approved the purchase of alcohol to give to the girls to loosen them up and he paid bonuses to cameramen for explicit scenes.

Francis, Selander said, also has a personal interest in child pornography.

"16-year-old blondes were the ideal target. Mr. Francis keeps a private kiddy porn collection of the out-takes," Selander said.

Another cameraman testified that GGW was in Panama City during high school Spring Break, but Francis just pushed for more and more scenes despite the younger crowd.

"What does all this amount to? Joe Francis had a business pattern and practice to take advantage of young girls, and doing that is the very essence of the intent to inflict emotion distress and pain," Selander said.

He talked about Plaintiff V and the masturbation.

"He took her hand and another girl's hand and performed that act by force. Imagine if that was your daughter. Think about that."

During cross-examination, Francis had asked Plaintiff V what she wanted from him.

"She said, 'I'd like you to be forced to stop this. I don't want this to happen to any more girls.' Make him stop," Selander told the jury.

Francis, he said, was personally involved. He selected B's footage for a video, and he placed J's and S's scene in a video surrounded by "hard-core pornography."

"He did that."

Then Francis blames the girls, saying they came up with a conspiracy to wreck their lives and sue him.

"It's just nuts."

Selander said the jurors got a first-hand look at Joe Francis the predator.

"You saw what Joe Francis feels for these victims – zero."

He went through the types of damages: mental and emotional pain, loss of income or earning potential and punitive.

"They've each suffered about a million dollars difference in earnings. Was that pain and suffering, that loss of income, caused by Girls Gone Wild? Yes."

Lebowitz said they'd need open-ended counseling.

"Fifty-thousand a piece sounds like a round number to me."

Medical expenses?

"This is not a big medical cost case. A lot of people tried to kill themselves and if they don't get some help, if they don't turn their lives around, we're going to see more of that. We already have one talking about killing herself just from her exposure to Joe Francis in court."

Selander again pointed out that there was no contradictory testimony to the fact that the plaintiffs in this case had been ostracized, isolated and suffered "toxic levels of shame."

"Sure, it is possible that other things contributed, but the law says if Girls Gone Wild was a substantial cause of damage to them then it doesn't make any difference."

Plaintiff V, for instance, had an abusive father and just lost her mother.

"Until the GGW incident, she was dealing with it."

Is she somehow damaged less, he asked, because she had other problems in her life?

It's time to welcome these girls back into the community. The first way, he said, was by announcing with their verdict that the plaintiffs did nothing wrong.

"Those were kids. What they did wasn't wrong. It would be nice to take away their pain, but we can't. We can only give them money. How do you value lost friends, lost family, lost youth, loss of fun? How do you value them trying to kill themselves? How do you value the fact that Plaintiff B feels responsible for the death of her father?"

The first way, he said, was to give them the money that GGW made off their videos, $17 million.

"I know that's a lot of money. Either that money goes to them or Joe Francis keeps it."

That amount was in compensatory damages, for pain and suffering. Selander then said the jurors would have to decide if punitive damages were appropriate.

He explained that punitive was meant to punish, to deter others from the same behavior that had victimized these girls.

"If you don't punish, if someone doesn't do something, if this jury that has the ability to do something doesn't, then the message goes out that this was OK and we'll keep doing this."

GGW made $160 million off the illegal videos. Joe Francis personally made $12 million in 2002.

"So how do we get his attention? How do we punish and deter him? He was fined $2.1 million, which was essentially nothing. He didn't notice it. I think we get his attention with a lot of money. A lot of money. How much is up to you."

He was close to wrapping up and touched on Francis' conspiracy theory, saying it didn't hold water.

"You saw a predator in action," Selander said, referring to Francis' cross-examinations of the plaintiffs, "a predator we need to stop from preying on young people. He has no remorse. Until you stop it, I believe nothing is going to happen. We need to do something for our society."

Their verdict, he said, could help these girls change the course of their lives.

"Help them come back into their community."

Chapter 54

"Moral cesspool"

Rachel Seaton-Virga wanted to get a laugh somewhere early in her closing, but she was afraid that joking was a bit of a risk.

"What if it falls flat?" she'd asked the night before.

But she managed to hit the jurors just right. When she got to the podium and looked at the women sitting before her, she introduced herself, something she wasn't able to do at the beginning of trial.

"This is the first time I've had an opportunity to talk with you," Seaton-Virga said. "This is highly, highly unusual. You don't have to have been around the courthouse for long to know that this is not generally the way a trial is conducted."

She introduced Gerard.

"Yes, we're married. Which may be, while he was testifying earlier, I may have sounded like a nagging wife. I can't help myself."

It got the desired laugh from all eight women on the jury.

That connection was what separated her closing from Selander's.

She told the jurors that before Thursday she'd never spoken with Joe Francis, but that had changed rapidly once she took the case.

"I've had a few days now to speak with him. I have a feeling that the way Mr. Virga and I have conducted this trial, stylistically, may be a little different than the way Mr. Francis proceeded.

"I would also imagine, based on my review of some of the testimony transcripts in this case, that he may have come off as an unlikeable person. And maybe you don't like him. There's a good chance you probably don't like him or like what he does or the entire arena in which he operates. But that's not what this case is about."

She said this case was about more than Mardi Gras beads and tank tops.

"It's about these plaintiffs playing the lottery and Mr. Francis and these companies are their lottery tickets. They are taking their chances at the big payoff. This is the big time for them."

She told them to rely on their own memories, not on what she or Selander said, in evaluating the evidence.

"Credibility is always at issue. It matters whether or not you believe what these young ladies are telling you. It matters whether or not you believe their damages and their testimony was inflated to sensationalize it. It matters. Because Mr. Selander is correct, this case comes down to damages."

She said Francis acknowledged that he made a mistake.

"The question becomes this: Were these mistakes intentional? Were they reckless? Did he set out to hurt these women? Do you believe it was his goal to derail these women's lives? Are you going to ignore their histories? Or are you going to push that to the side and say this was all Mr. Francis's fault?

"These women have taken no personal responsibility for anything that happened? That's the question you're going to have to go back there and ask yourselves."

She took up one of Francis' repeated points, that he had represented himself because he cared deeply about the case. But when it came time for him to hand the case off to a professional, she'd accepted the challenge.

"That's my personal responsibility to do so and I accepted that responsibility."

She asked the jurors if they remembered Pontikes asking any of the plaintiffs about their hospitalizations? Did they hear anything from the plaintiffs that these hospitalizations happened, in some cases, years after their encounters with Girls Gone Wild?

"Plaintiff V is the woman who claims that Mr. Francis forced her to masturbate him in a motel room with approximately eight other people in the room. Plaintiff V also testified that she flashed the camera. But what you also heard was that Plaintiff V thinks it's fun to flash. She does not morally object to flashing. I'm pretty sure she didn't say that when she testified. I'm pretty sure it was along the lines of, 'Flashing is traumatizing. I was horrified by the experience. It has scarred me for life.' What about the other time she did it that same day? Did that scar her? What about when she asked Mr. Francis for a ride in his Ferrari after it happened?"

She said V had taken Francis by her house and gotten his phone number so they could hook up again later that night to go to a party. That didn't work out, though, because her friends had already told their parents about what happened that day.

Plaintiff V was dealing with a lot in 2003: her mother's death, an abusive father and her father's new girlfriend.

When she was hospitalized, she talked about her mother's death and her father's abuse.

"She didn't mention Girls Gone Wild, she didn't mention Joe Francis."

Plaintiff B also was dealing with a lot: new schools, new friends and then her father died.

"Now, the implication is that somehow, I guess, her anxiety and her desire to come home resulted in her father's death. Plaintiff B said she did not think that Girls Gone Wild had anything to do with her father's death. And while it sounds sensational to discuss it in closing, or in opening, unfortunately the evidence just doesn't support it. That has nothing to do with this case."

Her father's death was the beginning of her problems.

"She was traumatized by the death of her father. It was unexpected and she was on the phone with him. Why wouldn't that be traumatic? How could it not be? Of course it was. Following that, she couldn't keep it together. I don't think anybody blames her for that."

In 2004, she is hospitalized for the first time and for the next six weeks she's in and out of treatment centers.

"Three different institutions in three different areas, treated by several different doctors. All of these doctors said she was suffering from bipolar disorder. She was suffering from hallucinations. The plaintiffs would have you believe that Plaintiff B's issues with bipolar disorder were caused by Mr. Francis. That doesn't make any sense. Dr. Lebowitz commented on the diagnosis, saying that, based on her review which did not include talking with other physicians, that she didn't believe B had bipolar disorder. Certainly, bipolar disorder doesn't fit in with the plaintiffs' theory of the case. It's not convenient."

During her treatment at these mental health facilities, she never mentioned Girls Gone Wild or Joe Francis. Instead, B claimed she didn't have a drug or alcohol problem. She talked about her father.

"Ultimately, the doctors formed the opinion that she was grieving and she needed to grieve.

"Her mother was aware of the Girls Gone Wild incident, she didn't disclose it to medical professionals. Her daughter has been institutionalized, something is very wrong with her daughter; I think that her mom would want to make sure she got the help she needed, but didn't see fit to include this information so that the doctors could perform an analysis on this."

Dr. Lebowitz testified that she disagreed with the bipolar diagnosis because B had not shown signs of bipolar in the last few years despite being off medication.

"What we didn't hear from Dr. Lebowitz was B's prescription was changed. She was medicated. And at that time she still hadn't disclosed, even once the medication was right, she didn't disclose anything about Girls Gone Wild or this incident."

As far as her self image was concerned, Plaintiff B appeared in two movies during her time in California, "Spider-Man" and "Starsky and Hutch."

"The incident with Girls Gone Wild was not so debilitating that she couldn't imagine herself ever being on film again. She certainly wasn't afraid of the attention, being in a movie, of pursuing an acting career. She was aware of what Girls Gone Wild was and what she was doing."

The plaintiffs' experts testified that people's brains don't fully develop until their mid-20s.

"This incident occurred on March 31, 2002. On June 1, 2002, B turned 18. In those two and a half months, did she develop that much?"

There are hundreds of thousands of women in these films, many of them are in their early 20s or late teens. Should they be compensated because they didn't know what they were doing?

"Do two months really matter? Three years, four years, five years?These women all certainly knew what a video camera was. It's not like they didn't know the camera was right there. Certainly when something is on film someone may see it. That's logical.

"My two-year-old knows what the video camera is for."

She turned her attention to plaintiffs J and S.

They'd seen the video. They could draw their own conclusion as to the girls' demeanor.

"The laughing, the giggling, the 'I'll do it too!'"

She said Plaintiff S's contention that a cameraman had badgered them for 30 minutes to get them to flash was ludicrous considering there were hundreds of willing women in the same area.

"Video doesn't forget. It doesn't make mistakes. It doesn't misrepresent. Take that video for what it is. That is an account of what happened that day on Front Beach Road, plain and simple. I didn't see any shame. Did you? Or did you see a girl sitting the front seat, smoking a cigarette, who thought it was cool, who wanted to fit in, whose sister was egging her on and daring her to do it?"

She said kids of this generation are exposed to more things, through the internet and cell phones, than past generations, and are therefore more worldly. Families living in this area are also more familiar with what goes on during Spring Break.

"These aren't innocent girls who aren't somewhat familiar with what goes on on Spring Break. It is a moral cesspool at Spring Break on Panama City Beach."

And Plaintiff S testified that she was smoking a cigarette that day, even though she was just 15.

"I'm not implying that makes her a bad person. But Plaintiff S testified that she was smoking because she thought it was cool. She wanted to fit in."

Plaintiff S failed ninth grade, she was already a bad student before she met Girls Gone Wild.

"What excuse did she give for that? She had a creepy gym teacher. Who didn't in high school have a creepy gym teacher or a creepy coach who taught biology?" Seaton-Virga said with a shrug and a smile. "Maybe it was just me."

S had an opportunity to go to summer school, but she declined and was held back.

"Her parents didn't think enough about education to jerk her up by the collar and say, 'You're getting your butt to summer school.'" Ultimately, she dropped out in the 11th grade. She then ended up in an abusive relationship and got involved with drugs.

"She testified, tearfully, that she even tried crack cocaine. Is that Mr. Francis' fault? Is that the fault of Girls Gone Wild? Or were there other contributing factors? That's for you to decide, if Plaintiff S's life problems are due to Mr. Francis. Would she have gone down that path but for Mr. Francis?"

"Plaintiff S also testified that for eight years she maintained employment. That's saying something, that someone had been able to do the same thing for eight years, especially in their 20s."

As a result of her abusive relationship, S ended up going to counseling, which was provided free to her by the state. "I don't believe that was mentioned on her direct by my esteemed colleague. And surprise, surprise, she didn't say anything about Girls Gone Wild or Joe Francis. She didn't realize what the reason for her poor choices and her situation in life was until she spoke to the plaintiffs' doctors. (Lebowitz) testified she wasn't a miracle worker, but, wow, they certainly became open once they started talking with Dr. Lebowitz. They really wanted to share their experiences then. But not to any of those other doctors. And that is consistent with each one of these women. If you ignore that, it is a travesty. It's an excuse."

And Selander's assertion that S and J's clip was "surrounded by hard-core pornography" on the DVD, "There's no evidence to support that. But it sounds good."

Plaintiff J also dropped out of school and, like her sister, she never told anyone about bullying, sexual bullying or being traumatized by Girls Gone Wild until she met with Lebowitz.

"She has three kids, but according to Dr. Lebowitz she has a fear of sexual contact and a fear of intimacy? I don't think I need to comment on that."

J also testified that she's been in a long-term healthy relationship and "she did that without hundreds of thousands of dollars in counseling paid for by Mr. Francis. Amazing. She testified that she likes her job, she's closer to her parents and that she's still daddy's girl."

Her two suicide attempts came three and four years after she flashed for GGW. And when she was committed for those attempts, she said problems with her boyfriend were the cause.

She was the child of an alcoholic father and had lived with a boyfriend in her parents' home when she was 15. When her parents separated for a time, J opted to stay with her alcoholic father to take care of him.

"This was a young lady with a lot on her shoulders who was growing up way faster than she needed to. But that is not the fault of Mr. Francis or Girls Gone Wild."

When she was committed again in 2004, after her second suicide attempt, she told the doctors she was distraught because her new boyfriend had broken up with her.

"She didn't tell that doctor she quit school because of Joe Francis or Girls Gone Wild or because she was teased and bullied. She told you that, but that's not what she told the doctor."

At that time, J said she wasn't depressed or abusing drugs and there was no trauma in her life.

"Mr. Selander suggests that the other stressors in their lives were not relevant. I'm sure that is what the plaintiffs' attorney would like you to believe because if they were relevant they would go to calculating damages. So he's asking you to ignore that. I ask that you don't. I ask that you look at the whole picture, that you look at the testimony both on the stand and the testimony elicited in deposition. When they weren't looking at you. When they didn't have their attorney here asking them the questions in front of you.

"Credibility is always an issue. If you feel like something was kept from you or you were somehow misled, that's relevant."

Seaton-Virga then started to talk about Dr. Leslie Lebowitz.

"Dr. Lebowitz was a talker, wasn't she?" That got a smile from a few jurors. "She liked to talk. She had a lot of things that she wanted to get out and that she wanted to tell you about and, gosh darn it, she sure was going to do it. She sometimes couldn't even remember the question by the time she was done talking. She had an agenda. She was going to hit all the talking points, every single one of them."

She said Selander claimed that none of their experts had an ax to grind, didn't have anything to gain by testifying the way they did. But Seaton-Virga pointed out that Lebowitz was paid $300 an hour while she conducted lengthy interviews, read through the volumes of medical records and depositions and then testified. "This was a very profitable experience for her."

It was obvious that Lebowitz disliked the adult entertainment industry as a whole. But what was astounding, Seaton-Virga said, was how she discounted the diagnoses of the other professionals who had treated the plaintiffs. She'd concluded that they were wrong and she was right without ever talking to them.

"And what was the catch-phrase she kept using, 'to a reasonable degree of medical certainty'? She could tell you with a reasonable degree of medical certainty the problems and obstacles encountered by these plaintiffs was due to the conduct of Mr. Francis, and that regardless of what they had told countless other trained psychologists and doctors, they were wrong. They didn't have the whole picture."

Lebowitz had said that wasn't unusual, the girls wouldn't open up to someone they didn't feel was understanding.

"What did she say? They know compassion when they see it. Let's talk about compassion. When you think 'attorney' do you think compassion? I am guessing that you probably don't. I don't. I deal with attorneys all the time. Compassion is the last word that comes to my mind. But who did they disclose to before Dr. Lebowitz, the compassionate doctor, the miracle worker? Their attorneys. But not the other trained medical professionals that had evaluated them previously."

She told the jurors not to take what she was saying as a personal attack on the plaintiffs. She gave the plaintiffs credit for seeing an opportunity and going for it.

"Good for them. They see deep pockets and they're going to try to dig right in."

She said this case, however, was about personal responsibility.

"Where is the personal responsibility? At what point do you own it and say, 'Yeah, I had something to do with that. Yes I had problems before this happened and they weren't because of Mr. Francis and Girls Gone Wild.'"

As far as being psychologically captured by Francis, "successful people attract other people, especially when it comes to litigation."

Seaton-Virga went on to discount the testimony of the cameramen, many of whom had been fired by GGW or were facing charges of their own when they gave their testimony.

Then she went back to personal responsibility.

"Imagine your daughter flashing, Spring Break, underage, smoking, drinking. Now imagine making her a millionaire for it. That's certainly a lesson in personal responsibility."

And, Seaton-Virga said, none of the girls could say how they'd been damaged.

"It's a good thing that Dr. Lebowitz was able to tell everybody how they were damaged, since they didn't realize they were damaged by Girls Gone Wild and Joe Francis."

She said Selander suggested that each plaintiff should receive a million dollars each in lost earnings potential because they didn't go to college. That number was only relevant if the jurors believed that all of these plaintiffs planned to go to college.

Seaton-Virga said one of the girls was skipping classes and failed a grade before she even met a cameraman.

"Look at these people as individuals, not as general statistics."

She went to the issue of punitive damages. She said GGW had changed since 2003, and changed even more since the company got hit with record keeping violations in 2006.

If they were to award punitive damages it would be punishing the company twice. "Are there any other changes that could possibly be made now?"

She addressed the Pilot Ware printout. She told them this was just one step in the process and didn't mean that Plaintiff B's footage was considered good to go.

Smoak interrupted Seaton-Virga's closing and told her it was getting late in the day.

"Are you saying, your honor, that I have five minutes to wrap up?" she asked. It was a pointed question and put Smoak on the spot. The defense would be even more sympathetic if the jurors believed the judge was shutting them down.

Smoak just told her to get to a good breaking point and she could resume in the morning.

She went back to the three-step identification procedures in place at Girls Gone Wild, but Selander objected. He said at sidebar that what she was saying in closing had not been testified to by a witness. Seaton-Virga pointed to Deutsch's testimony. Selander complained there had been a lot of objectionable things to her closing and it "just kept going on and on."

Smoak suggested they break for the night and Seaton-Virga could resume in the morning. She agreed and Smoak sent the jurors home.

"See everybody in the morning," he said as he left the bench.

It worked out perfectly for Seaton-Virga. Not only would she send the jury home with her message ringing in their ears, but she'd get the first word in the morning.

Chapter 55

"I don't appreciate being manipulated"

Rachel Seaton-Virga came over to Angela's house fairly early that evening. She wanted to load the kids up in the wagon and take them for a walk along the seawall-bordered Beach Drive. Vivi and I had been going out every evening after the trial with me pushing her wagon in front of me so we could talk the whole way. She was every inch her mother's daughter, she rarely stopped talking. With the azaleas in bloom, our latest thing was to go along collecting flowers that Vivi would alternatively hold, put on the bottom of the wagon, transfer back to the seat of the wagon and then, ultimately, ask me to carry because she couldn't find the best place for them.

All the while, Vivi and I would look for pelicans, boats and motorcycles. It was a blissful 40 minutes.

So when Rachel suggested a walk, I didn't think anything about it. I just loaded Vivi up in her wagon and we set off. I guess it was naive of me to think that we would talk about something other than Joe Francis.

"He really bothers me," Rachel began.

"Who?"

"Joe Francis. He calls like every 15 minutes. And every time, all I hear is, 'If you win this I'm gonna make you big. You're gonna be huge. You're gonna blow up.' I keep telling him I don't want to be huge. I like my business just the way it is."

"Why does that bother you?"

"I don't appreciate being manipulated."

"But he's like that with everybody."

"Is he?"

"Yes. Every time I've talked to him this week it's been, 'I'm gonna help you get published. If we win this case, I'll go on a book tour with you.' Blah, blah, blah."

"Doesn't that bother you?"

"No. Why would it? I find Joe Francis refreshing. I have to deal with so many people who are constantly trying to manipulate me in one way or another. Many of them don't even realize they're doing it. Those are the ones that bother me. Joe Francis is so obvious, so blatant that he makes me laugh."

"I guess."

"Just let it wash right over you."

With that behind us, and three or four flowers in the wagon, I thought Rachel would start to relax and take in the stunning view from Beach Drive: the wide teardrop shaped bay narrowing to a point at the pass, the long private dock, it's boards bent by the salt and sun, supported by pylons sunk in the sandy bottom, the distant mansions on Bay Point to the right and the wooded, untouched tip of Tyndall Air Force Base to the left.

"It's so nice out," Rachel said, breathing in the last chill of spring.

It was nice.

"So, can you believe Pontikes ...."

Chapter 56

"Extreme and outrageous conduct"

"Good morning," Rachel Seaton-Virga said to the jurors Wednesday as she resumed her place at the podium.

They responded with a hearty good morning, which made Rachel laugh.

"I hear enthusiasm. Perhaps because you see the light at the end of the tunnel."

Her closing, and especially this second half, had to touch on many issues. She had to continue introducing herself, to give the jurors a reason to trust her, address the issues that Selander raised and highlight the factors she felt the jurors should be focusing on.

She felt it was important, as a part of her introduction, to let the jurors know that she'd been a prosecutor for many years. So she told them a story about her first year as a prosecutor and how a judge told her an old adage: If you have the facts on your side, you argue the facts; If you have the law, you argue the law; If you have neither, you pound your fist on the podium.

Yesterday, she said, they'd talked about the facts. Today she wanted to touch briefly on the law.

"We talked about how some of the defendants have been found liable on certain elements as to certain counts. That is true."

But liability doesn't immediately lead to damages.

"What it comes down to is this with the damages: you have to believe that these plaintiffs were damaged by the actions of the defendants. Are there any real damages? Are these fabrications? Are these excuses? Is this what these women came up with once they'd hired an attorney and talked to yet another doctor?"

She talked again about the plaintiffs' prior hospitalizations that occurred without any mention of Girls Gone Wild. She said it wasn't until they hired lawyers and talked to Lebowitz that they had their breakthrough.

"The realization was that Mr. Francis, the Girls Gone Wild companies, had deep pockets. They were someone they could blame for their poor choices or for the position they found themselves in life, even though it may not have been their fault."

Those poor decisions could have been the result of bad upbringing, genetics, an abusive father or an alcoholic parent.

"All I can do is ask you to think about these things as you evaluate the facts and compare them to the law."

The jurors, she said, were going to have to find that Joe Francis intentionally inflicted emotional damage on these girls, that he set out with a course of action to destroy their lives.

"What the plaintiffs have to have proven to you by the greater weight of the evidence is extreme and outrageous conduct."

She said there was a legal definition of that conduct: "behavior which, under the circumstances, goes beyond all possible bounds of decency and is regarded as shocking, atrocious and utterly intolerable in a civilized community."

"What is emotional distress? They must show that the emotional distress is severe when it is of such intensity or duration that no ordinary person should be expected to endure it."

What the plaintiffs had to prove was that the plaintiffs' emotional distress was caused by the intentional, extreme and outrageous conduct of Girls Gone Wild and Joe Francis.

"But for the extreme and outrageous conduct, the severe emotional distress would not have occurred," Seaton-Virga explained. "The plaintiffs cannot prove that particular element to you. They simply cannot."

But, if the jurors were to find that any of the defendants did intentionally inflict emotional distress on the plaintiffs, they would next have to decide how the girls were damaged.

As far as damages, "You don't need me to tell you what constitutes a damage and what doesn't. Look at the facts of this particular case, then take the law and apply it to the facts."

To decide damages, Seaton-Virga said, they would have to rely on the credibility of the plaintiffs.

"Credibility is, of course, important. How could it not be? These women are asking you to give them, according to Mr. Selander, a minimum of $17 million. Of course it's important that you find them credible if you're going to even consider awarding them that type of dollar amount."

To decide if the plaintiffs are believable, look at their testimony and ask yourself, 'Do they have a reason to not tell the truth? Do they have a personal interest in the outcome of the case? Did they seem to have a good memory? Did they say something in court that was contradictory to what they said in their depositions or that conflicts with the evidence in the case?'

"I would like you to think about what they told you on the stand and what they didn't tell you."

She then went to punitive damages.

"Punitive damages are not meant to be a corporate death penalty. They're are not intended to bankrupt a company. It is only to deter future conduct. We know that they have stepped up their verification procedures for identification. This not the same company, in terms of verification, that it was in 2000, because a change needed to be made and they made it."

She questioned the $17 million figure the plaintiffs had thrown out as to profit on the films. She said that didn't include business expenses. That money, she said, isn't simply sitting in a bank somewhere.

"And while I'm thinking about it, I know I wasn't here for the entire trial, but what I have not heard and what I'm a little unclear on is what role Aero Falcon had in any of this. Who is Aero Falcon? What did they do? All we heard was Joe Francis, Joe Francis, Joe Francis. What about MRA Holdings, who are they? How did they allegedly damage these plaintiffs?"

It was time for a big finish and she knew it.

"Essentially, what I'm asking you to do is go back, evaluate the testimony, evaluate the inconsistencies in the testimony. Dr. Lebowitz, Dr. Constanzo, look at their motivations, look at what they considered and what they didn't consider. Evaluate the agenda.

"What I suspect is, what we'll be left with, is the plaintiffs pounding their fists because the evidence does not support that these women were damaged by these defendants. What the evidence points to is a convenience factor, a lack of personal responsibility, a blame game.

"If you believe that Mr. Francis caused these women all of these life problems, then I suppose you have to quantify that. But I submit to you that what they are entitled to is not a dollar. They had opportunities for counseling and they chose not to disclose this. Why? Because it wasn't that traumatic. When they saw dollar signs, they saw trauma.

"Remember what Dr. Lebowitz said, 'Trauma is one's own perception.' They certainly weren't perceiving it in 2003 when they were hospitalized. Or 2004 when they were hospitalized. Or when they were going through counseling free of cost.

"And that's relevant.

"Let me say this before I sit down: Thank you all for your attention. I know that this has gone on longer than expected. I know that you're tired. I would like to thank the plaintiffs' counsel, they have been extremely accommodating throughout this entire process. And also, your honor.

"With that, I will leave Mr. Selander to his fist pounding."

She gathered up her notes and turned from the podium.

Selander rose, took Seaton-Virga's place at the podium and started his rebuttal closing with the same story she told about arguing the law and the facts.

"When you don't have either, you blame somebody else. You try to put somebody else on trial. Their defense has been, let's put the victims on trial. They don't put any evidence on because you know they don't have anything to say.

"They forget that we know who has personal responsibility here, who is the actor in this whole drama, who caused the whole problem: Joe Francis."

Francis, he said, pled guilty and admitted in court that his business practice was to film minors. He did so 150 times over a number of years.

"Consistency shows intent. If you're consistently doing wrong then you are intentionally doing wrong."

He talked again about Schmitz's testimony that Francis had a private child pornography collection.

"Who had the personal responsibility for the harm done here? One person: Joe Francis."

The defense, he said, attacks the victims. They said these girls were hoping to hit the lottery. This was all a big conspiracy. He said it was hard to believe that these girls would destroy the last decade of their lives as a tactic to be used in a lawsuit against Joe Francis.

"Who already won the lottery here? Joe Francis won the lottery. He put millions of dollars in his pocket because he targeted minors. If it isn't taken away, he will keep it. There is an opportunity here. What is more outrageous conduct then child pornography? I can't think of anything worse."

He said a strong verdict would give teeth to the laws protecting children from pornographers.

"You looked into the eyeballs of all of these victims. Were they crying just for your benefit?"

He said the jurors were able to see Francis's true character in court as he questioned the girls on the stand.

"That was a predator in action in this courtroom."

The defense said the plaintiffs' experts were biased.

"Dr. Lebowitz is biased? Is she supposed to like Joe Francis? Is she supposed to like a guy who causes trauma to minors? Of course not. This is not about liking Joe Francis. This is about what he did and whether we need to punish him and take away the profit for what he did."

Lebowitz explained why the girls were reluctant to come forward earlier: trauma victims don't talk about the trauma.

The defense, he said, called the experts' testimony "excuses."

"This is just the predator trying to put the victim on trial. You heard the testimony. This was not an excuse. It's the truth."

He said the science was there to explain a child's lack of mental development and the reason why they are vulnerable.

"It's the mechanism by which someone like this predator can take advantage of these victims, of these minors, of vulnerable girls."

He said it was like saying a physical handicap is an excuse.

"A handicap is not an excuse," Selander said, sounding outraged that anyone could make that argument, even though he was the only one suggesting it. "A handicap is a condition that can be taken advantage of."

He lifted his fist as if to pound it on the podium, but caught himself.

Their experts, he said, were the people with the best knowledge of these issues, conditions and trauma. But since the defense couldn't bring any witnesses to contradict the plaintiffs' experts, they had to blame the plaintiffs' parents.

"They need to blame the parents for the intentional actions of a convicted child pornographer, a 150-time convicted child pornographer."

The plaintiffs had to prove that GGW and Francis acted outrageously.

"Is there anything more outrageous, anything more atrocious, than child pornography?"

He agreed with Seaton-Virga that punitive damages couldn't be used to bankrupt a company. He said there was little chance of crippling a company that made hundreds of millions from videos, internet, Pay-per-View, "A whole lot of different things.

"They have lots of money."

The base award, he said, should be what the company profited off the videos of the three plaintiffs.

"They keep it, they won."

He said Francis knew the laws prohibiting the use of minors in pornographic films.

"He had a choice to comply with the law and lose those vulnerable victims or ignore the law and make huge profits. He built this huge empire by employing a business practice founded on a consistent and intentional violation of the law. He made many, many millions of dollars by exploiting minors.

"The victims suffered diminished lives while Francis became enormously wealthy. Only you can right that wrong. Only you can change that result."

Chapter 57

"Who gets the money?"

It took Judge Smoak almost an hour to read to the jurors all the legal instructions and the verdict form they would have to use to come to a decision.

When he finished it was about 11 a.m. He was ready to send them into the jury room to begin deliberating, but one woman asked if they could be excused to go to lunch.

They'd bonded, she said, and their lunches were something they all looked forward to.

Smoak smiled and agreed.

• • •

They returned together at 12:30, trailing behind Dobos as he led them across the parking lot, into the courthouse and took the first group up the elevator. When the elevator reached the second floor, Dobos motioned for the women to wait. He'd done this every time he'd brought the jurors up the elevator throughout the trial. He had them wait, then he put one foot into the hallway, keeping the other inside the elevator, and looked both ways to see who was there, who he might have to clear out before he could let the jurors out. He then led them to a small room where they would spend most of their time deliberating.

Smoak set about trying to clean up some matters on his criminal docket that had been shifted around by the trial. Criminal defendants talked in the hallway while reporters stared out the window or read.

The country voice of a man who was preparing to go before the judge broke my reverie as I stared out at the bay.

"Did you know," he said slowly, with a rolling Southern drawl, to three people who looked like relatives, "that if you kill someone the most you can get in the federal system is 40 years? Then when you have a person who is in possession of a firearm, who'd been convicted 25 years ago, they want to put you away for three and a half years. It just don't make no sense."

I glanced up in time to see his gap-tooth smile. He was tall, with a prominent beer gut and raggedly cropped hair.

"I never left my house with my guns. I hunted on my own prop-tee. I had a gov'ment-issued huntin' license. Now, if they didn't want me ownin' no guns, why did the gov'ment issue me this permit?"

He shook his head.

"Well, you live and you learn."

"And then you die and forget it all," an older woman standing next to him said, too softy for him to hear.

"Huh?"

"And then you die and forget it all," she spoke up.

"Tha's right. Tha's right, you die and forget it all."

"Just read your Bible."

"Tha's right," the big guy said, nodding dramatically. "We in the beginnin' of the end of days and there're people out there who are too stupid to know it. We in the bee-GIN-in' of the end of days. Jus look at wha's goin on in the world today. All that nook-ler stuff going on in J'pan and blowin' over to Cal'forna."

"The Iranians killing all the Jews," an older man spoke up.

"I say kill em all," big guy said, leaning back and drawing out the last two words. "Kill em allll."

"The Jews and the Christians."

"They can kill em all, let God sorts em out. It doesn't bother me one bit."

"It does me, I'm gonna be one of em they's try to kill. Their God can't come back till they kill all the Christians and Jews."

Big gut turned to a younger woman who hadn't participated in the conversation and started instructing her on how to get along during his absence. He recommended that she file a claim against BP for damages suffered as a result of the oil spill a year before.

"A claim? For what?"

"I got a boat. Just push it into the water and file a claim."

"That oil ain't gone," older guy said pensively, "it's sittin' there on the bottom killin' all the fish."

"Kill em alllllll," big gut said, apparently lumping fish in with Jews and Christians. "Let it kill all the fishes."

Just then a bailiff came out and said the judge was ready to see them, bringing the conversation to an abrupt conclusion.

A television reporter had been trying to read a book but had long since put it down and been eavesdropping on the conversation as well. As the four went into the courtroom, he rubbed his eyes with the heels of his hands.

"You should've heard the conversation they had earlier," he said, slowly shaking his head from side to side as he tried to rub the exhaustion out of his eyes.

• • •

I had relocated to my truck by mid-afternoon and was typing on my computer when I saw four cars lurch into the parking lot and expel the lawyers in the civil case. They mingled together and filed up the ramp into the front door.

Do they have a verdict? I asked when I caught up to them at the metal detector.

Not a verdict, a question.

Three questions, actually: What is Aero Falcon? Where did the 2006 $2.1 million fine go? Who would get the money if we awarded punitive damages?

Smoak brought the jurors in and told them that Aero Falcon was a named defendant that had been defaulted against.

The fine went to the U.S. government.

And, the plaintiffs would get the money in a punitive damage judgment.

The women of the jury listened closely then filed out to resume their deliberation, leaving behind a rippling wake of speculation and discussion as to what those questions might mean.

"It looks like they're at least at the end," Seaton-Virga said to the other lawyers. "The punitive damage question doesn't come up till the end."

Actually, there were two places where punitive damages had to be resolved: halfway through and at the end. The juror's question could not be interpreted to mean that this would all be over soon.

Just the opposite. At 4:45, the jurors sent a note out to the bailiffs that said, "Call our husbands. We don't know how long we're going to be."

Smoak came out of his office and brought the note into court for the attorneys. He bypassed his seat on the bench and leaned against the podium.

"There's nothing we can do," he said, then grinned. "This is when you begin to subtly withdraw the comforts. Just wait till the air conditioning suddenly fails."

• • •

The light drained out of the evening sky in a glow of orange that deepened and enriched the blue of the bay. The moon was a sickle pointed toward the horizon, and as the evening turned into night, the sickle sank like the blade of guillotine.

It turned blood red as it severed the horizon.

The courthouse was lit from the inside by office lights that were rarely on this late, and on the outside by the glaring television lights from Channel 13's live truck.

Rachel Seaton-Virga was on the first floor, in a bailiff's chair by the metal detector, staring out the floor-to-ceiling picture window. Her movements showed the conflicting forces that were in control of her body: exhaustion and adrenaline.

"What do you think?" she asked without looking at me. She kept her chin in her hand and her gaze out the window. It was the same question she'd asked me a dozen times already since the jury had gone out, and had asked just as many times to anyone else she ran into.

"For what it's worth," I began. Speculating on jury deliberations, while the single most common activity for lawyers and reporters at this stage of a trial, is essentially pointless.

"For what's it's worth," she agreed, waving away any thought that she'd hold my speculation against me at a later date.

"When I first heard the punitive damage question I thought what they'd done was quickly go through and zero-out all the compensatory damage claims. Then they started thinking about punishing the company, but when they found out that the money would go to the girls, they went back to square-one.

"I think they've been back there the whole time trying to figure out a way to punish Joe Francis while not enriching the girls."

She nodded her head. She'd been thinking the same thing. It wasn't a far-fetched speculation considering how the jurors had reacted to both Francis and the girls. They didn't appear to like either.

So how do you impose punitive damages on the bad pornographer while not making millionaires of the bad girls?

"Joe's freaking out. He's calling me every five minutes."

"He's thinks it's bad. Hell, you think it's bad so why wouldn't he?"

She'd joked earlier that the jurors were probably trying to decide between the $100 million and $17 million judgments that Selander had suggested.

I thought that it was unlikely, even unfathomable, that the jury would not award a monetary judgment. Not after this amount of time.

The question remained: How much money would be considered a win by either side?

Seaton-Virga thought the judgment would be in the $5 million range. I thought they were spending their time crafting a judgment specific to each girl and what they thought would be beneficial.

"I think they'll come back with something that says, plaintiff whatever should get $250,000, something that can be used for counseling, and plaintiff whatever should get $150,000. But I think the total will come to less than a million."

The speculation continued as Wednesday night became Thursday morning.

Chapter 58

The Jury

Right about 1 a.m., the jury announced it had reached a verdict after 12 hours of deliberation.

Seaton-Virga had gone to pick up her son, Tre from Angela's house. Tre was sleeping in his car seat, so Seaton-Virga decided to drive to the courthouse and wait outside with Gerard as long as she could.

She'd been there just a minute when the bailiffs came out and called the lawyers into the courtroom. Seaton-Virga left Tre with Jim Batton and got into the courtroom as quickly as she could. She was no longer exhausted, the adrenaline was in charge.

She stood by her chair and watched the door that the jurors would walk through. It opened and bailiff Dick Hughes announced, as he always did, "Please rise for the jury."

Normally startling, his announcement was particularly jarring in the still courtroom. Seaton-Virga watched as the first two women came into the room and looked at her. She felt a small jolt. Jurors in criminal cases don't look at the defendants when they have decided to convict.

This could be a good sign.

The clerk took the verdict form and began to read:

"What is the amount of damage, including physical injury, pain and suffering, mental anguish, shock and discomfort or any invasion of a personal right that Plaintiff B suffered as a result of Defendants' sexually exploiting Plaintiff B as a minor by featuring her in the Girls Gone Wild video series?

"Amount, zero."

Holy shit. It wasn't the most sophisticated thought to cross Rachel's mind, but it was the most succinct.

Zero!

It was just the first question and Rachel couldn't immediately surrender to the excitement that was rising in her chest.

A few of the women on the jury began to sniffle into their tissues and dab their eyes. They didn't believe the girls deserved a reward, but they wanted desperately to punish Girls Gone Wild.

The rest of the questions went along the same path: zero damages.

The jury had sent a message with one finding in their verdict. They found that Joe Francis had "engaged in extreme and outrageous conduct or behavior that goes beyond all possible bounds of decency and is regarded as shocking, atrocious and utterly intolerable in a civilized community when Defendant Francis or anyone acting on his behalf (including independent contractors) filmed or produced or sold images of 13-year-old Plaintiff J or 15-year-old Plaintiff S or 16-year-old Plaintiff V or 17-year-old Plaintiff B flashing their breasts and/or Plaintiff B engaged in sexually explicit conduct and/or when Defendant Francis coerced 16-year-old Plaintiff V to masturbate him."

They also found that Francis or someone working on his behalf, took a motion picture of Plaintiff B while she was a minor engaged in sexual conduct.

But Francis didn't coerce her into prostitution and Francis did not act with intent to cause emotional distress or with reckless disregard of the high probability of causing emotional distress.

Count after count, zero damages.

Then came the big one, punitive damages. Rachel Seaton-Virga was nervous.

"Do you find that the evidence supports an award of punitive damages in favor of the Plaintiffs?"

"No."

Holy shit.

Clean sweep.

She didn't want to think that they'd won, but there it was. They'd won. Seaton-Virga barely heard Smoak dismissing the jury, with his thanks, and sending them home. She stood as they were leaving and looked each juror in the face, nearly bowing under the gratitude she felt.

She shook hands with Larry Selander and Rachael Pontikes, who looked sucker punched.

Then she called Joe.

Someone in his corporation released a statement later that morning.

"After eight days in trial, four of which Girls Gone Wild founder Joe Francis spent defending himself as his own attorney, a federal jury in a Panama City, Florida courtroom of eight women returned a verdict – and Joe Francis won!

"Francis won the federal case against him, while the four plaintiffs – who sought to cripple the GGW Empire to the tune of hundreds of millions of dollars – got nothing.

"Francis proclaimed, 'I am relieved that I have finally been vindicated from these slanderous, disgusting, and now proven false allegations in a federal court by a jury of eight respectful, conservative women.'

"The odds were definitely stacked against Francis, fighting for justice in the Panama City courthouse where he was previously jailed by the same judge for eleven and a half months, because he refused to settle a civil lawsuit brought against him.

"My legal team did an outstanding job and Girls Gone Wild will continue to take strident measures to avoid facing these false allegations ever again," said Francis. "On behalf of myself and my corporations I would like to thank the jurors and the people of Panama City for their continued support."

Chapter 59

"Serving justice"

The jurors first discovered the contempt of court order against Joe Francis when they began their deliberation and found the order in the file.

Before that, they had no idea why Francis was no longer in the courtroom.

Juror 6 found the order as she was leafing through a box.

"Ladies, that's why he isn't with us any longer," she announced to the rest of the panel.

Fairly quickly in the process they began to ask themselves some of the same questions that Rachel Seaton-Virga had posed: Who was Aero Falcon. So they decided they would ask the judge.

When Smoak called them in to court he could only tell them that Aero Falcon was a named corporate defendant in the case.

"We weren't given a straight answer on it, by no means. It was almost like, 'We're not gonna tell you.' All that did was make me mad. I asked a question, now answer the question. That's all you gotta do."

It was obvious that when they began deliberating the case they were split 6-2 or 5-3, with the majority in favor of finding that Girls Gone Wild had not damaged the girls. But two, definitely, were of the opposite opinion.

So what Juror 6 decided to do was start from the beginning of the verdict form, go through it count by count and decide which ones they could all agree on. When they reached one that they disagreed over, they would set it aside and come back to it.

The first thing they all agreed on was the issue of a minimum award for damages if they found Francis or his companies had intentionally inflicted emotional damage.

Everyone thought it was appropriate that Francis pay something.

"But we don't believe we should be told a minimum amount he should have to pay," Juror 6 said. "I said, 'I don't have a problem with a dollar, but a dollar meant $50,000.'"

She took a calculator out of her purse and put it on the table. She figured up $50,000 times the four defendants who would each have to pay – Mantra Films, MRA Holdings, Aero Falcon and Joe Francis – which meant that each plaintiff would receive $200,000.

"Everybody was not okay with the $50,000, times the four, times the four. So when we got through the first page it was like, it was 5-3, with 5 for zero and no and three for yes, but they didn't want to give them any dollars."

That led them to the question of punitive damages and who would get that money. Most of them felt strongly that they would like to punish, but they resisted the idea of rewarding the girls.

They would have been willing to find against Girls Gone Wild for some damages, but only if they could designate the money to counseling."But when it was told to us that that we couldn't tell them how they were gonna be able to spend their money, it all changed and it changed for everyone, all eight of us," Juror 6 said.

That issue came up four hours into the 12-hour deliberation. The next eight hours were spent crafting the appropriate verdict. That required negotiation.

"When we went through it initially it was basically 5-3. There was one or two questions that all eight of us ... well, it wasn't .... there was one person that stood alone, that was a holdout. The school teacher, on every one of them she was a yes."

The school teacher was even willing to give the girls money, if it meant punishing GGW. But even she balked at the $50,000 minimum.

The $17 million that Selander had suggested never even crossed their minds.

The question that took the longest to resolve was on the second page, about intentional infliction of emotional distress, and it nearly caused a mistrial.

"There were people who did not want to vote yes," she said. "He didn't cause the emotional distress. It got down to, it was 6-2. Besides the school teacher, there was the other one, the young black girl, Juror 1. It was Juror 1 and Juror 5, and Juror 5 said, 'It sounds like to me that it's a hung jury.' I said, 'No, it's not a hung jury.'"

That discussion happened around 10 p.m. and almost immediately after that, they were allowed to step out of the jury room and take a break.

The discussion continued outside.

"I said, 'We're not gonna have a hung jury,'" Juror 6 said.

She had an ally on the panel, Juror 3, a woman from Wassau, who agreed with her, "No, we're not going that way. They're not gonna get another chance."

They returned to the room, and that's when the negotiations really began. Juror 6 described it this way:

"It must have been about 12 o'clock, Wassau was telling the school teacher, 'I'm not buying it. I'm not buying it. You tell me how he can do that to them? You've seen everything.'

"The school teacher was very emotional, 'I just cannot let him off. I cannot let him off.' It's a debate back and forth and back and forth and, at this time, I just backed out of the conversation. I sat there and I listened to it. I was sitting at the end of the table, the school teacher was sitting here (to her right). The Wassau woman was sitting here (to her left). I looked at her and

I said, 'OK, let me ask you this school teacher: if I agree with you on 'yes' will you go for zero dollars?'

"And she looked at me and my Wassau friend said, 'I'm not buying that. And I said, 'OK, let me ask you this: do you not feel that you could vote for a 'yes' but not give them any money? Do you not think that that doesn't send a message?' At this point in time it was 6-2, six no and two yes, and everybody said, 'I'll go with what you go with, foreperson.'"

"I put it out there. And I looked at the school teacher and said, 'Can you go for that?' And she said, 'Yes, I can.' I said, 'I'm not going for 50 ($50,000) it will have to be zero.' And she said, 'I can go for that.' And I looked at Wassau and I said, 'Can you not go for that?' And she said, 'I'll do that.' I said, 'That's better than a hung jury and doing this again with taxpayers' dollars.'"

• • •

After the verdict was read, the jurors returned to the jury room to collect their things. There was very little conversation, the women were all drained by twelve hours of debate and the intensely emotional reading of the verdict.

Into this hush walked Judge Smoak with his usual quiet and purposeful walk which carried him unobtrusively through the doorway. He stopped and looked around as all eight sets of eyes settled on him.

"I appreciate your deliberation," he told the women, moving his eyes to the faces around the room. I believe you did a very good job and you have restored my faith in the judicial system."

Juror 6 recalled that moment as a justification of all her hard work, all her frustration. Smoak thanked them and left the room as quietly and purposefully as he had entered.

Juror 6 walked out behind him and felt for the first time in a week that she was breathing easily.

"I felt like I served justice," she said later. "I believe the judge believed we served justice."

• • •

Later that morning, Rachel awoke to a horrible noise and the blurry sight of someone standing by her bed. She didn't remember going to bed or even sleeping.

"Court! Got to get to court!" she jerked upright.

"You don't have court today," the figure by the bed said.

"What is that noise?" she groaned, focusing her vision on the person standing bedside.

"It's your alarm," Angela said. "I don't know how to shut it off."

"My what?"

"Your alarm," as in the house alarm that Angela set off, and couldn't disarm, when she used her key to open the front door.

Rachel rolled off the bed, padded across the floor, looked at the keypad and tried to bring her thoughts on line. Finally, she got the code and the shriek silenced abruptly.

"You didn't answer your door."

"What time is it?"

After 7. Angela was dropping off Vivi, who had spent the night with her.

"Oh, there's Vivi," Rachel said, still not clearing the sleep from her mind. But she was thrilled to see her daughter.

She felt like she was hungover, pounding headache and the real threat that she'd vomit. It took hours, as she worked her way into the morning, for her to shake off the physical effects of exhaustion. It would take days for her to fully recover.

Chapter 60

The end of the beginning

On May 9, 2011, Rachael Pontikes filed a motion asking Judge Smoak to grant the plaintiffs a new trial.

"The judgment entered in favor of Francis is fatally flawed, requiring a new trial. Many factors made it impossible for this jury to render a reasoned verdict: Francis's disruptive behavior; the de facto admission of unauthenticated medical records; and a closing geared to stigmatize these plaintiffs."

Pontikes said Seaton-Virga essentially characterized the plaintiffs as sluts, "a category of persons so fundamentally damaged that they could not be damaged further.

"This made it impossible for the jury to ignore the issue of consent as this court directed the jury to do and as the law requires."

She said stereotyping the girls as sluts implied that they could do nothing else but consent to the sexual performances "and a pornographer simply reveals her true nature no matter how young she is."

Pontikes cited three lines from Seaton-Virga's closing to illustrate this point: When she told the jurors that "these aren't innocent girls who aren't somewhat familiar with what goes on on Spring Break," and then said the Spring Break atmosphere was "a moral cesspool" and "these girls knew exactly what went on at Spring Break."

"No matter what Francis did to these girls," Pontikes wrote in her motion, "once they were painted as sluts, Francis could not damage them."

She pointed out that the jurors found that Francis had acted outrageously, even criminally, but had decided that he hadn't damaged these girls.

"This verdict is a miscarriage of justice. It finds that a pornographer can exploit teenage girls without damaging them, which declares open season on teenage girls and invites their sexual exploitation by adult men. This record requires this court to grant plaintiffs a new trial."

As of the date of this book's publication, the appeals court had not ruled on Pontikes' motion.

• • •

On September 10 and 11, 2012, Joe Francis' good fortune in court turned into a fortune in damages when a jury awarded casino mogul Steve Wynn $40 million in a slander suit against Francis.

Francis had said in court, then repeated several times to reporters, that Wynn had threatened to kill him and bury him in the desert because of $2 million in gambling debts Francis owed to Wynn. Wynn sued him in 2008 in an effort to collect the debt and Francis first made the comment during a court hearing in that case.

After the verdicts, Francis vowed to appeal, saying he still believed that Wynn intended to kill him.

"I'm the victim here."

Epilogue

The Q&A with Juror 6

Juror 6 is a handsome woman, a description most Southern women hate, somewhere in her 50s or 60s, with golden blonde hair, strong features and quick, appraising eyes. When she introduced herself in the lobby of O'Charlie's Restaurant on May 26, she gripped my hand quickly and firmly, looked me in the eyes with a genuine smile on her face.

While watchful of others she wasn't automatically distrustful and was also quick to say exactly what she was thinking.

She'd been the foreperson on the jury and agreed to talk to me as long as I didn't use her name. We sat in a booth in the bar. I ordered a tall beer and she had an amaretto sour, which she nursed through the 90-minute interview.

"When they first came in, when they first brought the plaintiffs in," Six said, getting into the interview after a small amount of small talk, "and I saw B, as in boy, before I knew anything about her, to me she looked like a rich girl that had got caught. The other three I figured they were just trailer trash, and that's what I thought."

She said she didn't think she'd be picked as a juror because she knew one of the lawyers, Robert Fleming.

"My son played football with him at Rutherford (high school) and they said, 'What do you think about this trial.' I said, 'I believe everybody deserves their day in court whether it'd been Joe whether it'd been the girls. I believe everybody deserves their day in court.'"

She made a bet with another woman in the jury pool as to which of the two of them would be picked for the jury.

"The girl that was sitting directly in front of me, when we had to come back in the jurors box, the girl in front of me said, 'You're gonna get picked.' I said to her, "I'll bet you a Coke-Cola I don't get picked." And she said, 'I'll bet you.'"

When juror number six was selected, the woman turned around and said with a smile, "Let me give you the money for a Coke because you're gonna need it.

"The one sitting next to me who got picked along with me, she said, 'You're gonna get picked.' And I said, 'Oh no, I'm not,' and she said, 'I'm not gonna picked. I know those girls.' And she had been one of the one's who had stated she knew the girls and they called her back into the conference room and she stated how she knew them and everything. Whenever I got picked she tapped me on the shoulder and she said, 'See, you're it.' When they called her name I said, 'Whoo and you're there with me.'"

Juror 4 was a surprise. She was young, had a 14-year-old daughter and said she had issues with GGW. Another woman on the front row was "very, very opinionated." When the jury was selected they were excused for a few minutes and they met together in the jury room for the first time as a group.

"We had to go back there in the back, the young girl from Graceville was very upset and the school teacher next to me was very upset. They both were crying. Before the trial ever started they said what a scumbag he was and everything else and what I said to them was, I could see myself there, where he was. We left and come back the next day and I figure you make the best of it is what you do, you make the very best of the situation. I was intent on it but I wasn't a prude about it. I think you can look at things in a different manner."

On the first day of testimony, Tuesday, Juror 6 began to take stock of the people around her. Not just Joe Francis and the Chicago lawyers, but the other women on her jury.

"We came in and that next morning, I kinda watched the different ones. I read people pretty pretty good and I figured in that point in time there was gonna be three people I was gonna have problems with and it was the young girl from Graceville, the older lady, and the one sitting next to me."

When you say, the ones you're gonna have problems with, what does that mean?

"They're not gonna look at the facts. They're not gonna look at the law. They're emotion driven. They didn't want to be there and I didn't want to be there either, but I still believe that everybody deserves their day in court. So when we first started out and they told us whatever jurors we were and what we'd have to do and everything, the next morning we went out there and Joe started. Do I like him? No, I don't like him. Do I think he's a scumbag? I think he's a scumbag. But a statement was made in the very opening by the opposite team and it still sticks to me today and I kept thinking this the whole time: There's someone in this community that believes that Mr. Francis should pay. That's almost verbatim what they said that day. I sat there and I thought about it. I was thinking about it as everything else was going on and the way that Joe handled himself. When we went back for our first break, the first time we got taken out of the courtroom later in the day, I just sat there, and there was things being said and I said, 'Everybody ... we don't know, so we don't know what it's all about.' And the school teacher was just very abrupt with me. And I told her, 'I'm gonna tell you something, to every one of ya'll right now, I am very straightforward. I will tell you what I think and I'm not easily swayed just because that's what you want. I think there's more to this story than we probably will ever know but I believe everybody deserves their day in court.'

"Joe, he reminded me of a cat or a lion that was caged up and he knew that someone was either fixing to cut his throat or shoot him and he was fightin' for his life. That's what I took of it. I then thought, I kinda figured he must've been ADHD. I often wondered if he was hyped up on coke. He might have been; he might very well have been.

"He went back to the jurors' room and I shared what I thought and I said, 'I can't say I would be any different than him.' If I felt like that everything I had and had worked for I was fixin' to lose, I would probably be worse than him. And one of the jurors, which was another one of the older ladies that was on the front row, she looked at me and she and I were on the same wavelength. I knew the one sitting next to me, the older lady, she had lost her husband, she knew those girls and she made a couple comments that those girls aren't what they are putting them out there to be.

"The school teacher said, 'We are not to discuss that.' I said, 'We're not discussing anything. They're talking freely, I believe I have the right to say what I think.' At that point, I knew that was my number one trouble right there (the school teacher). I knew that was my number one trouble."

It was obvious from early in the trial that you were going to be the foreperson.

"They had said early on, 'Do we need to pick a foreperson?' And I said, 'No, not till the end.' And they said, 'We already know who it is.' And I said, 'Nah, I'm not gonna be the foreperson.' The more I thought about it, I thought as the trial went on and I saw how certain individuals were going, in the manner that they did, I just thought, 'Okay, I'm not gonna say anything but if that's what it takes then that's what it takes.'"

I caught you more than once watching Joe and I didn't think you liked what you were watching.

"I didn't. Some of his stuff I didn't. But I will tell you, when it come up that he told Plaintiff V, is that the (does the handjob motion), okay, V as in victor, when he was talking to her it was very obvious that those girls had been coached. When he asked her how much money do you want, she didn't look at him. She looked at those attorneys. And when he said to her ... she had said, 'I took the money off of the bed' and he called her, 'Well aren't you a prostitute?' We got nicely escorted out but didn't know anything about the contempt of court at that point in time. That's where he brought things out that probably ... well, I wouldn't put it past Rachel, but I think probably it never would have come out.

"In that sense in the manner, I think he did himself a justice, not an injustice. He showed someone fighting for themself. I think he's always pretty much gotten what he's wanted, that's my take on it. I sat and I watched him. He was arrogant, but i could read that he was intently nervous. He was up against all these powerful lawyers. Probably the striking point for me was, he went over to the plaintiffs table and he asked, I call her Miss Poochy Butt ..."

Pontikes?

"Pontikes, he asked her for something. She scribbled it and he said to her, I can't read it. Could you write it out for me or something?' And she didn't, she pushed it at him. That right there said she wasn't going to be fair to him. Whether he is a lawyer or he's not a lawyer you have to be fair. I also noticed that every time they had to go to sidebar, when he started first she jumped her flat tail up in front of him and then sling her head and make her facial gestures. I don't hide my facial expressions very well, she doesn't either. She would do that every time and I watched that.

"When the (Virgas) come in, they were totally different. When I sat and watched them I saw Miss Po-Po said, 'Well, I got some real McCoys here. Now I gotta act in the manner that I should be acting as an attorney,' even though you didn't give that other person the same respect. That goes a long way for me."

What did you think of Lebowitz?

"She talked in circles and she chased her tail. When she compared those girls to men in combat ... (shakes her head in disbelief). When I first found out where they was from I went back and I told (the other jurors), 'I can tell you exactly where this come from, Robert Fleming went to Duke. Those Chicago big dogs thought they was dealing with a bunch of dumbasses. They was coming to the Redneck Riviera and all we was was a bunch of dumb dumbs."

That seemed clear even in the way that Pontikes and Selander spoke when they were at the podium.

"Yes, it was like you weren't smart enough to figure it out. More than one time when they had to go to sidebar and we had to go out I would sit back there and say, 'You know, they might think I'm a dummy, but I'm not a dummy and I'm not buying into this.' Early on I said there's more to this story; Like Paul Harvey used to say 'and the rest of the story is ...' My friend from Wassau over there said, 'You're right sister.' She's very educated. Juror 4 was emotional. She was so stern in her body language, everything about her, she didn't really have much of a poker face. It was just such a nice jury to have good solid people.

"One thing that the school teacher didn't like, she never went to lunch with us. She finally went one day. We didn't talk at lunch about the case. We talked about our kids and what we did for a living and how good the food was where we went. We went to different places and I think the reason the school teacher went was ... I think she went so she could ... thinking she would pick up on something we were saying that she could take to the judge.

"She kept talking about how she had a son, she had a daughter. Her husband was retired military. They were very, very big in the church. I said to her on more than one occasion, 'I don't believe he held a gun to their heads.'

"And probably the changing for the young lady with the longer hair was when they showed the tape of those girls, whenever they first showed the tape and there was no audio. My opinion, and its strictly my opinion, was that was on purpose and it may not have been that they didn't want any audio. The prosecution didn't. I felt like it was on purpose the reason the audio was not there because the prosecution said, 'You're honor, they've seen it.' And Rachel spoke up and said, 'Your honor, there was no audio.' And he took us out to the jury room. We stayed out there about 30 minutes and he brung us back in and he said, 'I apologize.' And we heard the audio. The audio was just more clarification that those girls were not under duress. Those girls were not being forced to do that. When they said those girls had never been to the beach, you know what I looked at? I looked at their swimsuits. Those weren't brand new swimsuits. Those were well-used swimsuits."

You were comparing their testimony to the facts?

"That's correct."

If they had come out and said something closer to what was shown on the video, would that have changed your opinion at all about this case?

"No, they had a choice in what they did. She said they were coerced, she only did it because I wanted them to go away. A big impact was when we got back into the jury room and we got all the evidence. We didn't get shown the evidence of the FBI seeking out these people. That's not something that was told us. So the first thing we did was we started going through the exhibits. (The FBI) started seeking these people out. These people didn't come forward, they were sought out. Why were they sought out? I still believe there is somebody behind this. That we might not ever know who it is, but somebody in the community's daughter that went out there and they are pissed off. That's what I honestly think because of the opening statement that they made.

"When I brought that up I said, 'Ladies, do you not remember the opening statement they made? I can tell you almost verbatim what they said.' And they just looked at me and I said, 'This right here tells you that they sought those people out. They were sought out and they were told that they were fixin' to get a bunch of money. We're a sue happy world. The more money they get the more money the attorneys get. So if they honestly were hurt and there is free help for you out there and you don't take it, and you tell me that a guy caused you an incomprehensible amount of distress and you go and get him a towel you picked the money up off of the table, and you go and you follow him and you want to ride in his car, and you take him to your house and you come back and you call him to get into another party. Tell me where's he's done all this at?' And it was like light switches that were startin' to come on.

"When it got brought out that (Plaintiff V) had followed him, close to the end, the next day when we come back in, the one that had always been so upset, she said to me, 'I want you to know I have peace about this.' She said, 'What you said is right, it is all in the choices that you make.'

"And she said, 'I don't have to like him but it doesn't mean that I have to persecute him and that's ... the law's the law and he broke the law and he paid criminally for what he did.' Are we here because they all were angels? No, they were not angels by no means. And they kept bringing into the fact that B's father dying and all that. B would've never had a problem if she had not got cut off financially and when it finally come out from the boyfriend that she got cut off financially, that's where it all come about."

Let me ask you about B's father. When Selander did his opening he very carefully crafted that opening to not actually say that GGW caused her father to die. But they kept coming back to it. When you heard that in opening what did you think?

"I honestly thought that ... when they brought the girls out before he did his opening statement ... there was more to that chick. Her body language. She would flip that hair back and back again. It was died jet black. She was very nervous. I watched her hands. I watched her mess with her jacket all the time, and that flipping of the hair. It was like, 'I don't really want it all to come out but I'm gonna do what I think I need to do.' That's what I took from her."

You felt like she was hiding something?

"Yes, I did. Her body language. The other young ladies that come out, every one of them had on skin tight clothes and skin tight pants. Every one of them. Why would you come dressed to court like that?

"When (plaintiffs J's and S's) mother come out, you can't tell me you've lived in this town you're whole entire life and you'd never been to the beach. I'm not buying that cup of tea. I'm sorry I'm just not buying that cup of tea. Now, one of our jurors shared with us that they went to Brother Hunt's church. When she said that, I'm watching people the whole time and I can tell you this, someone from Brother Hunt's church, a woman especially, she don't have tattoos on her. And the mother had a tattoo on her. Yes, they are pretty strict. Those girls, if they were pressed so hard, why didn't the driver do it? And I said that to the fellow jurors: 'If they were put under such duress why didn't the driver do it?' Neither one flinched in the little bit of audio we got.

How do you feel about never seeing the other videos?

"There was something to hide. We got to see the packages, the empty packages. That's what I feel was an injustice. If you want to admit, admit the whole thing. Don't admit bits and pieces that's gonna make me just think one way. And my thing was, a big part of it was, if it was as bad as the prosecution said, why don't you put it out there? That's the first thing I asked to my fellow jurors."

When you began deliberations, you started by going through the exhibits. That's when you found out why Joe Francis was no longer representing himself.

"That was the first time we saw the contempt of court. We couldn't figure out how, okay, he's here and then he's gone. We didn't know. So I'm looking through the exhibits and I say, 'Okay, here is a contempt of court. Ladies, that's why he isn't with us any longer.'"

It was obvious that when they began deliberating the case they were split 6-2 or 5-3, with the majority in favor of finding that Girls Gone Wild had not damaged the girls. But two, definitely, were of the opposite opinion.

The first thing they all agreed on was the issue of a minimum award for damages if they found Francis or his companies had intentionally inflicted emotional damage.

Everyone thought it was appropriate that Francis pay something.

"But we don't believe we should be told a minimum amount he should have to pay. I said, 'I don't have a problem with a dollar, but a dollar meant fifty-thousand dollars."

She took a calculator out of her purse and put it on the table. She figured up fifty-thousand dollars times the four defendants, which meant that each plaintiff would receive two-hundred thousand dollars.

"Everybody was not okay with the fifty-thousand dollars, times the four, times the four. So when we got through the first page it was like, it was 5-3, with 5 for zero and no and three for yes, but they didn't want to give them any dollars."

One of your first questions was: if we award punitive damages who does the money go to? Everybody thought what you were trying to do is, you wanted to punish him but you don't want to reward the girls.

"That's correct, because we said, if we can say that it went to counseling and only to counseling we would be willing to entertain giving some money. But when it was told to us that that we couldn't tell them how they were gonna be able to spend their money, it all changed and it changed for everyone, all eight of us."

That question came four hours into a 12-hour deliberation. What issue took you the rest of the way?

"The questions that we answered yes to and zero dollars."

What you guys were doing was trying to fashion a verdict that was going to send a message but not reward these girls?

"When we went through it initially it was basically 5-3. There was one or two questions that all eight of us ... well, it wasn't .... there was one person that stood alone, that was a holdout. The school teacher, on every one of them she was a yes."

So she believed that Joe Francis had damaged them and she wanted yes on everything?

"Yes."

What were her feeling as far as damages?

"She thought they deserved something but she didn't necessarily agree with the fifty-thousand dollars. That was too much."

Even that was too much? So the 17 million was probably something that didn't even cross your mind?"

"No. No. So I said, 'This is what I think we need to do: We need to start with each question and we'll see if we can come to a unanimous decision. If we can't we'll go on to the next one. And if we get to a point where we can't talk it out amongst ourselves, we can't come to a complete decision, then we'll leave those to the side and we'll come back to them, and that's what we did."

What was the question that hung you guys up the most?

"The first one on the second page that we finally voted yes to. I don't even remember what it was. That was a stickler."

There were people who didn't want to vote yes?

"That's right, there were people who did not want to vote yes."

Why didn't they want to vote yes on that?

"Because we didn't think he ... it was a no, no he didn't have the impact on them."

He didn't harm them to the point where they were damaged?

"That's right, he didn't cause the emotional distress. It got down to, it was 6-2. Besides the school teacher, there was the other one, the young black girl, Juror 1. It was No. 1 and No. 5 and No. 5 said, 'It sounds like to me that it's a hung jury.' I said, 'No, it's not a hung jury.'"

How late in the evening was it when she said that?

"Probably 10, 10 o'clock."

They'd been allowed to step outside to stretch their legs and get some air late in the evening. The hung jury comment was made just before they went outside, so it was a topic of conversation.

"I said, 'We're not gonna have a hung jury.' My Wassau friend (Juror 3) said, 'No, we're not going that way. They're not gonna get another chance.' We come back in and we started going through it again and at, was it at one o'clock when we finished?"

Yes.

"It must have been about 12 o'clock, Wassau was telling the school teacher, 'I'm not buying it. I'm not buying it. You tell me how he can do that to them? You've seen everything.'

"The school teacher was very emotional, 'I just cannot let him off. I cannot let him off.' It's a debate back and forth and back and forth and, at this time, I just backed out of the conversation. I sat there and I listened to it. I was sitting at the end of the table, the school teacher was sitting here (to her right). The Wassau woman was sitting here (to her left). I looked at her and, 'I said, okay, let me ask you this school teacher: if I agree with you on 'yes' will you go for zero dollars?'

"And she looked at me and my Wassau friend said, 'I'm not buying that. and I said, okay, let me ask you this: do you not feel that you could vote for a 'yes' but not give them any money? Do you not think that that doesn't send a message?' At this point in time it was 6-2, six no's and two yeses, and everybody said, 'I'll go with what you go with foreperson.'"

So you're the one that finally decided it was going to be yes and zero?

"I put it out there. And I looked at the school teacher and said, 'Can you go for that?' And she said, 'Yes, I can.' I said, 'I'm not going for 50 it will have to be zero.' And she said, 'I can go for that.' And I looked at Wassau and I said, 'Can you not go for that?' And she said, 'I'll do that.' I said, 'That's better than a hung jury and doing this again with taxpayers' dollars.'"

There were jurors that were crying during the reading of the verdict.

"I was one of them."

Why?

"Because I never knew I was gonna have to sit up front. That wasn't told to me until we got right there to the door. They told me, 'You have to sit up here at the very front.' And I said, 'They'll know who the foreperson is.' And they said, 'Yeah.'"

"It was emotional for me in two reasons. I think that the attorneys played and painted a big picture to them girls and I think those girls thought that was gonna be a nice payday for them with the money they were gonna get and I was fixin' to change their lives drastically because I wasn't gonna give them what they thought they wanted.

"I believe right's right and wrong's wrong and I believe that people make mistakes, but if that man hadn't a had any money would they have come after him?"

So you really didn't have any hard feelings even against the girls?

"No. No. I think they were just trying to make a fast buck. Their names were not published, so unless you were there, and it was 90 percent of Burke and Blue's office that were there, and Robert Fleming's father sitting there watching him, who knows me very well, and he made a lot of eye contact with me. I looked at him. I think they were truly upset.

"I was emotional, but I focused on the (plaintiffs' attorneys) as the things were being read and it was, (she drops her head incrementally as if she's being deflated with each finding). When that 'yes' was read it was like, 'Okay, here we go. We're finally fixin' to get into the money.' But when that zero dollars was read, I think I could have just (she blows gently through pursed lips) and they would have just fell over. They were some upset kitty cats.

"Did I want to be on the case? No I didn't. But in hindsight I was glad I was because I felt like I served justice. And I believe the judge believed we served justice because of the remark he made to us after it was all over with. We asked if we could speak to him. We wanted to thank him and he said to us, 'I appreciate your deliberation. I believe you did a very good job and you have restored my faith in the judicial system.' That's what he said. He said that to all of us jurors in the deliberation room after it was all over with and we were getting ready to leave. He come in there and said he appreciated what we had done and we had restored his faith in the judicial system."

What this case boiled down to was, the law could be read in a really, really specific way and those things were argued over and over again.

"Oh, those questions were very very tricky."

But you guys brought in a lot of common sense.

"We read it and we said, 'Okay, what do you think that means? Okay, where is the law on that? Did he prove that he broke the law?' And it's about the law. It's not about whether you like him or you don't like him because, I said that, I don't like him. I think he's a scumbag. But did he cause irreversible emotional distress? No he didn't. No he didn't, because it was brought out that those girls had a chance to change their lives and they chose not to."

Rachel (Seaton-Virga) really made an impact on you.

"Oh, she did. Oh she did. She made a real good impact and it said an awful lot about her when she had her husband on the stand and he was talking and she said, 'Move your hand.' My school teacher friend next to me said, 'Oh that was so rude' back in the jury room. When we come back in for nine-hundred and ninety-ninth-thousand time, (Rachel) said, 'I want to apologize for speaking to my husband the way I did.' When we went back again (to the jury room) I said, 'So tell me what that says about that attorney that got up there and apologized in front of the whole courtroom for what she did. What she was trying to do was give us the opportunity to understand it clearly.' (The teacher) said, 'I guess you're right and it worked.'

"I think (Rachel) Virga, the way she carried herself, I thought was very, very good. I thought she was very precise. Did I know if they'd been behind the scene the entire time? A couple of the jurors thought, 'Oh, they'd been there the whole time, you know. This is a drama deal.' And I said, 'Why would you risk that if that were the case?' I think the Chicago folks come in thinking it was a grand slam for them and it wasn't.

"I think if we had awarded money, and I made this statement, if you award money you just open the door for all the cockroaches to come out.

"I still believe there's somebody behind it that we don't know."

What did you think of Joe's cross examination of the plaintiffs, of the girls?

"Was he badgering? No. He wanted to get out there that he wasn't the one, he didn't hold a gun to their head. He was trying to do the best he could as an attorney. I probably would have been worse than him if it had been me because I would have been saying, 'Hey now, let's be honest about this.'

"When he asked V, did that make her a prostitute? When you accept money, you are a prostitute. It don't take a rocket scientist, not a lawyer, to figure that out, so did he bring something to the table? He did.

"What I couldn't figure out was the hispanic lookin' lady and the little pimp looking guy, I couldn't figure them out.

"The only question I had and I never could figure out was: Why was the guy who testified that he worked for Playboy (Eric Deutsch), how in the world would he ever get mixed up with Joe Francis?"

Juror 6 asked: "Who did he make mad in the very beginning? did he make Lee Sullivan mad?"

Lee Sullivan saw this as a political opportunity, and Joe, in 2003, saw this is as great publicity.

"Wet T-shirt contests, (bars) doing simulated sex acts on the beach, this is Spring Break. I'm not a dumb old girl."__

Acknowledgments:

Thank you to Angela Seaton, Laurie Hughes and Greg Wilson for reading and editing the manuscript and all the advice they included in those edits.

A special thank-you to David Demarest, the editor who came in at the last minute and did what he could to salvage the manuscript and infuse life back into the project.

www.ingramcontent.com/pod-product-compliance
Lightning Source LLC
LaVergne TN
LVHW020519100826
845148LV00010B/1283

9780615705804